IMPROVING
COLLEGE TEACHING

IMPROVING
COLLEGE TEACHING

Peter Seldin

Lubin School of Business
Pace University
Pleasantville, NY

and Associates

Anker Publishing Company, Inc.
Bolton, MA

Improving College Teaching

ISBN 1-882982-08-8

Composition by Deerfoot Studios.
Cover design by Deerfoot Studios.

Anker Publishing Company, Inc.
176 Ballville Road
P.O. Box 249
Bolton, MA 01740–0249

THE AUTHORS

Peter Seldin is Distinguished Professor of Management in the Lubin School of Business, Pace University, Pleasantville, New York.

Susan A. Ambrose is Director of the University Teaching Center and Lecturer in the Department of History, Carnegie Mellon University.

Linda Annis is Professor of Educational Psychology, Ball State University.

Robert A. Armour is Assistant Secretary General for Higher Education for the Board of Higher Education and Ministry, The United Methodist Church. He is also Professor Emeritus of English at Virginia Commonwealth University.

Raoul A. Arreola is Professor and Director of Educational Technology, University of Tennessee, Memphis.

Ann E. Austin is Associate Professor and Coordinator of the Higher, Adult, and Lifelong Education Program, Michigan State University.

Roger G. Baldwin is Associate Professor in the School of Education, College of William and Mary.

Beverly Black is Director of the TA Training and Development Program, Center for Research on Learning and Teaching, University of Michigan.

L. Dee Fink is Director of the Instructional Development Program, University of Oklahoma.

Walter H. Gmelch is Professor and Chair, Department of Educational Leadership and Counseling Psychology, and Director of the Center for the Study of the Department Chair, Washington State University.

Judy A. Greene is Director of the Center for Teaching Effectiveness, University of Delaware.

Irene W. D. Hecht is an independent educational consultant and Senior Associate, the American Council on Education.

William K. Jackson is Associate Director of the Office of Instructional Development, University of Georgia.

Carolee Jones is Professor of Business Education and Office Administration, School of Business, Ball State University.

Barbara Beigun Kaplan is Coordinator of Faculty Development, University of Maryland University College.

Barbara J. Millis is Assistant Dean, Faculty Development, University of Maryland University College.

Joseph M. Pastore, Jr. is Professor of Management in the Lubin School of Business, Pace University, Pleasantville, New York.

Ronald D. Simpson is Professor of Higher Education and Science Education, and Director of the Office of Instructional Development, University of Georgia.

Mary Deane Sorcinelli is Director of the Center for Teaching and associate adjunct faculty in the Department of Educational Policy, Research, and Administration, University of Massachusetts, Amherst.

Emily C. (Rusty) Wadsworth is Associate Dean for Humanities, McHenry County College, Crystal Lake, Illinois.

Kathleen Wagschal is Associate Professor in the School of Education and Human Services, National University, San Diego, California.

Peter H. Wagschal is Vice-President for Research at National University and Director of the National University Research Institute.

John Zubizarreta is Professor of English and Director of Honors at Columbia College, South Carolina.

CONTENTS

PREFACE

There's never been a more promising time to improve teaching. At long last, after years of mounting criticism and cries for reform, more and more institutions are reexamining their commitment to teaching and exploring ways to improve it. The movement to take teaching seriously today is growing exponentially. Interest in improving teaching is marked by overflow crowds of faculty and administrators at national and regional conferences, generous financial support from major foundations and government agencies, and books on improving teaching that quickly need reprinting.

What's behind the new emphasis on teaching? The rapid growth of the faculty development movement plus recognition of the validity of different teaching styles played a part. Then too, there was the changing demographics of those attending college and the emergence of new educational technology. And the insistence that teaching is actually an expression of scholarship, that it lives and thrives in intimate knowledge and dissemination of research in the classroom also contributed. But perhaps the most compelling force for the new seriousness about teaching came from the insistent public demands for teaching accountability from newly aroused legislatures and institutional governing boards.

Since college professors are hired with the expectation that they will offer effective instruction, providing them with assistance to improve their instruction is no more than a logical extension of this expectation. Just as students deserve guidance as learners, professors are entitled to helpful direction in their teaching. No matter how good a teacher is in the classroom or laboratory, he or she can improve. No matter how effective a particular teaching method, it can be enhanced.

What do activities to improve teaching look like? Among others, they include programs to: 1) develop different teaching skills needed for different kinds of students; 2) develop skillful use of current educational technology; 3) assist teachers to find greater intrinsic satisfaction in their teaching; 4) encourage teachers to evaluate their own teaching and assist each other's teaching; and 5) provide feedback to instructors on their teaching performance.

Improving College Teaching offers teachers and administrators the practical, ready-to-use, research-based information required to foster truly effective teaching at their institutions. The book is a reasoned, well-grounded guide for achieving needed changes in campus culture, teacher training programs, evaluation and development of performance, faculty motivation, and genuine commitment to teaching. Earlier books on improving teaching effectiveness have mainly been collections of instructional techniques, often focused on a specific academic discipline. The thrust here is different. This book:

✦ Details in depth time-tested strategies and specific activities to improve teaching of faculty and teaching assistants

✦ Provides case studies from different institutions to examine campus cultures that contribute to good teaching

✦ Describes the key role for administrators, especially department chairs

✦ Discusses productive approaches to enhance faculty motivation for teaching

✦ Spells out successful low-cost or no-cost instructional development activities

✦ Identifies key issues, red-flag dangers and benchmarks for success.

In short, *Improving College Teaching* offers college and university administrators and faculty the kind of pragmatic, hands-on information about specific strategies and state-of-the-art techniques required to improve teaching.

It is written for presidents, provosts, academic vice-presidents, deans, department chairs, instructional development specialists, and faculty. They are the essential partners in evaluating and improving teaching. The practical suggestions and recommendations presented should prove of value to these administrators and faculty whether they are in public or private institutions. The book will also be helpful to students of higher education, whether they are planning careers as academic administrators or faculty.

OVERVIEW OF THE CONTENTS

Part I, Key Influences on Teaching Quality, examines key influences on teaching quality in colleges and universities and how they affect the faculty.

In *Chapter One,* Seldin weighs reasons for improving teaching, cites barriers to improvement, and offers examples of specific programs. He ticks off characteristics of successful teaching improvement programs and describes the kinds of concrete action available to administrators to support a higher priority for teaching.

In *Chapter Two,* Armour discusses how institutions can improve instruction by paying closer attention to the culture that fosters teaching on their campuses. He uses case studies from four disparate institutions to illuminate the role of campus culture in creating a positive atmosphere for teaching and explores the building of this supportive culture.

In *Chapter Three,* Hecht examines the vital role of administrators in upgrading the quality of teaching. She details how administrators can shape the campus dialogue, encourage faculty team skills and collaborative work, apply institutional resources, and facilitate connections with external audiences.

In *Chapter Four,* Austin and Baldwin describe how both intrinsic and extrinsic rewards can support faculty motivation for teaching. They are persuaded that different types of teaching opportunities and support are needed to motivate faculty at successive career stages, and they lay out the key components of a comprehensive plan to enhance faculty motivation to teach.

In *Chapter Five,* Pastore argues that the creation of a culture of commitment to "teaching space" is fundamental to any program, policy, or leadership effort to enhance teaching effectiveness. He also argues that efforts to create such a culture of commitment must include a systemic (students, faculty, administration, and governing boards) exertion to raise teaching and learning to an active, rather than rhetorical, manifestation of institutional purpose.

Part II, Programs to Improve Teaching, focuses on specific programs for improvement and the successful methods of their implementation.

In *Chapter Six,* Black tells why it is essential to give graduate teaching assistants (TAs) the training and support they need to effectively do their jobs and launch their teaching careers. Drawing on the literature and her practical experience, she explains what works and what does not and recommends a TA training model successfully used at the University of Michigan.

In *Chapter Seven,* Ambrose probes how and why success in improving teaching depends in large part on how well the program is integrated into the institution. She describes the establishment of the University Teaching Center at Carnegie Mellon University and identifies sixteen crucial tenets as essential to the creation and maintenance of every successful teaching improvement program.

In *Chapter Eight,* Simpson and Jackson offer evidence that volunteer peer consultants are a key to effective low-cost or no-cost instructional improvement activities. Drawing on their experience at the University of Georgia, they offer concrete examples of inexpensive programs designed both for individual faculty and faculty groups.

In *Chapter Nine,* Greene points to the college teacher's pivotal role as change agent in creating a campus climate that values diversity in the classroom. She discusses how teachers can recognize, value, and use diversity issues as an integral part of their classroom teaching. She also describes the "Welcoming Diversity" workshop developed by the National Coalition Building Institute.

In *Chapter Ten,* Wadsworth finds that the traditional community college focus on teaching creates the kind of institutional climate in which instructional development is perceived as integral to the mission of the institution. She offers concrete examples of teaching improvement activities and describes the opportunities for instructional development coordinators to encourage teaching improvement.

Part III, Strategies for Teaching Improvement, is devoted to real-world examples of strategies needed to improve teaching and the crucial roles of the department chair, faculty peers, and teachers, themselves, in strengthening classroom performance.

In *Chapter Eleven,* Sorcinelli analyzes how mentoring programs improve the teaching of new and junior faculty members. She presents four model mentoring programs and discusses seven important lessons to keep mentoring healthy.

In *Chapter Twelve,* Millis and Kaplan describe the use of peer classroom observations to enhance teaching. They delineate the role of carefully-selected, well-trained observers, and discuss key factors in successful peer assessment programs. Also discussed is the highly regarded peer visit program at the University of Maryland University College.

In *Chapter Thirteen*, Gmelch outlines the department chair's pivotal role in improving teaching. He presents key elements of chair behaviors that create and maintain teaching excellence, draws on the research literature and his own experience in revealing what works and what does not, and offers practical strategies for department chairs.

In *Chapter Fourteen*, Zubizarreta discusses how the teaching portfolio can be adapted as a concise course portfolio to raise classroom performance. He explores the possible contents of a portfolio, discusses the key role of a mentor in guiding the process of teaching improvement, and offers practical recommendations to faculty who want to develop a course portfolio to improve their teaching.

In *Chapter Fifteen*, Annis and Jones consider student portfolios as a vehicle for improving teaching and learning. Drawing on their practical experience, they explain how to plan, implement, and evaluate a student portfolio assignment, and they make recommendations to those considering using such an assignment.

In *Chapter Sixteen*, Fink discusses a successful approach for teachers to evaluate their own classroom performance. He cites five sources of information that can be used to evaluate teaching, and the unique value, recommended frequency, limitation, and appropriate response to each limitation. Fink offers a case study showing how comprehensive evaluation works to identify teaching weaknesses and improve performance.

Part IV, Approaches to Nontraditional Teaching, focuses on nontraditional teaching and includes a chapter-by-chapter summary and key recommendations for improving teaching.

In *Chapter Seventeen*, Baldwin and Austin examine the continuum of collaborative teaching arrangements and the important benefits and potential problems inherent in team teaching. They sort out what works and what does not and offer eight key recommendations to those considering joint teaching with colleagues. Baldwin and Austin also offer six practical recommendations to administrators who want to promote classroom collaboration.

In *Chapter Eighteen*, Arreola discusses the rapidly growing use of telecommunication technology to deliver instruction (distance education). Noting that distance education forces teachers to sharpen their presentation, he offers practical guidelines for effectively doing so. Also discussed are the profound implications of distance education for teaching load, faculty evaluation, and teacher productivity.

In *Chapter Nineteen*, Wagschal and Wagschal examine successful approaches to teaching adult learners. They offer practical strategies not only for creating an appropriate learning environment but also for using a mixture of teaching techniques to take advantage of the adult learners' wealth of experience.

In *Chapter Twenty*, Seldin summarizes chapter-by-chapter key points and recommendations for faculty and administrators to bring about needed changes that encourage teaching excellence throughout the institution.

Peter Seldin
Pleasantville, NY
February, 1995

ONE

IMPROVING COLLEGE TEACHING

Peter Seldin

Teaching in colleges is marked by historic paradox: though institutions constantly talk up its importance, they evaluate faculty primarily on the basis of scholarly achievements outside the classroom. Teaching is what almost every professor does, but it seems to suffer from that very commonness. It occupies the greatest amount of most professors' time, but rarely operates at the highest level of competence.

There seems to be an ingrained academic reluctance to regard teaching in the same way the profession regards every other set of skills: as something that can be taught. Professors who take painstaking care for method within their discipline of chemistry, history, or psychology, for example, all too often are unreflective when it comes to teaching.

Some professors even regard teaching as so straightforward that it requires no special training. Others find it so personal and idiosyncratic that no training could ever meet its multiplicity of demands. But most share the common folk belief that teachers are born and not made. "He (or she) is a born teacher," is said of too many good teachers as a cop-out by those who aren't. And some good teachers fuel this belief by agreeing, "I guess I'm a good teacher. Things seem to go well in the classroom. The students say they like what I do. But I don't really know how I do it."

In fact, the marginal truth in this belief applies no more to teaching than to any other profession. If there are born teachers, there are born physicians, born attorneys, and born engineers. Yet those who are naturally great at these professions invariably spend an unnatural amount of time acquiring skills and practicing in the vortex of intense competition. Potentially great teachers become great teachers by the same route:

1

through conditioning mind, through acquiring skills, and through practicing amidst intense competition (Eble, 1988).

The interest in improved teaching has mushroomed rapidly in recent years, burrowing into all areas of the country and all types of institutions. Colleges and universities are moving from lip-service endorsements of the importance of teaching to concerted and sustained efforts to improve programs. Faculty and administrators flock to teaching conferences; government agencies and private foundations offer financial support, and a wave of new books on the subject appear.

Yet the concept of improving teaching is hardly new. Years ago its emphasis was to improve subject matter competence. To further such competence, sabbatical leaves and attendance at professional meetings were encouraged. Claimed as rationale was a deeper understanding of the content of a discipline. Practically no attention was paid to how that understanding could best be imparted to students. Today, this early approach has been turned around. Now the concept is based on three assumptions: first, the primary professional activity of most professors is teaching; second, instructional behavior is not inborn, but rather a learned web of skills, attitudes, and goals; and third, faculty can be taught how to improve their classroom performance.

The "new" emphasis on teaching stems from "new" social and political forces. Demographics have changed the student population and their educational needs. The advent of educational technology has forever altered concepts about teaching and learning. And public outcries demanding teaching accountability have roused legislators and governing boards to actions. All forces rally for improved teaching.

BARRIERS TO IMPROVEMENT

How have the faculty responded to efforts around the nation to develop their teaching competence? Regrettably, they have mostly dragged their heels. Why? Several reasons come to mind. First, there is a core belief embedded in many teachers that only someone knowledgeable in a discipline can talk meaningfully about it. They believe that general ideas about teaching don't easily translate into the discipline-specific terms and concepts that a teacher of a particular course can readily act upon (Angelo, 1994).

Second, some teachers fail to recognize the need for improvement in their own teaching. They think that they are already doing a good job in the classroom, a perception that reduces their interest in teaching improvement programs. For example, in a survey of nearly 300 college teachers, Blackburn et. al (1980) found that 92 percent believed their own teaching was above average. For Angelo (1994, p.5) that finding evoked Garrison Keillor's Lake Wobegon, "a place where all the woman are strong, all the men are good-looking, and all the children are above-average."

Third, the generic nature of many teaching improvement programs sometimes doesn't respond to a given teacher's highly personal and specific needs. Said a Wisconsin professor, "Why should I invest time and energy in programs that don't directly relate to the teaching problems I face?"

Fourth, many faculty have yet to be motivated to cross the threshold of a teaching improvement program. Inertia more than opposition has kept them on the sidelines. As a California professor said as she shrugged, "Some day I'll probably take part in a teaching improvement program. But not right now."

WHY IMPROVE TEACHING?

The reasons for improving teaching are found in four different yet interconnected areas. They are reasons related to: 1) institutions of higher education, 2) faculty members, 3) students, and 4) society and societal forces (Cole, 1978; Seldin, 1993).

Institutional Reasons

Today, there is virtually endemic dissatisfaction with the faculty reward system. The typical system overvalues research and scholarship and undervalues teaching. One by-product of this tilted reward system is the inattention paid to teaching by graduate schools in their doctoral programs. (For a report on one institution that does pay attention, see the chapter by Black.) At bottom, the values predominant in higher education generally do not support teaching. Yet the intensified competition for students today requires that institutions strengthen their claim of offering outstanding teaching. Colleges where superior teaching is the rule rather than the exception, and where it is sufficiently recognized and rewarded, enjoy a distinct advantage in the competition for students.

Faculty

Despite the growth of the faculty development movement over the past two decades, as a practical matter, only a relatively small percentage of faculty take advantage of available teaching improvement programs. That is most unfortunate since so many teachers have never studied the history of the teaching profession, are unaware of the professional literature in teaching and learning, and have never systematically developed their own teaching philosophies.

Teachers, like other professionals, should have a hungering need to update themselves, to engage in professional growth, to expand and deepen their understanding. They must be attentive to fresh pedagogical techniques, student learning theories, and technological advances. Even the best teachers must continue learning in order to remain the best.

Students

College students today are quite a different mix than they were even two decades ago. Today, there are more students from minority groups, more older students, more students who are working full-time, more students with physical handicaps, and more students without a college-going tradition in their families. And those who teach today's students must learn to gear instruction to a new classroom dynamic.

Society and Societal Forces

Lastly, we come to societal reasons for improving teaching. Telecommunications and computer technology have emerged as powerful forces in teaching and learning, especially when in the form of live, two-way video connections. With these connections, the classroom experience is essentially brought into the students' homes or offices. Clearly, distance education via electronic telecommunications technology poses special requirements on the professor who must design and deliver instruction in a manner very different from teaching a traditional class. If their teaching is to be effective, faculty delivering distance education courses using telecommunications require formal training in using the new technology (see the chapter by Arreola).

APPROACHES TO IMPROVING TEACHING

Since college professors are hired with the expectation that they will offer effective instruction, providing them with assistance to improve their instruction is no more than a logical extension of this expectation.

Just as students deserve guidance as learners, professors are entitled to helpful direction in their teaching. No matter how good a teacher is in the classroom or laboratory, he or she can improve. No matter how effective a particular teaching method, it can be enhanced.

The argument has been raised by some that we still lack the final answer to the question of what constitutes effective teaching. That may well be true, but the key ingredients of effective teaching are increasingly known. We have no reason to ignore hundreds of studies that are in general agreement on these characteristics. They include a deep knowledge of the subject, an ability to communicate with and motivate students, enthusiasm for the subject and for teaching, clarity of presentation, and fairness.

What might activities to improve teaching look like? Eble and McKeachie (1986, p. 14) suggest that growing as a teacher, "...may be a matter of enlarging a faculty member's knowledge of learning theory and pedagogical practices, of increasing the professor's interest in and commitment to teaching, of reinforcing and rewarding excellent teaching, and of providing opportunities to bring about this kind of growth."

What might such opportunities for growth look like? Seldin (1993) and Eble and McKeachie suggest that they include, among others, emphasis in the following areas:

1. Programs to develop the repertoire of teaching skills needed by the professor to be effective for different kinds of students and different kinds of learning goals. Included are skills in using a variety of teaching methods, skills in the use of current technology, and discipline-related skills in teaching particular concepts or materials (see the chapter by Ambrose).

2. Programs to build bridges between what the teacher knows and what the student is trying to grasp. Students differ in experience, ways of thinking, and motivation. For that reason, no single method of teaching is equally effective for all students. Skills are required to recognize where individual students are and how to reach them.

3. Programs to develop skills and understanding having to do with interpersonal relationships with students. Vital to most students' learning is the sense that the teacher cares about them. Research tells us that the most effective teachers are available to students and work closely with them both inside and outside the classroom.

4. Programs to help teachers gain greater understanding of how their disciplines' organizational structures facilitate or inhibit student learning. Teachers must communicate differently to students who are taking introductory classes than they do to those in doctoral seminars. Learning how to communicate at the proper student level is a key component of effective teaching.

5. Programs to assist teachers to find greater intrinsic satisfaction in their teaching. Such enhanced motivation may be individually fostered or may arise from a campus climate that inspires commitment and enthusiasm.

6. Programs that help teachers learn how to continue learning from their experiences as teachers. That means achieving skill in monitoring one's own effectiveness and adapting one's methods to a particular class and teaching situation (see the chapter by Fink).

7. Programs that encourage faculty to support, critique, and assist each other's teaching (see the chapter by Millis and Kaplan), that foster conversation about teaching, that assert a sense of common purpose, and rally dispirited or isolated faculty to a greater commitment to teaching and learning (see the chapter by Pastore and by Hecht).

8. Programs that provide feedback to instructors on their teaching performance. This approach is particularly advantageous to teachers needing more individual help than can be obtained from workshops. Feedback sources vary but generally used are student ratings, videotapes of performance, and classroom observers. Simply giving the diagnosis of classroom problems is not enough; instructors must also be given remedies for the problems. Teaching improvement is much more likely when the feedback is discussed with the teacher by a sympathetic and knowledgeable colleague or teaching improvement specialist who helps interpret results, provides encouragement, and suggests specific teaching-improvement strategies.

Because teachers may need different kinds of help at different career stages, instructional improvement efforts must be geared to particular faculty needs. For example, new teachers fresh from graduate school will likely need help in lecturing, leading discussions, and constructing tests. Those at mid-career will likely value learning new skills, taking part in interdisciplinary work, and adopting new technologies in the classroom. Those in the latter stages of their careers will likely benefit from systematically reflecting on their teaching and becoming mentors for their more junior colleagues.

A cautionary note. Regardless of the professor's length of teaching experience, there is no single best way to improve teaching. What is effective for some may be ineffective for others. But something works better than nothing, and certain programs and approaches work very well. Programs and approaches work well to the extent that they fit both the character of the teacher and the culture of the institution (Weimer, 1990; Seldin, 1993).

CHARACTERISTICS OF
SUCCESSFUL TEACHING IMPROVEMENT PROGRAMS

The guidelines and strategies suggested in the literature are the product of a wealth of experimentation and experience. They are worth careful consideration. Institutions that are considering the introduction of a teaching improvement program or that are anxious to overcome remnants of resistance or ease sticking points in an existing program would do well to give serious consideration to this advice. What are the benchmarks of successful teaching improvement programs? Eble and McKeachie (1986), Menges (1991), Seldin (1993), and Seldin (1994) suggest the following:

✦ Tailor the program to the institution's culture.

✦ Design it for long-term impact but build it for short- term payoffs.

✦ Structure it with multiple approaches to meet individual preferences, schedules, and styles.

✦ Gain clear and visible support from top-level administrators and be sure this support is publicly articulated.

✦ Use advisory groups to design and manage the program.

✦ Start small and rely on pilot projects targeting specific needs or groups.

✦ Approach the improvement of teaching positively and offer opportunities for the solid contributors and the stars, not just those who have been ineffective.

✦ Enable teachers to participate as partners and let them exercise significant autonomy and initiative in shaping their development experiences.

✦ Enlist substantial numbers of faculty in planning and administering the program.

✦ Stimulate faculty enthusiasm and a high rate of participation in various aspects of the program. Set up a feedback mechanism to learn of tangible changes in courses, teaching strategies and methodologies, or curricula resulting from the program.

✦ Challenge teachers to stretch their individual efforts.

✦ Reduce resistance to the program not by fiat or muscle but by being willing to listen to others, explain and modify the program, and allow enough time for the program's acceptance.

✦ Recognize and reward excellence in teaching.

THE KEY ROLE OF ADMINISTRATORS IN IMPROVING TEACHING

To bring substantive improvement to college teaching requires a campus climate that supports and rewards teaching, giving it equal status with scholarly research and publication. If institutions are going to embrace superior teachers and superior scholars equally, the initiative and guidance for such transformation falls to administrative leaders. As Seldin (1990, p.9) argues: "They must champion the importance of teaching and personally crusade for this idea. In a sense they must stake their careers on this point and actively seek and find forums from which to broadcast to academia the importance of teaching. They must introduce and promote appropriate institutional polices and practices."

What kinds of concrete action might be taken by administrators in support of a higher priority for teaching? Experience suggests that the following approaches, used in combination, work well.

Making the Campus Environment More Responsive to Teaching

Each professor should be encouraged to set personal professorial goals in the classroom. Experimentation should be encouraged and viewed as a normal part of professional growth. Teaching loads should be kept to reasonable limits so the teacher has time to keep abreast of changes in the discipline.

Providing the Proper Setting and Tools to Support Instruction

Unfortunately, in many colleges, classroom conditions—including light, heat, air, and noise—are no better controlled today than they were in less technologically advanced times. Floors are not swept. Equipment doesn't work. Chalk and erasers are in short supply. Failure to pay attention to these details suggests to instructors that teaching is considered a second-class activity by the institution.

Rewarding Improved Teaching

Many teachers argue that the biggest roadblock to improved teaching is the reward system that pits teaching against research. Many institutions give lip service to the importance of teaching but then turn around and reward scholarly research and publication. Clearly the reward system needs to be reworked so that there is greater recognition of superior teaching. If teaching is not given a central role in hiring, promotion, and tenure decisions, faculty will correctly perceive that only research and publication are considered important.

CONCLUSION

Until recent years, the widespread institutional bias toward research and scholarship outside the classroom discouraged and rendered pointless efforts to improve teaching. Today, however, teaching is being taken more seriously. Swelling pressure from such diverse sources as the Carnegie Foundation for the Advancement of Teaching, the American Association for Higher Education, state legislatures, faculty, and students have moved institutions to reconsider the importance of teaching and the role of the teacher in the classroom. Countless institutions are reexamining their commitment to teaching and exploring ways to improve and reward it.

Teaching is an art and not a science. Yet, every artist needs a grounding in technique before setting to work, and there is no artist—or teacher—who cannot improve his or her skill.

No one would make light of the hurdles confronting professors intent on improvement. Progress may be slow. For some, the effort may possibly fail. But the stakes for teaching and learning are high, and the effort is imperative.

President John F. Kennedy was fond of telling a story about the French Marshall Louis Lyautey. When the marshall announced that he wished to plant a tree, his gardener responded that the tree would not reach full growth for more than one hundred years. "In that case," Lyautey replied, "we have no time to lose. We must start to plant this afternoon."Administrators and faculty intent on improving teaching also have no time to lose. They, too, must start to plant this afternoon.

In the succeeding chapters in this book, readers will find pragmatic advice on key influences on teaching quality and successful programs for improvement.

AUTHOR

Peter Seldin is Distinguished Professor of Management in the Lubin School of Business, Pace University, Pleasantville, New York. A specialist in the evaluation and development of faculty performance, he has been a consultant to more than two-hundred colleges and universities throughout the United States and in twenty-five countries around the world.

Seldin is a frequent speaker at national and international conferences and regularly serves as a faculty leader in programs offered by the American Council on Education and the American Assembly of Collegiate Schools of Business.

His well-received books include *Successful Use of Teaching Portfolios* (1993, with associates), *The Teaching Portfolio* (1991), *How Administrators Can Improve Teaching* (1990, with associates), *Changing Practices in Faculty Evaluation* (1984), *Successful Faculty Evaluation Programs* (1980), *Teaching Professors to Teach* (1977), and *How Colleges Evaluate Professors* (1975). He has also contributed numerous articles on the teaching profession, student ratings, and academic culture to such publications as *The New York Times, The Chronicle of Higher Education,* and *Change* magazine.

He has won awards both as an educator and as a grower of cherry tomatoes.

REFERENCES

Angelo, T.A. (1994). From faculty development to academic development. *AAHE Bulletin,* 46 (10): 3–7.

Blackburn, R.T., Bober, A., O'Donnell, C., & Pellino, G. (1980). *Project for faculty development program evaluation: Final report.* Ann Arbor, MI: University of Michigan, Center for the Study of Higher Education.

Cole, C.C. (1978). *To improve instruction.* ASHE-ERIC Higher Education Research Report, No. 2. Washington, DC: American Association for Higher Education.

Eble, K.E. (1988). *The craft of teaching.* 2nd ed. San Francisco, CA: Jossey-Bass.

Eble, K.E., & McKeachie, W.J. (1986). *Improving undergraduate education through faculty development.* San Francisco, CA: Jossey-Bass.

Menges, R.J. (1991). The real world of teaching improvement. In M. Theall and J. Franklin (Eds.), *New Directions for Teaching and Learning: No. 48. Effective practices for improving teaching.* San Francisco, CA: Jossey-Bass,

Seldin, P. & Associates. (1990). *How administrators can improve teaching.* San Francisco, CA: Jossey-Bass.

Seldin, P. (June, 1993). Improving and evaluating teaching. Paper presented at the American Council on Education Department Chairs Seminar, Washington, DC.

Seldin, P. (March, 1994). Improving college teaching. Paper presented at Hong Kong University, Hong Kong.

Weimer, M. (1990). *Improving college teaching.* San Francisco, CA: Jossey-Bass.

TWO

USING CAMPUS CULTURE TO FOSTER IMPROVED TEACHING

Robert A. Armour

At large and diverse institutions, which often set the tone for education, it is common knowledge that teaching is undervalued in favor of research. In the years following World War II, research and its attendant perquisites (revenue, recognized faculty, national reputation) became the most widely acknowledged measures of institutional merit. Even smaller institutions cast envious eyes on the resources and reputations of larger, research-oriented universities. First-hand experiences among faculty, as well as research data, demonstrate the validity of the assumption that research counts for more than teaching.

Change, however, is in the air, and the impetus to change this situation comes from all directions. Legislators at the federal and state levels, accrediting bodies, parents, and students themselves all demand and expect reform.

Faculty are at the center of the movement to shift their emphasis more squarely onto teaching. A nationwide survey conducted by Syracuse University found that faculty widely support a more equal balance between teaching and research, and two independent surveys of different groups of faculty from Virginia found strong support for increased attention to teaching. Faculty, however, can easily feel conflicted about their roles. They appreciate the joy that comes from conducting a stimulating class and take genuine pride in the accomplishments of their students. Yet there is joy in good scholarship too, and some faculty believe that the quickest road to career success lies in research, particularly in the larger universities. As long as faculty perceive that research is the key to success at their institutions and the primary criterion for recognition within their disciplines, teaching will remain in a subservient position.

13

Therefore, restoring teaching to first importance at some institutions will not come easy. It is, nevertheless, possible to build a campus culture that encourages good teaching and insists that teaching be given at least equal attention when compared to research. Even institutions that already emphasize teaching, such as liberal arts colleges, can improve instruction through deliberate attention to the culture that fosters teaching on their campuses. This chapter will deal with the role that the campus culture has in creating a positive atmosphere for teaching. It will use examples from four widely different campuses to illustrate the major principles that support teaching, and then it will explore the building of this supportive culture.

FOUR CASE STUDIES

Four institutions of higher education have been chosen for the study of the impact of campus culture on teaching. The four were selected for the diversity of their missions, their differing sizes, their geography, and their acknowledged valuing of teaching. Since the reward system is one of the most visible and important components of campus culture, the study of these institutions has examined messages the reward system delivers about teaching. What the reward system values will become the dominating characteristic of the culture. An adjunct to the reward system is the institution's commitment to developing teachers. Like all reflective practitioners, good teachers can become even better through deliberate training, and faculty development programs can complement the best reward systems. The studies that follow will, therefore, concentrate on reward systems and on faculty development.

Syracuse University

Among major research universities, Syracuse University stands out as one committed to teaching. With fourteen schools and colleges, over seventy-five departments and academic divisions, 15,859 students (all figures are 1993 FTE), and 1,051 faculty, Syracuse is too large and too complex to have a unitary reward system. Instead, each school or college is responsible for developing its own criteria for promotion and tenure and its own program of faculty evaluation. The university has established broad guidelines within which schools and colleges must operate, and these parameters clearly call for a renewed emphasis on teaching.

In 1992 the first major address to the campus community by the new chancellor, Kenneth A. Shaw, stated the need for the faculty reward system to create a more equal balance among teaching, research, and service. Shaw asked that academic units revise their systems to assure "an increased emphasis on teaching and advising; an improved set of procedures for both formative and summative annual evaluation of teaching and advising for tenured and non-tenured faculty; and a description of the appropriate balance, with teaching holding equal emphasis with research, scholarship and professional activity" (1992, p. 1). He called for these guidelines to influence the next round of merit salary increases.

Three years earlier, Syracuse had received a small grant from the Sears-Roebuck Foundation to fund a project that would rebalance teaching and research at the university. The project grew and expanded over the next years and became a major source for campus renewal. The involvement of high ranking officers of the administration demonstrated the university's commitment to the task.

The first goal of the project was to improve the perception on campus of the importance of teaching. The project focused on the roles of deans and departmental chairs in influencing attitudes toward teaching. These administrators were viewed as the most efficient and effective agents of change, in part because faculty perceive them as setting standards for the reward system. Over the first year of the project, numerous meetings of the deans and chairs educated them about their roles and developed in them skills for bringing about change. A book on improving teaching was prepared for their use. The deans and chairs then led their divisions in developing standards and procedures for evaluating teaching. In the third year of the expanded project, departmental faculty worked to create procedures for evaluating teaching and set standards for promotion, tenure, and merit salary increases. At this stage the project accommodated differences in need among the various disciplines.

It was into this climate that Kenneth Shaw entered as chancellor. He saw the necessity to modify the size of the student body and to reconfigure the administration to make it more effective and cost conscious. The project on teaching fit in neatly with his own goals, and he endorsed the initiatives already underway.

In increasing the balance between teaching and scholarship, the university rethought what it meant by scholarship. Shaw called for the revised guidelines to provide for the "integration of research into teaching" (1992, p. 1). In addition, he asked for "an expanded definition of research, including the relative weighing of the scholarship of discovery, the scholarship of integration, the scholarship of application, the scholarship of teaching and, where appropriate, creative professional activity" (1992, p. 2). His language was borrowed from Ernest Boyer's 1990 proposal for the reconsideration of scholarship, but the desire that the definition of scholarship be broadened to include pedagogical research took on special meaning at Syracuse. Various departments at Syracuse, as well as at other institutions nationwide, have rewritten their guidelines for evaluating faculty in order to increase the range of activities considered the scholarly, professional, and creative work of faculty. Research into the teaching of a discipline is now receiving credit in disciplines that hitherto have placed small value on such work.

Shenandoah University

Shenandoah University is a regional university located in Winchester, Virginia. In two decades it has grown from a little-known college and conservatory to a university which is beginning to develop a fine reputation, especially for its professional preparation programs. In the fall of 1993, it had 1,367 students and 128 faculty.

President James A. Davis has long been an articulate advocate for Shenandoah University as a teaching university that appreciates excellent scholarship and service as complements to the teaching mission. Provost Joel Stegall maintains that the culture there is in part due to the president using public forums to emphasize the value teaching has at the institution. Stegall says that it is important that members of the campus community talk about teaching and that the president, provost, and deans stimulate these discussions.

For the past two years the faculty assembly has been working to revise the institution's plan for faculty evaluation and development. As of this writing, the new plan has been approved by the assembly and is awaiting its expected adoption by the administration. Its principles clearly articulate the accepted attitudes on campus: "It is expected that every faculty member should be involved in teaching, in scholarly activities, and in service. In keeping with the mission of Shenandoah, the primary role of the faculty is teaching. Therefore, for most faculty, the largest portion of time will be devoted to teaching responsibilities" (Shenandoah,1994, p. 3). Later the document elaborates on this concept: "The prime responsibility for all faculty is teaching. Teaching effectiveness is considered the most important element for promotion in rank. It is also understood that scholarship, creative activities, and university and community service contribute to teaching effectiveness..." (p. 4). The faculty define teaching in broad terms: course and curricular development, class preparation and grading, various forms of student contact, and advising. All these components will be assessed during a review of a faculty member; and teaching effectiveness, as the cumulative effect of all of them, will always receive the greatest weight, when compared with research and service. According to provost Joel Stegall, the guiding question in any evaluative process is "How good is this person as a teacher?" To demonstrate teaching effectiveness, faculty are expected to present portfolios, based on the procedures outlined by Peter Seldin (1991, 1993) in his books on portfolios.

Nebraska Wesleyan University

Despite its name, Nebraska Wesleyan is a liberal arts college. When founded over a century ago, it was called a university with expectations that it would offer graduate courses, but it has instead, most recently under the leadership of current president John W. White, Jr., discovered its niche as a liberal arts college, recognized nationally for the excellence of its programs. Located in Lincoln, in 1993 Nebraska Wesleyan had 1,449 students and 113 faculty.

The faculty development plan is designed to keep faculty engaged in the process of teaching throughout their careers. From the time they are hired until their retirement, faculty are provided opportunities to grow and develop as teachers and scholars. During this time, teaching remains at the center of their careers. Draft guidelines (1994, no page) for portfolio assessment state: "The central focus at Nebraska Wesleyan University is teaching."

According to provost Janet Rasmussen, the first critical period in the career of a faculty member at Nebraska Wesleyan is the hire. The intent is to be clear at this stage about teaching expectations. As the draft (p. 1) of a new document from the faculty task force puts it, "The focus of creating a vibrant faculty is to hire excellent people and to support their continued development."

During the first year on campus, new faculty participate in a seminar coordinated by the provost. In these weekly sessions they discuss teaching, study the campus ethos—which includes the emphasis on teaching—and come to understand something about the students they will be teaching. In their second and fourth years, new faculty undergo formal reviews conducted by the Faculty Evaluation Committee. These reviews are based on portfolios and include classroom visits from their department chairs. Extensive documentation of teaching abilities is expected to be part of the portfolios. In the sixth year, the new faculty member is considered for tenure.

Once tenured, the faculty member and the university work developmentally to assure a long and fruitful career. Evaluation and development are closely connected. As Provost Rasmussen puts it, at this stage "conversations turn to providing needed resources for the faculty member." The goal is to increase cooperative work among faculty. (See the chapter by Sorcinelli, this volume). To this end, faculty collaborate in Professional Development Plans. According to a draft proposal currently working its way toward approval, all tenured faculty will file with their chairs a plan for their professional growth over the following one to five years. The plan must be developed in consultation with two or three colleagues, one of whom must be from outside the faculty member's department. This is to be a brief, but specific, plan that addresses professional growth in teaching, collegiality, scholarship, and service. Part of the plan should be a request for needed support, including financial, from the university. At the conclusion of the time specified for this plan, the faculty member must file a report on his or her success in meeting the goals of the plan. This report must be signed by the colleagues who have supported the faculty member during the process.

Huntingdon College

With 595 students and 50 faculty, Huntingdon College is smaller than some of the departments at Syracuse University. Located in Montgomery, Alabama, the college is gaining respect as a small, regional liberal arts college.

Wanda Bigham came to Huntingdon as president in the summer of 1993. As she says, the culture at the college communicates to faculty and a new president alike that teaching is important. It exerts influence—both formal and informal—on faculty to teach well. Her insight is that the culture belongs to the faculty; they are the ones who have created and sustained it. It is, therefore, the faculty who support and demand good teaching.

The formal statement of this attitude is in the Faculty Manual. Its introduction forcefully establishes teaching as the driving motivator of the faculty: "To fulfill its purpose, Huntingdon College expects its faculty members to be fully prepared academically, to excel in their teaching performance, and to excel in their ability to encourage students and other faculty members to develop in accordance with the aims of the college" (Huntingdon,1989/1990, p. 12). Later, the manual goes on to say, "It should be clearly understood that all of the criteria [for promotion and tenure] should contribute to the primary goal of excellence in undergraduate teaching. Huntingdon has been historically a teaching college and primary emphasis in decisions of promotion and tenure should be based on the teaching skills of the candidate" (p.14).

In this culture research receives scant attention. The teaching load is heavy—at least four courses a semester—and most faculty who conduct research for publication do so during the summer. Some faculty even suspect that publications would count against them in a promotion and tenure review.

One might expect, therefore, that in this environment conversations about teaching would dominate faculty relations, but such is not the case. Expectations for teaching so permeate the culture that they are taken for granted, and some new faculty wish openly for more opportunities to talk with colleagues about teaching.

As with the other institutions studied, the process of inculcating a new member of the faculty into this teaching environment begins during the hiring. One recently hired faculty member described at length her conversations with her prospective chair and dean in the weeks in which she and the college were negotiating over her accepting a position there. These discussions clearly impressed on her mind that this is a teaching college. As Dean William Top explains, after going through this process, these faculty come to the college because they want to be at this particular institution and because they want to teach.

Dean Top has been at the college twenty-four years and has put his stamp on the culture. Faculty give him credit for creating the teaching atmosphere. Not only does he hire the faculty, but he also visits with each one annually to review her or his teaching and to discuss development.

IMPORTANT LESSONS LEARNED

From these cases we can extrapolate some important lessons which define the relation between the campus culture and the emphasis on teaching:

✦ *A positive environment for teaching takes a committed president and provost or dean, who can articulate the university/college's mission in terms of teaching.* They must be able to convince faculty that this attitude is not merely polite language to satisfy various external constituents and that it will indeed drive the reward system.

✦ *The faculty have to be equally accepting of the attitude.* They are the ones who serve on promotion and tenure committees and who set standards for their disciplines. They must take pride in the teaching and learning accomplishments of their institution.

✦ *There must be clear statements in print that forcefully make public the institution's position on teaching, especially as it affects promotion, tenure, and salary.* Most often these are found in faculty handbooks or similar documents, but one wonders why the institutional mission statement might not also be an appropriate forum for such a position.

✦ *The hiring process is one of the most valuable points for establishing this culture; if you hire people who want to teach and emphasize with them the institutional attitude, important first steps have been taken.* Joel Stegall points out that involving students in the hiring, especially during a presentation by the candidate in a classroom-like setting, will demonstrate the importance the institution places on student learning.

✦ *Once hired, faculty members should be provided developmental opportunities to increase their skills as teachers.* The development plan at Nebraska Wesleyan might be used as a model for an intentional effort to keep even the best teachers growing and expanding. Faculty may come to the institution with good teaching instincts and skills, but great teachers are made, not born. (See the chapter by Ambrose, and also by Black, this volume.)

✦ *Both the institution and individual faculty members must find an appropriate balance between teaching and scholarship.* What is appropriate will vary by institution, by discipline, and by personal inclination; it will also vary at different times in a faculty member's career. Calls from Eugene Rice, Ernest Boyer, and others for a redefinition of scholarship will aid those who want to engage in forms of research that have been traditionally devalued by some academics. Diamond (1994), of Syracuse, has demonstrated that many disciplinary associations are recommending standards for scholarship in their fields that encourage the broader definition of scholarship, including research on teaching in the discipline. In emphasizing teaching, institutions must be careful not to dismiss relevant research; in particular, faculty should be encouraged to engage in research which informs and enhances their teaching.

✦ *Observations at these institutions reinforce research at Stanford University which identified departmental attributes which hinder improved teaching.* Massey, Wilger, and Colbeck (1994) have demonstrated that some aspects of departmental culture can be detriments to faculty working together to improve teaching. The major problem areas they identify are faculty isolation, fragmented communication, over-specialization, generational splits, personnel policies, constrained resources, inappropriate evaluation and reward systems, indefensible salary differentials, and superficial assessment of teaching. What is true for departments also holds more generally for institutions. Institutions laboring under the constraints of these hindrances will not easily change their culture in favor of enhanced teaching. Once institutions identify these hindrances, however, they can deliberately work to lessen their impact.

BUILDING A CAMPUS CULTURE IN SUPPORT OF TEACHING

It is possible, as Syracuse University and other institutions have done, to build deliberately a culture that values good teaching. For this to happen, certain circumstances must exist at the same time. First, there must be a commitment to change and an investment in the process. It is said that the rebellious Americans fought the American Revolution with the support of only one-third of the population. It is hard to imagine that a college could bring about fundamental changes in its culture with such thin support. Those who first see the necessity for change must document the needs and articulate them in such a convincing manner that involvement in change becomes widespread. One of the contributions from the quality movement is the question, "No matter how good we are now, what can we do to become even better?" Even very good institutions can bring credit upon themselves by trying to become better.

Second, the administration must assume central roles. There must be a vision of an improved culture, one in which teaching is more prominent or conducted to higher standards. At Syracuse someone had to say "Teaching should have equal place alongside research." At Nebraska Wesleyan, someone had to say: "We can create a climate in which even senior, tenured faculty can find renewal in teaching." The process has the greatest chance for change when this someone is the president and when he or she is closely supported by the chief academic officer.

Third, this commitment has to spread across the entire campus community. Faculty want to teach as well as they can, as good teaching leads to great personal satisfaction, but support for change is not automatic among the faculty. Some will believe that they are teaching as well as they can (and some will be right). Others see the road to career success leads through research (and some will be right, but probably not as many as think so). Others will be satisfied with the comfortable niches they have created for themselves and will not want anyone suggesting something new that will disturb their peace (these faculty need to be renewed, retired, or replaced). Despite the objections of some, however, leaders among the faculty and administration can generate strong engagement in the process of change if the need is great and their arguments invigorating.

Once the circumstances favorable for change are in synch, leaders can begin to work toward their vision of a changed culture. It will vary according to the mission of the institution and the personnel available, but there are generic traits:

✦ *Attention must be paid to the process for change.* Leaders must understand how to bring about change on this particular campus. They must know whom to involve, when to make critical statements, and what the taboo issues are. They must have a sense for timing and must be flexible. They must know which committees can be most effective in dealing with these topics, and they must have a realistic view of the costs involved.

✦ *We create culture through our stories, and a culture that encourages good teaching will be one that permits and celebrates stories about teaching.* Joel Stegall has begun to use stories about teachers at Shenandoah to build the university's reputation. Virginia Commonwealth University in Richmond published *VCU Teaching*, an attractive biannual magazine that told the stories of good teaching on campus, both past and present.

✦ *Faculty and the administration must set high standards for teaching.* In an era characterized by accountability and assessment, we can no longer be satisfied by the assumption that faculty teach well just because they have done it for years. Departments must set standards for excellent teaching which consider, among other things, student learning, the ability to motivate students, contact with students outside the classroom, and advising.

✦ *The campus culture should also recognize that faculty can be motivated by both extrinsic and intrinsic rewards.* Adequate salary, sabbaticals, faculty development opportunities, support for teaching innovations, etc. are important extrinsic motivators and will substantially improve faculty morale. A good system, however, will also seek faculty who relish the intrinsic rewards: the joys of teaching and learning, the stimulation of discovery and innovation, the satisfaction of knowing that you make a difference in someone's life. (See the chapter by Austin and Baldwin, this volume.)

VISIONS OF THE FUTURE

As difficult as it is to predict the future, it remains useful to scan the horizon to determine ideas now being discussed that have the potential for modifying campus culture and teaching in the not-too-distant future. Two such ideas brought to national discussion by the American Association for Higher Education (AAHE) in separate publications should be mentioned briefly here as examples of shifts in the way we might think about teaching. The ideas are probably controversial in some quarters, but are cited here as stimulants to further discussion.

The first is what Wergin (1994, p. 1) calls "collective responsibility." In a monograph for AAHE, Wergin calls for institutions to sharpen their missions and for members of academic units—departments, usually—to decide together how they can work to meet the institutional mission. Individual faculty within the department will work differently to meet this collective responsibility. As Wergin (p. 3) writes, "If departments define themselves in ways that contribute to the mission of the institution, and if faculty define how they can contribute to the mission of the department, the potential exists for connections that can revitalize senior faculty careers, and energize new ones." Teaching would benefit from such an arrangement because those who choose to teach will be able to devote time and energy to teaching, while others, less inclined to classroom performance, can devote themselves to other departmental activities which satisfy other components of the institutional mission. As long as the collective responsibility is met, it would little matter at the institutional level who does what within the department. The best teachers could devote themselves to their craft.

Second, an issue of the AAHE magazine *Change*, (November/ December, 1993) was devoted to the idea of "Opening the Classroom Door." As Russell Edgerton, Lee S. Schulman, Parker Palmer, and others explain it in a variety of essays, the time has come to stop thinking of teaching as something that takes place behind a closed door. Instead, teaching should become a community activity which is discussed openly, openly valued, and openly evaluated. The key to opening the door is to encourage good conversation about teaching, a theme that is echoed elsewhere in this chapter.

In conclusion, there is urgency in the need for higher education to redirect its energies. Society is probably not willing to continue to support the type of research common in many departments at most universities and colleges, and many people express concern about the quality of graduates from our institutions. Research is essential to education and must continue to occupy a critical role in the mission of higher education, but a more even-handed balance between research and teaching must be achieved. Even colleges which traditionally claim to value teaching must take seriously the opportunity to use assessment methodologies, new technologies, and advanced understandings of how students learn to improve teaching. Campus cultures must encourage commitment to teaching and must support the many faculty for whom Chaucer's description of the Clerk is apt, "And gladly wolde he lerne, and gladly teche."

AUTHOR

Robert A. Armour is Assistant General Secretary for Higher Education for the Board of Higher Education and Ministry of the United Methodist Church. He is also Professor Emeritus of English at Virginia Commonwealth University. In addition to his books and articles on higher education, he has written on literature, film, and mythology.

REFERENCES

Armour, R., Caffarella, R., Fuhrmann, B., & Wergin, J. (March,1989). Senior faculty careers and personal development: A survey. A paper presented for the American Education Research Association.

Boyer, E.L.(1990). *Scholarship revisited.* Princeton, NJ: Carnegie Foundation for the Advancement of Teaching.

Diamond, R. (1994). *Serving on promotion and tenure committees: A faculty guide.* Bolton, MA: Anker Publishing.

Huntingdon College. (1989/1990). *Faculty Manual.*

Massy, W.F., Wilger, A., & Colbeck, C. (1994). Overcoming "hollowed" collegiality. *Change* 26 (4): 10–20, 1994.

Nebraska Wesleyan University. Various draft documents from the Faculty Task Force.

Opening the Classroom Door. A thematic issue of *Change*, November/December, 1993.

Seldin, P. (1991). *The teaching portfolio: A practical guide to improved performance and promotion/tenure decisions.* Bolton, MA: Anker Publishing.

Seldin, P. (1993). *Successful use of teaching portfolios.* Bolton, MA: Anker Publishing.

Shenandoah University. (1994). *Faculty evaluation and development* (a draft document adopted by the Faculty Assembly).

Shaw, K. (Feb., 1992). Restructuring Syracuse University: Introducing a more learning-and student-centered culture. A special supplement to the *Syracuse Record 22(24).*

Survey Research Laboratory. (1991). *An Overview of results from the Virginia faculty survey.* Richmond, VA: Survey Research Laboratory, Virginia Commonwealth University.

Wergin, J. (1994). *From my work to our work: Developing cultures of collective responsibility.* Washington, DC: American Association for Higher Education. (Used in draft form).

THREE

QUALITY TEACHING: WHAT ROLE FOR ADMINISTRATORS?

Irene W. D. Hecht

I n the coming decades the quality of teaching taking place on our college and university campuses is going to be a matter of concern as never before. Those concerns emanate from within our institutions and externally from both legislatures and citizens. The public's interest in the effectiveness of university teaching is a source of stress to the academy in that it forces an examination of assumptions about quality which had not been brought into question before. While this may not mean that all past activities and standards have become obsolete, it does mean explaining the value of things once thought to be self-evident.

This focus on the quality of education, and in particular the quality of teaching, demands change in administrative behavior as well as in faculty practices. The current crisis means that administrators need to see the enhancement of the quality of teaching within their institutions as a key concern to them as administrators. Issues of budgeting and management remain important, but as the means of supporting good teaching, not as concerns with independent merit.

These changes in the landscape of higher education have induced me—as one of those who moved gradually away from teaching and research into the "exile" of administration, first as program head, dean, and eventually president—to reflect on how an administrator might focus on encouraging quality teaching.

There is a well-understood and vocally-articulated standard in higher education that the curriculum is strictly the prerogative of the faculty and that the classroom is the personal "castle" of each instructor. This is such an ingrained value that administrators are wary of treading into terrain affecting teaching for fear of violating this unspoken taboo.

However, there are legitimate ways that administrators can help lead a renewed focus on the quality of teaching without violating the prerogatives of the teacher.

There are three important areas in which administrators can strengthen the quality of teaching in their institutions. These are:

✦ helping set the agenda and tone of dialog on the campus

✦ affecting faculty behavior through the application of institutional resources

✦ encouraging awareness of and connections with external audiences and developments

Shaping the Campus Dialog

A visit to any campus lunchroom or attendance to questions asked at public lectures will begin to reveal some of the concerns and attitudes prevalent on a campus. Human beings who work and associate together develop a pattern of dialog, sometimes puzzling to outsiders, but utterly comfortable and predictable to the participants. The longer one "lives" in a particular environment, the more one becomes an unthinking participant in that grooved conversation. In a time of rapid change and crisis such as we are now seeing, it may become desirable, in fact necessary, to apply conscious effort to reshape campus conversation. Administrators should participate in, if not lead, that process.

A good place to begin for an administrator who sees a need to encourage a change in campus dialog is with a conscious effort to describe the dialog as it exists. What is talked about? Are faculty primarily concerned with turf? Are they primarily worried about keeping resources for their department? When faculty meet with administrators, what subjects do they bring up? How much administrative dialog is concerned with issues of pedagogy? Of student achievement? Of curriculum development? Of faculty development? If little administrative time is spent speaking about topics that affect the quality of teaching, it may be time to look for ways to change that reality. How might one affect the tone of campus dialog, and encourage a focus on teaching?

Because of the centrality of the department, it is an excellent place to begin. An administrator can send a strong signal of interest in the quality of teaching by asking the department to prepare a seminar where the administrator can learn something about the discipline and how it is taught. Among the topics that might be discussed are: What are the current key questions in the discipline? Are there particular schools of thought which are dominant? What are the most important concepts that the department seeks to impart to beginning students? What concepts from this discipline are important for students to master if they are to be responsible public citizens? What pedagogical methods do they find work best? What are the department's goals with their majors? What do their students do upon graduation? If there are graduate students, are they educating them as teachers as well as researchers? Are they satisfied with the quality of their students? How could they enhance student achievement?

A vital department will already be talking about these questions and will be pleased to find that an administrator is interested in these same issues. If the department has not considered these questions recently, the above can be a productive way to initiate such reflection. The dialog will benefit any department, and it will give a clear signal that the administrator is seriously interested in teaching. Furthermore, in answering these questions, a department will be reflecting on the quality of its teaching and may discover steps to improve its quality.

Other topics can be productively pursued across the campus. Chief among these is the subject of pedagogy. On every campus, there are individuals who use non-standard teaching methods. For example, on one campus a professor taught a basic methods class in sociology by pursuing a group research project in the neighboring town. Students learned together the standard research methods by applying them to a real problem. As a group they dealt with a question of interest to the local governing body, and they had the satisfaction and stimulation of presenting their findings at the conclusion of their work. An administrator can go beyond simply knowing about such work. He or she can encourage public dialog around such efforts as a means of ensuring that thinking about pedagogy is of central interest to the campus.

A specific step in encouraging such dialog can be to find funds to host seminars on pedagogical experiments on the campus or in collaboration with neighboring campuses. Two things are accomplished through that kind of initiative. First, public recognition is given to the "innovator." Second, others are encouraged either to draw from the particular innovation described or to bring forward their own. The more this occurs, the more one builds an ambiance in which pedagogical experimentation is encouraged.

Closely related to discussions on pedagogy are conversations about research. In recent years there has been a growing drive for institutions to ratchet up their quality by requiring faculty to do research. For institutions whose historical mission has been teaching, this shift in gears has been especially painful. Frequently a chasm develops between older faculty recruited in a different era for whom research was never an expectation and new, young faculty fresh from graduate school where they learned to see research as the key professional activity.

In 1990 the Carnegie Foundation for the Advancement of Teaching published Ernest Boyer's *Scholarship Reconsidered: Priorities of the Professoriate*. Boyer opened up the question of the definition of research. He made the insightful observation that in a blind dash for quality, all institutions have defined "scholarship" as the expansion of knowledge, a definition used by research universities. But this is a limited definition, and one that is *not* readily applicable in comprehensive teaching universities or liberal arts colleges.

Administrators must send the right signals concerning research in their institutions. Is the relevant definition "expanding the horizons of knowledge?" Are faculty expected to publish in refereed journals? Are other forms of research more appropriate for a particular institution? For example, classroom research, as described by Boyer, is directly related to considerations of the quality of teaching and may, therefore, be far more appropriate at a teaching college or university than is a program to support research geared to expand knowledge. An administrator can and should help to legitimate discussion of these research issues.

Another important area of pedagogy is that of technology. Ever since computers began appearing on campuses in the 1960s, we have heard talk of the communications revolution. Eventually we may see that that revolution has come quickly. For those of us living through it, the process appears frustratingly slow. A major block for a long time has been the dearth of useful academic software. That reality is changing (see Arreola, this volume). Furthermore, the advent of the personal computer, as common today as the typewriter a generation ago, has opened the possibility of applying technology to teaching in all disciplines.

Campus response to the possibilities presented by the communications revolution is uneven. For administrators there are hazards as well as opportunities. A major concern today is the expense of up-to-the-minute technology. With budget recisions an annual fact of campus life, administrators need to push for real benefits as they make expensive investments in hardware.

Again, it is administrators who can help set the tone of discussion. They can encourage the initiated to lead the novices (and recalcitrants) by demonstrating the benefits to the quality of pedagogy. It is important to open a dialog that includes consideration of the impact on teaching of these new technical tools.

Perhaps the ultimate point of influence on campus dialog is the system of faculty assessment being used. Beginning in the 1960s, universities and colleges began using student evaluations and developing systematic reviews of faculty for appointment, promotion, and tenure. Much of that process has become quasi-standardized. However, we are also hearing suggestions for developing and applying some other processes, which may give a more sophisticated measure of the quality of teaching.

One such approach is the teaching portfolio (see Zubizarreta, this volume). Portfolios can be very useful in supporting good pedagogy. By their very nature, portfolios look at an instructor's activities over time allowing teacher and reviewer to note development. Portfolios also make it possible to see in-depth the differences in presentation to small groups and large, and they provide a means of seeing the development of students as they proceed through a course. (See Annis and Jones, this volume.)

A second approach is assessment that looks at the department, instead of exclusively at the individuals teaching in the department. This approach acknowledges that the individuals forming the department create a synergy that affects the quality of the departmental experience for students. This in no way suggests that there should be an homogenized style cultivated by the individuals in the department. What it does mean is that the curriculum should be thought of from the *student's* perspective, rather than from the point of view of instructors' idiosyncratic—even esoteric—specialties. It means that the connections between courses will be discussed. It means that the work of each individual will be looked at not only for itself, but also as it helps create a coherent curricular pattern for the department.

INFLUENCING BEHAVIOR

Although establishing an ambiance in which issues of pedagogy are discussed is important as a basis for improving the quality of teaching, action will be necessary for improvement to take effect. Thus, as an administrator, one needs to look for ways to encourage changes in behavior. Or to put it another way, one needs to encourage action as well as debate. Because taking action *ipso facto* involves risk, administrators are important in lending encouragement to the taking of risks.

The kind of action vital in today's climate may require drastic modifications in very old habits. A recent issue of *Policy Perspectives* from the Pew Higher Education Roundtable (April, 1994, p. 6), points out one of the important public concerns about the effects of current styles of pedagogy.

> What troubles public officials, commentators, business leaders, and policymakers is their sense that too many institutions too regularly graduate students without sufficient skills to be either effective workers or informed citizens. Even the best and the brightest, they argue, too often exhibit a self-centered aggressiveness rendering them incapable of working with others—the sense that today's graduates can compete but not collaborate.

This observation suggests that there is a need to foster the development of team skills within higher education. Without doubt this is a difficult issue for the academy, because meeting this need would require fundamental change in academic behavioral norms. Academic training most often is an exercise in individual development. It is individual achievement which is valued. It is individual creativity and insight that is rewarded. We study alone. We write dissertations alone. We teach alone.

Why should we set a premium on team work and collaboration? We should do so because, as many of us already realize, today's problems are often interdisciplinary and can only be solved through coordinated effort. It is, therefore, not only appropriate but necessary that we hone our collaborative skills and that we impart such skills to our students.

How might an administrator encourage the development of collaborative skills within a faculty? While the means of fostering collaborative work will vary from campus to campus, here is an example of a campus team-project.

Several deans and faculty members at one institution were convinced that greater effort was needed in acculturating and mentoring new faculty. Because it was a commuter university teaching both day and night students, the campus lacked the traditional collegiate focus that could be counted on to mentor and assist new faculty. With administrative backing, the planning group went as a team to an Annual Meeting of the American Association for Higher Education (AAHE).

Although the sessions did not speak specifically to the question of mentoring new faculty, the joint attendance at a stimulating meeting gave the planning group an opportunity to share a valuable intellectual activity. They also used dinners, evenings, and break times to meet together, share impressions, and develop plans for a new faculty "curriculum."

The group returned to campus ready to function as a team. They designed their curriculum and launched it that fall. While the meeting itself did not provide specific components for the new faculty curriculum, the fact that the group had traveled together and reserved time to meet and work together on their plan helped shape them into an effective team.

The composition of the team was also helpful in building collaboration. Deans as well as faculty were team members, a fact which helped transcend the usual faculty/administrative barriers. The fact that administrators were part of the planning team guaranteed their continued support after the group returned to campus.

In addition to encouraging collaborative efforts between individual faculty, it may also be desirable to foster a broader vision of the institution at the departmental level. When institutional budgets are developed, a common practice is to stop the give and take of negotiation at the "school" level. Thus, deans will struggle within the provost's or president's staff meetings to hang on to their piece of the budgetary pie, or—with luck and persistence—to expand their share. Deans are less likely to bring chairs together to look at the school budget as an entity.

Furthermore, the components of department budgets do not often include anything but maintenance monies. There is money for supplies and student workers. Rarely do departments ever see capital improvement budgets. The effect is to limit departmental planning to academic-year cycles. Long-term planning is not encouraged. In addition, the proclivity of departments to think narrowly of their own limited interests—apart from the interests of other departments—is strengthened.

Opening the budget process at the department level may seem risky. Will it augment pressure at the dean level? Possibly, but it may also have the effect of reducing that pressure by sharing the problems along with the burdens for making tough choices. Although this may reduce some of the budgetary autonomy at the dean level, the loss may be more than compensated by greater departmental awareness of the cross-currents of pressure and desires throughout the institution. It may help departments adjust to more community-focused behaviors.

Long-term strategic thinking can also be encouraged at the department level whenever a faculty search is initiated. Never should one settle for opening a search to replace the same disciplinary talents that are being lost. A departmental vacancy is a golden moment to review the mission and goals of the department compared to its base of human resources. What does the department lack? How can existing gaps be filled through the new hire? What skills will best complement the talents of the existing department? How will this personnel decision affect cognate departments that rely on this department for course support? All of these questions should be examined in some detail both as they impact the department and for their effect on the school or institution. To do so may require allaying the department's fear that by taking the time to examine these questions, they will lose a slot. If a vacancy is going to result in a position loss, it is better to be clear about that fact at the outset and not look to a review of the department's goals as a means of justifying the recision.

BUILDING EXTERNAL CONNECTIONS

The third general area in which administrators are particularly well-positioned to encourage quality teaching is by bringing new ideas to the campus and by fostering interaction between the campus and the external community locally and/or nationally. For example, racial conflict is a source of strain on many campuses, and these frictions extend into the classroom.

Encouraging productive dialogue is a delicate and difficult matter. One resource which administrators can introduce is to bring leaders from other racial groups to the campus on an informal basis to meet with chairs, particular departments or selected individuals. A model from which one might borrow is that of the eighteenth century Parisian salons which were a productive meeting ground for individuals of varied talents. Within a purely social setting, people who would not normally have crossed paths had the opportunity to meet each other. There are times when informal social interaction can be a better resource in implementing behavioral change than anything afforded by Blue Ribbon Committees, Task Forces, or Crisis Teams. Informal social contact is a source of learning. It can also build a human resource base to which one can turn for assistance with particular problems.

Administrators should also make a point of bringing new ideas to the campus community. Because they spend some of their professional time away from campus, administrators are in a good position to see what other institutions are doing. For example, if an administrator thinks TQM might provide inspiration to the campus, she can make a point of getting to know an institution that is applying TQM, and can share that knowledge on the home campus. Administrators can facilitate visits to their campus and encourage their faculty to visit neighboring campuses.

Administrators are also in the right spot to think about innovative ways to solve problems. Does the campus need a physical chemist but lack the demand to keep such a person occupied for a full load? Would a neighboring institution be willing to arrange for a shared appointment? These are the kind of innovations that require administrative leadership.

Is the institution engaged in collaborative projects with neighboring secondary or primary schools? Are departments linked with work settings in the environs? If these external connections do not already exist, administrators can be important catalysts for initiating such cooperation. If collaborative projects do exist, administrators can see that they are maintained and strengthened. In all cases such collaborations should be reviewed to ascertain their pedagogical impact on the institution's students. One should expect it to be positive, and if it is not, it is important to ascertain how it can become so.

It is also appropriate to look at what faculty members do exceptionally well and to find ways to get those faculty out to share with others. Here I am not thinking about the traditional kind of paper writing *cum* presentation at a professional meeting. What I have in mind is featuring some of the exciting teaching that is taking place on the campus. If pedagogical change is to take place, administrators must hunt for its occurrence, recognize its existence, and provide the means of publicizing these accomplishments. It means "learning" one's institution in a different way.

In conclusion, it is time to scotch the notion that to become an administrator means that one ceases to be engaged with the classroom and hence with the quality of teaching. Teaching is the only reason for the existence of most educational institutions and is a core activity even in research universities. If administrators have become disengaged from questions of quality of teaching, it is because they and the faculties they lead have lost sight of the fact that administrators as well as faculty determine the quality of teaching at an institution (see Pastore, this volume). It is time to build effective faculty-administration teamwork in the interest of realizing the mission of excellence in teaching.

AUTHOR

Irene W. D. Hecht is an independent educational consultant. She is a Senior Associate with the American Council on Education for whom she directs a series of national workshops for department and division chairs. Formerly, she was president, dean, or faculty member at institutions in different regions of the country.

REFERENCES

Boyer, E. (1990). *Scholarship reconsidered: Priorities of the professoriate.* Princeton, NJ: Carnegie Foundation for the Advancement of Teaching.

Policy perspectives. (April, 1994). Pew Higher Education Roundtable, vol 5, #3, Section A.

Four

Faculty Motivation
for Teaching

Ann E. Austin and Roger G. Baldwin

College and university faculty members perform a variety of roles, including teaching, research, advising, consulting, and fulfilling additional duties for their departments and institutions. Given this range of responsibilities, what motivates faculty to take their teaching seriously, especially in the face of messages that often suggest that research and publication are more likely to be rewarded than time spent improving one's teaching or helping a student understand a concept with which he or she is struggling?

Many college faculty members are attracted to the profession especially because of the intrinsic aspects of faculty work. Professors can pursue their scholarly interests, share their ideas with students and colleagues, and enjoy a degree of respect for their expertise. Their work enables them to experience autonomy, complexity and challenge, responsibility for others, and interpersonal interactions (McKeachie, 1979, 1982), each of which contributes to intrinsic satisfaction and motivation. A variety of issues and pressures currently confronting colleges and universities, however, have the potential to diminish the intrinsic satisfactions that may motivate faculty members. Budget constraints sometimes lead administrators to exert more control over decision-making; for example, faculty members may have less opportunity to decide what courses they will teach, when their courses will be offered, and how many students can enroll. External demands for accountability also often result in heightened emphasis on faculty evaluation. Such trends can leave faculty members feeling a sense of diminished autonomy coupled with greater anxiety about their work. Larger classes, which make interpersonal interaction and ongoing student feedback more difficult, and greater diversity in students' abilities in courses, which create conflicting challenges for the professor, are other current trends which can threaten intrinsic rewards and motivation. Additionally, tight budgets which result in frozen or decreasing salaries relative to other professions and or in poorly maintained classrooms and equipment may be interpreted by faculty as indications that they and their teaching efforts are not sufficiently valued by their institutions. Each of these factors, not uncommon in higher education today, can threaten the intrinsic motivation that faculty members bring to their classrooms and other work (Csikszentmihalyi, 1982; McKeachie, 1982).

This chapter considers the issue of faculty motivation, particularly in regard to teaching. Following a brief comment concerning the implications of several theoretical perspectives on motivation, we discuss a variety of strategies and ideas through which colleges and universities can nurture faculty members' motivation as teachers.

THEORIES OF MOTIVATION

Several theoretical perspectives on motivation offer guidance to those wishing to design incentives to encourage effective teaching. In particular, expectancy theory (e.g., see Vroom, 1964; Porter and Lawler, 1968; Lawler, 1973; Oldham, 1976; Mowday, 1982) implies that teaching rewards must accommodate individual differences in what professors find to be motivating. Additionally, standards for teaching excellence should be set at levels that can be reasonably achieved. Need theories of motivation (e.g., see McClelland and others, 1953; White, 1959; deCharms, 1968; Deci, 1975; Deci and Ryan, 1982; and Schneider and Zalesny, 1982) imply that faculty motivation to take teaching seriously can be enhanced by environments that foster autonomy, that provide opportunities to try new ideas in the classroom, and that offer new instructional challenges. Flow theory (Csikszentmihalyi, 1978, 1982) asserts that people feel motivated when they are deeply involved in their work; for faculty, such an experience requires a balance between the individual's skills and the challenges presented in the classroom.

Theoretical Perspectives on Intrinsic and Extrinsic Rewards

The several theoretical perspectives noted above provide useful insights concerning the issue of faculty members' motivation as teachers. It also is important to point out that theorists are in some conflict concerning the role of extrinsic rewards as motivators. According to expectancy theory, both intrinsic and extrinsic rewards can be useful as ways to encourage motivation. Expectancy theory posits that the expectation of receiving rewards that are valued (whether they be intrinsic or extrinsic) enhances motivation. Mowday (1982, p. 68) explains that "expectancy theory assumes that intrinsic and extrinsic outcomes influence motivation in an additive manner. In other words, adding extrinsic outcomes to an intrinsically rewarding task (or vice versa) should serve to increase the overall level of motivation."

Others, however, believe that too much reliance on external rewards can diminish intrinsic motivation, thus having the opposite effect than desired. McKeachie (1979, 1982), for example, argues that the use of extrinsic rewards can have a negative impact on motivation over time; once motivation is based on external rewards, he asserts, the extrinsic rewards must be continually increased in order to maintain the same level of motivation. Bess (1982, p.103) explains that the use of heavy external rewards may be seen by faculty as "compensatory"— as "payment for an unpleasant activity." This perspective could cause faculty to discontinue viewing teaching as exciting and stimulating, the source of considerable intrinsic motivation. Bess also explains that, for those faculty for whom teaching is not an intrinsically motivating activity, external rewards may only prevent dissatisfaction, not necessarily encourage motivation.

Despite these serious cautions about too heavy an emphasis or over-reliance on extrinsic rewards, McKeachie (1979) acknowledges that such extrinsic rewards as salary and promotion also have the symbolic importance of indicating that a faculty member is valued by the organization. The absence of such rewards can lead professors to feel that their teaching and other efforts are not appreciated and can thus diminish their sense of intrinsic motivation. Additionally, Deci and Ryan (1980, cited in Mowday, 1982) indicate that rewards used to recognize high competence, especially in work involving considerable autonomy, may enhance motivation. In sum, while theorists caution about heavy or exclusive use of extrinsic rewards as a way to motivate faculty, a reasonable conclusion seems to be that extrinsic rewards can be useful as symbols to recognize effort and affirm institutional valuing of teaching as an activity. Of prime importance, however, seems to be the cultivation of institutional environments that convey the importance of teaching excellence and that encourage faculty to experience intrinsic rewards from their teaching efforts. (See the chapter by Armour, and also by Pastore.)

Career Stages and Motivation to Teach

While all faculty members are individuals with their own valuing of activities and sense of motivation, those interested in ways to nurture professors' motivation toward their teaching should consider the literature on the experiences that characterize faculty at different career stages (see Baldwin and Blackburn, 1981; Fink, 1984; Sorcinelli, 1988; Boice, 1992, 1993; Olsen and Sorcinelli, 1992). For example, junior faculty tend to report feeling uncertain about their ability as teachers coupled with a desire to do a good job with their teaching. Efforts to support the motivation of these junior colleagues might productively be directed to helping them develop a set of teaching skills that enables them to feel confident that they can excel at this aspect of their professorial duties. Mid-career and senior faculty members may be most encouraged by opportunities to teach in new areas, to experiment with new strategies, or perhaps to team-teach with colleagues of differing perspectives or experiences. These new challenges may enhance the intrinsic reward of teaching for these more senior faculty by increasing the level of challenge, and thus, the sense of perceived self-competence of the professor.

STRATEGIES FOR SUPPORTING FACULTY MOTIVATION

The discussion that follows offers a variety of ways that faculty and administrative leaders, and in some cases, faculty members themselves, can provide institutional environments that nurture faculty members' motivation to be good teachers. These strategies take into account key implications of motivation theories, including the importance of nurturing faculty members' need for achievement, sense of self-competence, and feelings of autonomy and self-determination. Other key factors addressed by these strategies include the importance of opportunities for intellectual and collegial exchange, for experiencing challenges, and for receiving feedback about one's work. The strategies offered are based on the premise that attention to organizational design is an important way to help faculty maintain their intrinsic motivation as teachers (Bess, 1982; Nord, 1982). The ideas below (some of which were developed by Austin in collaboration with R. Eugene Rice at a 1992 meeting on faculty motivation to teach) are organized around the themes of strategies concerning the organizational culture, strategies involving institutional structures and policies, strategies for faculty development, and strategies for institutional leaders. All these strategies nurture and support faculty members' motivation to take teaching seriously.

Organizational Culture Strategies

If faculty are to feel motivated as teachers, it is important that the institution's commitment to teaching excellence is widely known and shared by administrators, students, and faculty members themselves. Especially at research-oriented universities, faculty members receive many messages about the importance of research and publication. An organizational culture that nurtures professors' own intrinsic motivation to teach is one where teaching is a highly valued part of the institutional mission. Among the ways to convey the valuing of teaching to faculty members and others is through symbols, rituals, and ceremonies. Prominent awards, special banquets and events to celebrate teaching excellence and faculty and students committed to high quality teaching, stimulating and widely attended faculty development activities, and buildings named in honor of distinguished teachers are examples of symbols and ceremonies that nurture an organizational culture that values teaching excellence and supports the motivation of professors as teachers. Wide publicity about teaching-related events, opportunities, and issues adds to the strength of the organization's message about teaching.

A key ingredient at a university or college committed to a culture that supports faculty members' motivation as teachers is the development of networks around teaching issues. Opportunities to talk with colleagues about teaching successes, failures, ideas, and innovations contribute to faculty motivation. Among the ways to create and sustain such networks are Teaching Fellows Programs that bring together small groups of faculty for a term or academic year to discuss teaching-related topics (see the chapter by Simpson and Jackson) (Austin, 1992), Master Faculty Programs (Katz and Henry, 1988) that link colleagues from different departments for ongoing visits to each other's classes and discussions about what is observed (see the chapter by Millis and Kaplan), and informal brown-bag lunches organized around issues of common interest. Such regularly scheduled programs create networks where groups of faculty become accustomed to talking with each other about their teaching concerns. The network provides support for their dedication to teaching, even in the face of academic cultures that often elevate the importance of research and knowledge production over involvement with students and knowledge sharing.

Structures and Policies

While an organization's implicit culture is a key variable that relates to faculty members' motivation as teachers, the organization's more formal structures and policies are highly important also. While extrinsic rewards should not be too heavily emphasized, as already discussed, institutions that value teaching will ensure that effort and success at teaching are included in criteria for evaluation and reward. As Cammann (1982) points out, evaluation systems that work effectively are clear about the institution's goals and standards. However, feedback systems that encourage faculty members' motivation need not only be associated with the reward structure. An increasing number of faculty members are learning about classroom research techniques that enable them easily, quickly, and informally to get information about their students and their teaching (Angelo and Cross, 1993).

Faculty members are motivated in different ways and by different factors. Thus, one policy implication is that faculty members should understand that different kinds of contributions are valued and rewarded. While one faculty member may be motivated and talented when working with a small group of graduate students, another may have a gift for teaching large classes or lower level students. Both should be recognized and valued in the formal and informal reward structures of the organization. The key point, however, is that if a college or university wants to provide a message that it values the intrinsic motivation that faculty feel as teachers, it must be sure the reward structure indeed recognizes and rewards teaching efforts. In fact, the notion of "shaping" suggests that professors should be recognized not only for teaching successes, but also for their efforts to improve as teachers, through attending conferences and meetings, trying new ideas (even when they fail), and taking time to plan new courses or teaching strategies (Nord, 1982).

Several other structural and policy strategies can enhance teaching motivation. Since the motivation research has shown that challenge (in balance with skill) and self-determination are likely ingredients in faculty motivation, faculty members are likely to feel more motivated when they have the opportunity to choose their own teaching assignments and to vary these assignments over time. Also, classes that are small enough to ensure some degree of meaningful student-faculty interaction typically provide more opportunity for student feedback to the professor and for stimulating interaction, both of which are factors related to professors' motivation. Another way to encourage interaction and stimulating intellectual exchange that may contribute to the motivation of some faculty members is through departmental, college, or institutional projects that concern teaching issues or the curriculum. Of course, the reward system should recognize work on such projects.

Faculty Development Strategies

Faculty development programs can contribute to creating a culture where teaching is valued and can be part of the formal structures and policies of the college or university. Faculty development opportunities can strengthen faculty members' motivation to take teaching seriously by helping professors develop their sense of competence as teachers and their ability to seek and use student and colleague feedback, by supporting them as they seek new challenges in their teaching, and by providing avenues for collegial interchange and support. Effective faculty development programs are multi-faceted, including opportunities for professors at different career stages, with different career emphases, and in different disciplines. In particular, faculty development programs that enhance professors' motivation as teachers should include programs to help graduate students develop teaching competencies, support for junior faculty to help them manage time and stress and to increase their teaching self-confidence, and encouragement for senior faculty to take risks and to try new approaches in their teaching. Mentoring programs, through which more senior faculty share ideas with junior colleagues about teaching, can provide benefits for all involved (see the chapter by Sorcinelli). Institutional support for faculty members to attend professional meetings and conferences that pertain to teaching-related issues are additional strategies for encouraging professors' intrinsic motivation as teachers.

Strategies for Institutional Leaders

The commitment of senior institutional leaders, deans, and department chairpersons is essential for carrying out the strategies already presented. In particular, institutional leaders who wish to encourage professors' motivation to teach well should frequently articulate the institution's valuing of teaching effort and excellence and find opportunities to recognize such efforts in formal and informal ways (see the chapter by Gmelch). For example, the attendance of provosts and deans at events that celebrate teaching or at seminars concerning teaching issues conveys a strong message about what the institution values.

Department chairpersons have a particularly important responsibility to help junior faculty members get established as teachers.

Concluding Thoughts

Faculty in higher education tend to be motivated by the intrinsic rewards associated with doing professorial work. The opportunity to direct one's efforts, to interact with interesting students and colleagues, to pursue stimulating lines of thought, to help others learn, and to feel a sense of achievement are all rewards that faculty often experience as they teach. Faculty will feel most motivated as teachers when the institutions in which they work nurture environments in which teaching is both valued and rewarded. In such environments, teaching will be both intrinsically and extrinsically motivating for professors.

Authors

Ann E. Austin is an Associate Professor and Coordinator of the Higher, Adult, and Lifelong Education Program at Michigan State University. Her research interests include improving college teaching, faculty careers and professional development, and colleges and universities as workplaces. Austin's publications include *Developing New and Junior Faculty* (co-edited with Mary Deane Sorcinelli) and *Faculty Collaboration: Enhancing the Quality of Scholarship and Teaching* (with Roger G. Baldwin).

Roger G. Baldwin is Associate Professor and Coordinator of the Higher Education Program at the College of William and Mary. His publications focus on the faculty career development process, conditions in the academic workplace, and faculty collaboration. He is coauthor, with Ann E. Austin, of *Faculty Collaboration: Enhancing the Quality of Scholarship and Teaching*.

REFERENCES

Angelo, T.A., & Cross, K.P. (1993). *Classroom assessment techniques: A handbook for college faculty*, 2nd ed. San Francisco, CA: Jossey-Bass.

Austin, A.E. (1992). Supporting junior faculty through a teaching fellows program. In M.D. Sorcinelli and A.E. Austin, (Eds.), *New Directions for Teaching and Learning: No. 50. Developing New and Junior Faculty*. San Francisco, CA: Jossey-Bass.

Baldwin, R.G., & Blackburn, R.T. (1981). The academic career as a developmental process: Implications for higher education. *Journal of Higher Education 52* (6): 598–614.

Bess, J.L. (1982).The motivation to teach: Meanings, messages, and morals. In J.L. Bess (Ed.), *New Directions for Teaching and Learning: No. 10. Motivating professors to teach effectively*. San Francisco, CA: Jossey-Bass.

Boice, R. (1992). *The new faculty member: Supporting and fostering professional development*. San Francisco, CA: Jossey-Bass.

Boice, R. (1993). Primal origins and later correctives for midcareer disillusionment. In M.J. Finkelstein and M.W. LaCelle-Peterson (Eds.), *New Directions for Teaching and Learning: No. 55. Developing senior faculty as teachers*. San Francisco, CA: Jossey-Bass.

Cammann, C. (1982). Feedback systems for teachers. In J.L. Bess (Ed.), *New Directions for Teaching and Learning: No. 10. Motivating professors to teach effectively*. San Francisco, CA: Jossey-Bass.

Csikszentmihalyi, M. (1978). Intrinsic rewards and emergent motivation. In M.R. Lepper and D. Greene (Eds.), *The hidden costs of reward*. Hillsdale, NJ: Erlbaum.

Csikszentmihalyi, M. (1982). Intrinsic motivation and effective teaching: A flow analysis. In J.L. Bess (Ed.), *New Directions for Teaching and Learning: No. 10. Motivating professors to teach effectively*. San Francisco, CA: Jossey-Bass.

Deci, E.L. (1975). *Intrinsic motivation*. New York, NY: Plenum.

Deci, E.L., & Ryan, R. (1982). Intrinsic motivation to teach: Possibilities and obstacles in our colleges and universities. In J.L. Bess (Ed.), *New Directions for Teaching and Learning: No. 10. Motivating professors to teach effectively*. San Francisco, CA: Jossey-Bass.

Deci, E.L., & Ryan, R. (1980). The empirical exploration of intrinsic motivation processes. In L. Berkowitz (Ed.), *Advances in experimental social psychology. Vol. 13.* New York, NY: Academic Press.

deCharms, R. (1968). *Personal causation: The internal affective determinants of behavior.* New York, NY: Academic Press.

Fink, L.D. (Ed.). (1984). *New Directions for Teaching and Learning: No. 17. The first year of college teaching.* San Francisco, CA: Jossey-Bass.

Katz, J., & Henry, M. (1988). *Turning professors into teachers: A new approach to faculty development and student learning.* New York, NY: Macmillan.

Lawler, E. (1973). *Motivation in work organizations.* Monterey, CA: Brooks/Cole.

McClelland, D.C., Atkinson, J.W., Clark, R.A., & Lowell, E.L. (1953). *The achievement motive.* New York, NY: Appleton-Century.

McKeachie, W.J. (1979). Perspectives from psychology: Financial incentives are ineffective for faculty. In D.R. Becker and W.E. Lewis, Jr. (Eds.), *Academic rewards in higher education.* Cambridge, MA: Ballingcr.

McKeachie, W.J. (1982). The reward of teaching. In J.L. Bess (Ed.), *New Directions for Teaching and Learning: No. 10. Motivating professors to teach effectively.* San Francisco, CA: Jossey-Bass.

Mowday, R.T. (1982). Expectancy theory approaches to faculty motivation. In J.L. Bess (Ed.), *New Directions for Teaching and Learning: No. 10. Motivating professors to teach effectively.* San Francisco, CA: Jossey-Bass.

Nadler, D., & Lawler, E. (1977). Motivation: A diagnostic approach. In J.R. Hackman, E. Lawler, and L.Porter (Eds.), *Perspectives on behavior in organizations.* New York, NY: McGraw-Hill.

Nord, W.R. (1982). Behavior modification in a loosely coupled system: Thoughts about motivating teaching performance. In J.L. Bess (Ed.), *New Directions for Teaching and Learning: No. 10. Motivating professors to teach effectively.* San Francisco, CA: Jossey-Bass.

Oldham, G. (1976). Job characteristics and internal motivation: The moderating effect of interpersonal and individual variables. *Human Relations* 29: 559–569.

Olsen, D., & Sorcinelli, M.D. (1992). The pretenure years: A longitudinal perspective. In M.D. Sorcinelli and A.E. Austin (Eds.), *New Directions for Teaching and Learning: No. 50. Developing new and junior faculty.* San Francisco, CA: Jossey-Bass.

Porter, L., & Lawler, E. (1968). *Managerial attitudes and performance.* Homewood, IL: Dorsey-Irwin.

Schneider, B., & Zalesny, M.D. (1982). Human needs and faculty motivation. In J.L. Bess (Ed.), *New Directions for Teaching and Learning: No. 10. Motivating professors to teach effectively.* San Francisco, CA: Jossey-Bass.

Sorcinelli, M.D. (1988). Satisfactions and concerns of new university teachers. *To Improve the Academy* 7: 121–131.

Vroom, V.H. (1964). *Work and motivation.* New York, NY: Wiley.

White, R.W. (1959). Motivation reconsidered: The concept of competence. *Psychological Review* 66: 297–333.

FIVE

CREATING A CULTURE OF COMMITMENT AS A FOUNDATION FOR TEACHING EFFECTIVENESS

Joseph M. Pastore, Jr.

Passages. It seems tolerable if not appropriate for one to reflect on thirty years of teaching, including twenty-three as Dean, Provost, Executive Vice-President and, more recently, four as Trustee. After all, for most academicians introspection and the search for meaning in one's work is often at the methodological core of academic life. Understanding what we do and how we do it is fundamental to improvement as well as a sense of fulfillment.

Reflections pose pitfalls, of course. One can succumb to the temptation to wax nostalgic and allow the positive illusions of early memories to suggest that academia is indeed in a state of crisis and a return to the college of two or three decades ago is the only salvation for the future of higher education. Or, one can wax narcissistic, engage "war stories" that boldly pronounce a correlation between one's own experience and the way things are (or ought to be) in higher education. Or, one can wax instructive and describe for those who may follow what it is like to return to the classroom after more than two decades of administrative life.

Fortunately, the urge to engage nostalgia seems terribly premature; the personal sense of excitement about teaching and living in an academic community is as alive today as it was in 1965. No nostalgia here. And, too many years of knowing that one's personal experience is rarely indicative of the larger community's sense of things urges a refrain from narcissism—as compatible as such an exercise may be with the academic human condition. Thankfully, the self-serving wisdom to continue to

49

teach through nearly every year of a twenty-three year administrative tour has blunted an opportunity to measure the effects of a chasmal shift from the administrative suite to the classroom. Besides, the latter experience has been described eloquently elsewhere (Schuman, 1994).

Though hints of nostalgia, narcissism, and personal lessons from the past are apt to seep into any retrospective analysis, the real incentive for this chapter is the urge to capture and recount some measure of the changed landscape in the culture and climate of academia and, most critically, the significance such changes suggest about the quality and effectiveness of what the academy is all about: teaching and learning. This urge comes from the not so surprising two-fold logic which counsels, first, that a college or university is nothing if it does not engage as its primary work the instruction of young and not so young minds (see the chapter by Wagschal & Wagschal) and, second, that the quality and effectiveness of such teaching is conditioned upon a variety of variables but none so necessary as the fertility of an academic community's culture of commitment. It is the latter and its changing impact which offer the focal point for what follows.

TRANSCENDING TECHNIQUE IN THE IMPROVEMENT OF TEACHING

The spectrum of tactics to improve teaching is reasonably recognized throughout the higher education community (Rice & Austin, 1990; Seldin, 1990; Angelo, 1994). Such tactics range from pure scholarship to formal faculty development programs to shaping institutional climate through policy formulation to emphasizing the nexus between leadership and teaching effectiveness.

Each, of course, has its limitations. For example, a mere leap of academic faith urges that teaching cannot be without scholarship nor scholarship without teaching; when one "wrastles" with the other it defines what a real university is all about (Healy, 1988). But there is something limiting and naive about the assumption that if one knows a discipline through scholarship one need only write and lecture about it to teach it. Similarly, efforts to formalize the development of teaching are necessary but constrained in that such programs are rarely sufficiently tailored, must endure the present day preoccupation with cost effectiveness and, unfortunately, too often fail to reach those who need it most (Seldin, 1990, p. 7-8). Managing institutional climate through policy formulation supportive of teaching (e.g. changes in the balance between teaching and research; reward systems; governance systems) moves us closer to fostering teaching improvement, but even such efforts fall prey to dysfunction, especially when policies are politicized, malevolent or punitive in tone, poorly crafted, or inappropriately administered.

It is tempting to conclude, therefore, that if basic teaching and scholarship, formal faculty development, and the creation of policies and strategies designed to enhance institutional climate are necessary, but not sufficient to meet teaching effectiveness objectives, one must nudge the logic a notch more, as some have done, and establish a dependency between leadership and teaching effectiveness (Green, 1990; Birnbaum, 1992). A cogent premise. But the purpose here is not to suggest, in the wake of a near quarter century of personal experience as a university administrator, how the attainment of effective teaching reduces to effective leadership. In fact, it may be fair to say the intent here is quite the opposite; it is exactly the preoccupation with academic leadership and the consequent understatement of the need for more systemic commitment within academic institutions that is at the core of concerns facing higher education. The idolatrous age of managers as heroes may finally be fading (Huey, 1994).

What this chapter will argue, therefore, is that foundational keys for teaching effectiveness will not be found so much among the debates over teaching and scholarship, nor the mechanics of faculty development, nor the reconstruction of institutional policy, nor even the heroics of leadership. Rather, until our college and university communities come closer to creating an inherently renewed sense or culture of commitment within their own communities by better understanding how larger systems influence (positively or negatively) our academic institutions, we cannot hope to lay a sufficient foundation upon which effective teaching may be built. Just as economists have come to understand that no nation's economy can be managed merely by economic technique and understood independent of global political, cultural, and economic forces, academicians must also transcend the temptation to seek solutions to such fundamental needs as teaching effectiveness without first understanding how campus culture is shaped by the culture of larger systems (Fallows, 1993; Boyer, 1994).

THE LARGER SYSTEM AND ITS INFLUENCE ON INDIVIDUAL ORGANIZATIONS

There is a road in the middle of a small village in Westchester County, New York which wends a serpentine path up a slight hill to a plateau on the fringe of the village's main business district. The curves are pronounced and fun to drive when one is not in a hurry. But there are moments, especially in inclement weather, when vehicles and bikers have been known to skid into trouble and cars moving too fast have crossed the median line bumping or crashing head on with opposing traffic. From a bird's eye view, one wonders why this road ever assumed such a dramatically curved configuration; clearly this is a case where a straight line would have been both the shortest and safest path and the nature of the gently sloping terrain would have permitted such a route.

It is not until one pauses to understand the effect of larger systems upon smaller and often dependent systems that apparent anomalies, such as the existence of a serpentine road where a straight road appears equally feasible and desirable, become less contradictory. In this case, the serpentine road is the result of the pre-mechanized turn of the century need to ease the burden of horse-drawn milk wagons from the center of town to a major dairy situated at the crest of the hill. In effect, the nature and design of one system (e.g., the road) is the result of impediments and forces imposed by a larger system (dairy logistics) and the matter as to which of the two systems will be controlling in the design and behavior of the other reduces to factors of power, costs, benefits, traditions, and trade-offs. In this case, the dairy which was quite large in its service to a major portion of the New York City area and therefore quite central to the economy of both the village and the region, would come to dictate the conditions under which most "support systems" would be designed and operated.

The notion of dependency and interdependency between systems has been explored in a variety of ways (Boulding, 1961) and has received renewed interest in recent years through the work of Peter Senge and his colleagues at the MIT Center for Organizational Learning. Senge, author of *The Fifth Discipline* (1990), joins with Fred Kofman in an exploration of the "primacy of the whole" and the relationship of the whole of an organization to the wholeness of larger systems when they observe the human tendency to see solutions in myopic rather than systemic ways:

Decomposition is a time honored way of dealing with complex problems but it has big limitations in a world of tight couplings and nonlinear feedbacks. The defining characteristic of a system is that it *cannot* be understood as a function of its isolated components. First, the behavior of a system doesn't depend on what each part is doing but on how each part is interacting with the rest....

Second, to understand a system we need to understand how it fits into the larger system of which it is a part....

Third, and most important, what we call the parts need not be taken as primary. In fact, how we define the parts is fundamentally a matter of *perspective and purpose* (emphasis added), not intrinsic in the nature of the "real thing" we are looking at (Kofman and Senge, 1993, p. 7).

The use of systems-based thinking has been a cornerstone of scientific analysis for years. In recent decades, such thinking has found its way into the management of organizations in a variety of forms to include service or product design, marketing, information management, and organizational development. What, one might ask, is its relevance to teaching effectiveness?

Systems, Commitment, and Teaching Effectiveness

The somewhat subtle reasoning with respect to systems and their interdependencies should not be lost in the effort to find ways to improve teaching. Teaching, too, is a system with its own parts. Teaching involves subject matter, skills, reasoning, learning objectives, and communication. But, teaching also involves a relationship to other systems. Teaching requires a teacher who often is part of a community of scholars or teachers and students who are part of a community of learners. Together, teachers and learners form a college which requires a variety of support components. Most critically, however, a college or academic community is not an entity unto itself, but as Kofman and Senge suggest, a system that is part of a larger system.

It is not until we define "parts" of the academic system in terms of what Kofman and Senge cite as "perspective and purpose, not intrinsic in the nature of the 'real thing' we are looking at" that we begin to understand, as suggested earlier, that the foundation for the improvement of teaching is not likely to be found in teaching itself, nor scholarship, nor faculty development programs, nor institutional policy, nor leadership, but through a focus on and commitment to a larger "perspective and purpose." Commitment, in this case, simply means a willingness to work hard, to strive to understand what one's academic institution and pursuits stand for, and ultimately to behave in a manner which leavens the likelihood that an institution's credo will be achieved even in the midst of larger countervailing systems. In academia, heroism and commitment to a credo translate to a willingness to devote and even risk one's professional (and sometimes personal) life in the service of teaching others.

The notion of teaching effectiveness and a sense of commitment to teaching and learning and to academic organizations as systems has been addressed in a compelling fashion by Parker Palmer in his fascinating spiritual exploration of teaching effectiveness, *To Know As We Are Known* (1983). In the chapter entitled "To Teach is to Create a Space...," Palmer suggests that "learning space" (one might substitute the term system for space) has three major dimensions: openness, boundaries, and an air of hospitality (Palmer, 1983, p. 71). Among these three characteristics, the notion of openness and the need to assure teaching and learning a free, uncluttered, unfettered learning environment (e.g., free of classroom logistical clutter or inordinate institutional politics), seems axiomatic and easily understood. Similarly, the characteristic of hospitality is equally digestible as a component of good teaching, for good teaching requires debate over dogma within the context of political tolerance—a space wherein learners feel free to express ideas, not without creative challenge, but without rancor and ridicule. But Palmer's notion of "boundaries" prompts pause because notions of learning spaces (systems) with simultaneous characteristics of openness and boundaries appear contradictory.

Palmer dramatizes the need for and dynamics of boundaries when he cites Benedicta Ward's passage from *The Desert Christian* (1975) which characterizes the sense of limits, boundaries, and discipline found among monastic teachers who lived in "cells," caves, or huts:

> The cell was of central importance in their asceticism. "Sit in your cell and it will teach you everything," they said. The point was that unless a man [sic] could find God *here*, in this one place, his cell, he would not find Him by going somewhere else. (Ward, 1975, p. xxiii).

And Palmer continues to note:

> For this reason, many monks to this day make a "vow of stabili-
> ty" as part of their monastic life. With this vow, they renounce
> the temptation to believe that some other monastery would be a
> better place to learn and grow. For that temptation often arises
> just at the point where the true knowing begins, the point where
> we are forced to face our illusions. Good teachers know that dis-
> comfort and pain are often signs that truth is struggling to be
> born among us. Such teachers will not allow their students, or
> themselves, to flee from the "cell." They will hold the boundaries
> firm… (Palmer, 1975, p. 73).

It is the marriage of Kofman and Senge's discourse on systems within
systems and Palmer's prescription of a "teaching space" characterized by
openness and hospitality, but with boundaries, which introduces the need
for a culture of commitment as a foundation for the improvement of
teaching. Boundaries prompt focus. Focus spawns commitment. Commitment mitigates thoughtless distraction by the forces of larger systems.

How Are We Doing?

To bring practical meaning to the notion that academic systems or
cultures are part of and influenced by larger systems as well as the idea that
a sense of bounded commitment to the "cell" which is academia is fundamental to effective teaching "space," it is useful to survey ways in which the
academy's culture of commitment, and therefore effective teaching, has
been or is penetrated by the forces of larger systems and cultures.

What are some major points of boundary penetration and what
should be done about them? A reflection on the past thirty years in higher education calls attention to four major exogenous forces which,
together, represent a larger system capable of undermining academic
commitment and, therefore, teaching effectiveness: (1) forces which
define quality; (2) forces which define leadership; (3) market forces; (4)
forces which erode faculty commitment.

The Measurement of Quality

The world, surely the competitive Western world, is immersed in
the quest for quality and universities are part of the effort. Terms such
as "assessment," "value added," "quality circles," and "total quality
management" (TQM), or "total quality improvement" (TQI) have

found their way into the language of educators as much as they dominate the rhetoric of corporate managers. Sometimes the preoccupation appears compulsive; I once witnessed a full morning of debate among educators from throughout the United States as to which of the two terms, "TQM" or "TQI," is more appropriate.

Traditionally, the measurement of quality in higher education has been and, for the greater part, remains elitist. "Prestigious" is the operative term for quality. But the meaning of "prestige" comes from the Latin "praestigium" which translates to "magic," "illusory," or "full of deceitful tricks." And so, it is little wonder that our society has been lulled into measuring the quality of an academic institution (and implicitly its teaching effectiveness) by such popular measures as longevity, name recognition, wealth, alumni networks, and athletic prowess. Regrettable is the tendency on the part of the public, but professional educators as well, to rely disproportionately on journalistic assessments of "quality" as reported in popular magazines, college guidebooks, and other similar publications. The result is that the larger world's (system's) measure of quality has been reduced to a search for "designer label" degrees or, as an outgrowth of our society's fascination with a "Super Bowl" standard, a search for "number one."

The point is that our waxing tendency to judge quality through imprecise, popular, external measures serves only to drag educators away from Palmer's "teaching space" or Ward's "monastic cell" and is hardly helpful to the development of teaching effectiveness. Comparing one college against another merely on the basis of popular standards breeds costly, self-serving competition which rarely serves the public interest. The temptation for faculty, for example, to judge themselves more in relation to the larger, external system lifts Palmer's requisite "boundary" and causes the focus to shift from a concern for the student and his or her learning to a focus on oneself in relation to others and by a standard of measure often irrelevant to teaching effectiveness.

But quality measurement requires comparison. The corporate world, for example, is constantly measuring quality through "benchmarking" and "best case" comparisons. Unfortunately, the focus is almost always external. Instead, the key to effective teaching and its recognition, is to spend more time in one's "cell" and to measure quality in terms of student development (rather than faculty development) and to do so as an internally comparative measure of performance—individually and institutionally—over time. An institution's ability to demonstrate a level of faculty and student achievement today which surpasses that attained yesterday and all in the interest of serving its special mission and societal niche is the only effective measure of teaching performance. All else is illusory and merely in the service of bugling prestige.

A personal story and footnote. A predecessor as dean, now 85 and a volunteer reading teacher for elementary school children, attracted the interest of *The New York Times.* When the interviewer posed a question as to why his universally acknowledged success was so, my colleague and friend responded very simply, "Rapport with my pupils." That, it seems, is what teaching effectiveness and a culture of commitment—staying in one's "cell"—are all about.

FORCES WHICH DEFINE LEADERSHIP

As noted earlier, the correlation between teaching effectiveness and leadership is generally established. But, that is not to say that leaders consistently spawn effective teaching. In fact, there appears to be some evidence (Birnbaum, 1992), to show that to the extent teaching is less effective, changes in the definition of academic leadership may be part of the cause.

While there are no doubt a variety of reasons why academic leadership is less than it ought to be, there appears to be a pattern or thread of reasons which have one aspect in common: they each reflect a tendency on the part of leaders to stray from the "cell" and to channel commitment not to "teaching space" but to "spaces" influenced by systems outside or peripheral to the academy.

Central to the external distractions appears to be the influence of corporate culture upon academia. There are a variety of fronts where the "boundary" of the academy is pierced by corporate culture:

✦ Boards of Trustees are typically dominated (by influence if not number) by corporate executives.

✦ A "management by idolatry" culture spawned in part by management journals and executive biographies which describe leadership models in corporate terms through the glorification of corporate heroes.

✦ The formal preparation and in-service education of higher education administrators shaped, in part, by trainers, educators, and curricula adopted essentially from business school models.

✦ The dramatic shift in the proportion of academic enterprise which is not central to teaching and scholarship, but to the management of auxiliary services, athletics, institutional advancement, student life, student recruitment, information technology, and the need for creative financial strategies.

✦ A seemingly national preoccupation with careers and career development, especially in management and leadership circles.

✦ A preoccupation with the real need to ratchet down the cost of higher education and the temptation to mimic the transformational restructuring strategies of the corporation without fully understanding that corporate "transformation" is essentially fictional. The classical *raison d'être* (maximization of owner wealth) in fact remains unchanged in the midst of corporate restructuring. Academic restructuring, however, threatens institutional purpose because so much of what an academic institution is about is not markets, but the fundamental infrastructure of specific people, curricula, and institutional history.

The apparently overwhelming influence of the larger corporate system upon the academic appears to have recast academic leaders in ways which place them beyond the boundary of academic enterprise. College presidents, judged more and more in terms of corporate measures of performance, are forced to decide whether they will leave their academic "cell" or hold true to an ideology which may seem to some inordinately altruistic in the midst of difficult managerial issues. Increasingly, college presidents and other academic leaders are reduced to demonstrating their allegiance to the "cell" in ways which distill to inspirational platitudes mouthed through undifferentiated ceremony, rather than a lived experience actively reflective of "respect for my pupils." Images of power are more frequently expressed (to use Ken Boulding's taxonomy) on the basis of threat or at best exchange, rarely in terms of integrative or love-based power so fundamental to teaching (Boulding, 1990). Conversations about cost overshadow conversations about credo, and leadership behaviors focus more on the seemingly heroic transformational rather than mundane, but fundamentally important, transactional (Burns, 1978). Too often administrators seek, or so it seems, to be served rather than to serve, and career administrators seem more intent on getting a job than doing one (a view echoed by Clark Kerr, 1994, p.14).

As academic leadership tends to stray more and more from its "cell," the ability of trustees and other campus leadership to even recognize much less understand the level of commitment to the "cell" required to assure effective teaching is likely to fade, giving rise to the probability that, as followers are apt to do in response to leadership, others, especially faculty and students, will also leave their "cells" like Norway lemmings.

MARKET FORCES

If our tendency to use "prestige-based" external measures of quality causes us to lose a student-based measure of quality so fundamental to teaching effectiveness and if our corporate-based models of leadership cause academic leaders to drift from discourse on credo to discourse on cost, it is the forces of the marketplace which threaten to separate our students from the "boundary" of our teaching "cell."

At the core of marketplace concerns is the dramatic shift in college admissions from a mostly selection and "admission" function to a marketing and sales function. Predictions offered by Dick Chait that "market conditions will radically alter the landscape and ground rules of college admissions" (Chait, 1992, p. B-1) are emerging as woefully true. The impact transcends marketing communications, advertising, and colorful, promise-laden brochures. Examples are mounting to demonstrate that U.S. colleges have evolved strategies for recruiting blocks of foreign students, for negotiating financial aid packages on a real-time reiterative basis in response to counter-offers (*The New York Times*, July 6, 1994), and for devising pricing strategies which attract the attention of the U.S. Justice Department and its concern for price fixing and collusion. Freshman enrollments at two-year community colleges have outstripped private sector four year colleges—a clear indication that "price sensitivity" has arrived in higher education.

The concern about the effect of market mechanics on the academy is not limited to a merely philosophical tug between one's definition of an academic community as an intellectual center versus that of an economic center. No, the issue strikes directly at the likelihood that efforts to improve teaching can be as successful as we may hope. The essential import of a market-centered relationship between a college and its students is that it, again, separates students from teaching "space" and places them more in an adversarial role as customers rather than to embrace them as partners or shareowners in the learning process.

The contagion of the marketplace does not stop with students. Faculty, like students, are also seen in economic rather than human terms. Price sensitivity breeds a cost-consciousness which in turn tempts trustees and administrators to view faculty as short-term assets and long-term liabilities which in turn prompts contentious and distracting debates about the need for tenure. Students become pitted against faculty when each spring the major documentation for tuition increases is announced in terms of the need for incremental funding to provide faculty salary increments—a major budgetary pressure given the labor intensive nature of academic entities. Hardly a relationship conducive to effective teaching.

Few doubt the need for colleges and universities to become more responsive to stemming the cost of higher education and striving to reap some of the efficiencies of a market driven environment. What we have not yet learned, however, is how to avoid the economic pitfalls of a cloistered cartel by opening our economic boundaries to a more efficient market system of management while at the same time insuring that the boundaries we require to define our teaching space as opposed to our economic space are clearly defined and respected.

FORCES WHICH ERODE FACULTY COMMITMENT

The plot thickens. As members of the academic community (especially alumni and, to some extent, parents) seek prestigious bragging rights which distill to functional measures of quality, as academic leaders more and more seek to mimic corporate leaders, and as students embrace an economic rather than intellectual alliance with their college, it should come as no surprise that the "cell of intellect" many faculty seek when they first decide to enter a "teaching space" too often appears as a confused, distracted system in search of perspective and purpose. Scan the pages of commentary on the current state of faculty and it is littered with themes of conflict, bashing, a preoccupation with the economics of the profession, retirement incentives, questionable ethics, sexual and gender politics, and other forces larger than the teaching "cell."

In the short term one wonders if we will ever "hear faculty voices" as Ted Marchese (1992) suggests we should; in the long term, the real fear is that beyond those faculty who will leave the "cell" in response to larger distractions, the next generation of faculty may never even know that such a "cell" exists. Clark Kerr cautions "…it is more difficult than it once was to get university teachers to take seriously their departmental and college responsibilities…They wish to concentrate more on their own affairs and not those of the institution" (Kerr, 1994, p. 14). One wonders whether "their own affairs" includes a commitment to teaching.

WHAT CAN WE DO?

It is not enough to merely accept the need for commitment as a foundation for teaching effectiveness. The challenge is to determine how to foster a committed community and leavened teaching climate. Ted Marchese (1992, p. 4) suggests that "you can trash a profession and wind up losing it. Another way to lose it is to ignore the harder work of renewal." What form might renewal and efforts toward assuring teaching effectiveness take? Each campus must do what it can, but the following observations may help to set the tone and spirit for what might be done:

✦ Commitment must be more to ideals and credos, not to mechanistic techniques or synthetic policies. Purpose, not process, will be a major source of resolve in difficult moments (whether financial crisis or a down day in the classroom).

✦ There should be no false images. Reasoning and research (Pascarella and Terenzini, 1991) indicate prestige does not assure teaching effectiveness and learning.

✦ There should be no false idols. Teaching effectiveness will not be found in good leadership alone. Commitment to teaching must be systemic; every aspect of the institution must commit, in its own way, to teaching space.

✦ Preserve rituals of commitment to teaching and allow everyone, especially students, to participate and celebrate in some way; don't assume main celebrants must always be individuals of hierarchical authority.

✦ Honor the past (especially teaching successes) through daily discourse. Consider everyone as bard; note the frequency with which tales of past academic achievement (distilled to student performance) are laced throughout the campus—including trustee meetings (and wonder why, if they are not). Stories shape commitment (Greeley, 1994; Campbell, 1988).

✦ Wonder why there is no such thing as a national ranking for teaching effectiveness, but avoid the urge to create one.

✦ Establish clusters of teaching rally points. Create departmental commitment, where appropriate, to teaching which results, for example, in student scholarship and publication, exemplary performance on licensure or certification examinations, or the encouragement of students to pursue careers in teaching.

✦ Ask students if they know who "owns" the college (it is assumed, with some reservation, the question need not be directed elsewhere). If their response includes the trustees, president, or basketball coach(!), find ways to instruct on the meaning of campus ownership, both *de jure* and *de facto*.

✦ Beware of transformational leadership without systemic understanding. Run the college efficiently, downsize if you must, but wonder why it had to be and recognize that academic restructuring, unlike corporate restructuring, means the loss of institutional memory, myth, and personalities which shape commitment.

✦ Do not expect presidents to leave their "teaching cell" and conform to a corporate model of leadership. When presidents leave their "cell," the rest of the administration is at least expected to follow. The result is segmented commitment or, if everyone follows, none at all.

✦ Engage the world through consultations, professional and corporate affiliations, and service, but always return to the teaching "cell" to translate such experiences in ways which promote learning and scholarship.

✦ Respect criticism but ignore critics. Bashing the academy is an unnecessary distraction and saps commitment. Maintain the obligation to revisit and renew on a good faith and continual basis *what* the institution stands for, *who* it serves, and *how* it operates; realize that what the institution stands for should change very little, that who it serves should change only in response to whom the institution can serve best, and that how it operates affords the greatest opportunity for change and innovation, providing the "what" is not violated.

The call for a culture of commitment as a foundation for teaching effectiveness is genuine. Commitment is not a euphemism for a return to a cloistered academy indifferent to worldly matters. Commitment is a threshold to excellence and performance. The academic community should find ways to test the premise of commitment as a foundation for teaching excellence. Ask the question: who are our best teachers and why? Be prepared to find the best among those who do not become tangled in the distracting debate between teaching and scholarship; who have come to balance the need for purpose with the need for process in teaching; who are respectful of leadership, but not dependent upon it for teaching effectiveness; and who have learned to remain quietly in one place with their students.

AUTHOR

Joseph M. Pastore, Jr. is Professor of Management in the Lubin School of Business at Pace University in Pleasantville, New York. Since 1965, he has integrated teaching and administration, having served over a twenty-three year period as dean, provost, and executive vice-president at St. Bonaventure University, Pace University, and Boston College while continuing to teach and engage in scholarship. He has also served as a member of the Alumni Council of the Institute for Educational Management, Harvard University, and is currently a trustee at Siena College. His scholarship has bridged business policy and strategy, dispute settlement, and the management of higher education.

REFERENCES

Angelo, T. (June, 1994). From faculty development to academic development. In *AAHE Bulletin*, p. 3.

Birnbaum, R. (1992). *How academic leadership works.* San Francisco, CA: Jossey-Bass.

Boulding, K. (1961). *The image.* Ann Arbor, MI: Univ. of Michigan Press.

Boulding, K. (1990). *Three faces of power.* Newbury Park, CA: Sage.

Boyer, E.L. (March 9, 1994). Creating the new American college. *The Chronicle of Higher Education,* p A-48.

Burns, J.M. (1978). *Leadership.* New York, NY: HarperCollins.

Campbell, J. (1988). *The power of myth.* New York, NY: Doubleday.

Chait, R. (May 20, 1992). The growing hucksterism of college admissions. *The Chronicle of Higher Education.* B1.

Colleges caught in the middle as parents seek best deal. (July 6, 1994). *The New York Times,* p. A1.

Fallows, J. (1993). Looking at the sun. *The Atlantic Monthly,* p. 69.

Greeley, A.M. (July 10, 1994). Why do Catholics stay in the church? Because of the stories. *The New York Times Magazine*, p. 38.

Green, M. (1990). Why good teaching needs active leadership. In P. Seldin (Ed.), *How administrators can improve teaching*. San Francisco, CA: Jossey-Bass.

Healy, T. (June 1988). 'Wrastling' at the university. *Higher Education and National Affairs*, p. 7.

Huey, J. (February 1994). The new post-heroic leadership. *Fortune*, p. 42.

Kerr, C. (January/February 1994). Knowledge, ethics and the new academic culture. *Change*.

Kofman, F., & Senge, P. (August 1993). Communities of commitment: The heart of learning organizations. *Organizational Dynamics*, p. 5.

Marchese, T. (November/December 1992). Hearing faculty voices. *Change*, p. 4.

Palmer, P.J. (1983). *To know as we are known*. New York, NY: Harper-Collins.

Pascarella, E., & Terenzini, P. (1991). *How college affects students*. San Francisco, CA: Jossey-Bass.

Rice, R.E., & Austin, A.E. (1990). Organizational impacts on faculty morale and motivation to teach. In P. Seldin (Ed.), *How administrators can improve teaching*. San Francisco, CA: Jossey-Bass.

Schuman, S. (April 1994). Gladly teaching. *AAHE Bulletin*, p. 3.

Seldin, P. (1990). Academic environments and teaching effectiveness. In P. Seldin (Ed.), *How administrators can improve teaching*. San Francisco, CA: Jossey-Bass.

Senge, P.M. (1990). *The fifth discipline*. New York, NY: Doubleday.

Ward, B. (1975). *The desert Christian*. New York, NY: Macmillan.

Six

TA Training: Making a Difference in Undergraduate Education

Beverly Black

Graduate student teaching assistants (TAs) play a major role at many universities in providing a high-quality learning experience for undergraduate students. At large institutions, TAs typically instruct between twenty-five and fifty percent of the undergraduate classes, usually in small groups or in one-to-one situations. In this setting, they have a unique opportunity to enhance the educational process. They make it possible to personalize undergraduate education and to introduce students to active learning situations. Well-run discussions, lab sessions, and individual work during office hours encourage students to practice thinking in the discipline. It helps them develop the skills necessary for analyzing material, solving problems, and grappling with difficult questions. TAs also provide much of the assessment and feedback that students receive. Teaching assistants need training and support to effectively fill the role of TA as well as to launch their careers as teachers.

The University of Michigan Mathematics Experiment

The Center for Research on Learning and Teaching (CRLT) at the University of Michigan has a number of programs that have been developed over the years to train and support graduate student teaching assistants. All of our programs are designed to enhance or supplement departmental TA training programs. Departmental training provides TAs with the assistance and support they need to teach in their disciplines. For the past few years, I have been working with the Mathematics Department to develop a comprehensive training and support system for TAs and new faculty. I will use this project as a case study for some of my later remarks on what I think is important in TA training programs.

My involvement in the Mathematics Department began when CRLT staff conducted midsemester assessments (using student discussion groups) to gather data at midterm on students' perceptions of the first semester of the introductory calculus course. The outcome of that process helped to stimulate a project that is changing how mathematics is taught and learned at the University of Michigan. Over the past several years, I have collaborated with the department to revise the curriculum and pedagogy in the two-semester introductory calculus course (called the New Wave Calculus Course). An essential part of this revision is the development of a comprehensive teaching development program and support system for all TAs and faculty teaching the course.

The "New Wave" Course

The project has moved the course away from a dependence on rote learning. Instead, the program uses real life story problems and graphing calculators to help students understand calculus graphically, numerically, algebraically, and through writing. Students are given more responsibility for learning from reading, writing about mathematics, participating in cooperative learning activities in the classroom, and through working collaboratively with a small homework group. Emphasis is on helping students learn to think, read, and talk about mathematics.

Teacher Training

The course is taught in sections of about 30 students and has common midterm and final exams. The 50 to 75 sections of the the course are taught by new TAs, experienced TAs, new faculty, and some more experienced faculty. Since the course requires a drastic change in the way mathematics has been taught at the University of Michigan, everyone teaching New Wave Calculus is required to participate in the teaching development programs. All new TAs and new faculty go through the course. In addition, the department is rotating senior faculty through the course so they will learn the new methods and strategies for teaching. Most of the instructors find that the teaching development program is essential in helping them develop the new skills they need to teach the new calculus course. The program includes a week of intensive workshops before classes begin, with instructors actively discussing and practicing the various methods and strategies they will be using in their classrooms. The program continues throughout the semester with all of the instructors meeting once a week in small groups. The groups discuss different aspects of teaching the course and exchange successes and concerns. Instructors receive midterm assessments from their students coupled with a discussion of the results with a teaching consultant. In addition, they visit and discuss each other's classes.

Because the project required a dramatic change in the calculus course, we started early in our attempts to gain the confidence of others in the department. We invited several faculty and experienced TAs to help develop and facilitate the training. Some of the early delights of the project were in the intense discussions about the teaching and learning of mathematics among those of us planning the program. In addition, we videotaped math instructors who were already using active learning strategies in their classroom. Segments of these videotapes shown in the early training sessions helped convince instructors that cooperative learning was feasible in a math class.

Training Techniques

Although teaching mathematics has been a largely private pursuit, we have found ways to make the teaching in the course visible to everyone. For example, we videotape all of the classes and watch and discuss them together (we have subsequently used some of these discussions in the training sessions). At departmental meetings, we show and discuss portions of the videotapes, allowing us to share our experiences with others in the department. We use the results of the students' mid-semester assessments to generate discussion among the instructors. The patterns of responses over all the sections and the course-wide suggestions give us information that is useful both to the instructors and in subsequent training.

Results

There are many departmental repercussions. Discussions about teaching and what it takes to learn math have become common in the department lounge. Many faculty and TAs take what they have learned about teaching and learning in the New Wave course and try the new strategies in their more advanced courses. A camaraderie has developed among those faculty and TAs who are teaching the course, and new faculty and TAs are being socialized into the department more rapidly and effectively. The New Wave course has also affected other courses. Both the precalculus course and the third-semester calculus courses are being changed to complement the philosophy of teaching and learning in the New Wave Calculus. Course-specific training programs have been added. Faculty and TAs who taught in the new and exciting course felt they had a part in helping the department to be recognized by the college for improving undergraduate education.

The Mathematics Department at the University of Michigan is developing a model of TA training that is working, though it is hard to separate its effects from the many other departmental initiatives aimed at improving undergraduate education. What started out to be training for new TAs and new faculty teaching the new course has become a vehicle for changing the teaching culture within the department. (See the chapter by Armour, and by Pastore, this volume.) During the first few years of teaching, graduate students go through at least three course-specific training programs and receive constant monitoring, feedback and assistance as they work to become effective teachers. They receive the support and help they need to teach undergraduate students as well as preparation for their careers as teachers.

Observations About TA Training

From helping to develop this model and working with and observing many other models of training, I have come to believe the following about TA training:

1. Most TA training should be located within the department with as many departmental faculty and TAs as possible planning and facilitating the training.

2. TA training and development needs to be connected with what TAs are actually doing in the classroom (both in content and pedagogy).

3. TA training and development are ongoing processes—not something that can be done in one week (or year) at the beginning of a TA's career as a teacher.

4. Teaching development opportunities should be provided for TAs whenever they are expected to do something they haven't yet done in the classroom.

5. TA training and development is generally separated too much from faculty development.

6. Teaching and learning centers are essential as a resource to help departments as they develop and improve their TA programs.

7. Mid-semester feedback both from students in individual sections and from TAs teaching in large courses can give a wealth of information for improving both the course and the training.

DEPARTMENTALLY-BASED TRAINING

There are many reasons for locating TA training in the departments. Two comments made by TAs who participated in a central (non-department) teaching orientation for new teaching assistants illustrate why:

"The teaching orientation was great, but it somehow seems unrelated to what I will actually be doing in the classroom. It isn't the fault of the presenters, there are just too many people having too many different responsibilities to be able to hit the mark for everyone."

"I left the teaching orientation after two-hours to see if I was going to be in charge of a class or be seated at the side 'assisting' the professor as I had thought I was going to do. It ended up I was in charge. It's a good thing I found out before I faced my class—so I could be prepared."

It is essential that TAs get explicit directions regarding course goals and objectives for the course they will be teaching, and that they learn the teaching strategies that are effective within that discipline. Although teaching tasks may be similar across departments, social practices, collective understandings, attitudes and values take on a cultural flavor unique to specific departments (Staton & Darling, 1989). Departmental training can help new TAs learn the norms of the department and help them develop a social support system.

Graduate students do not work in isolation. They receive many messages—both spoken and unspoken—about the importance of teaching from faculty and other graduate students in their department. These messages affect how the graduate students see their roles as teaching assistants. They tend to take teaching more seriously when faculty within the department are committed to helping them become more effective teachers.

Focusing on What TAs are Doing

A training program must address several areas of TA responsibility: what they teach, how they are expected to teach, the students they will teach, the expectations of the faculty member in charge of the course, etc. (Nyquist and others, 1989). In my experience, even generic teaching strategies are learned best in the context of learning to teach a particular course.

It is important that new TAs get critical information about departmental expectations, policies, procedures, and new ideas for teaching. Although much of this is included in departmental training, new TAs always need more information, and they are more likely to ask questions of experienced TAs than of course instructors (Staton & Darling, 1989). Thus, it is vital to have sessions in the initial training where new TAs get a chance to talk with and know experienced TAs within their department.

Departmental training works less well when the training is separate from the courses TAs will teach and the faculty in charge of those courses. But even in this case, the training gets closer to the language and norms of the department than it does with central training programs.

Faculty and TAs Assisting with Training Programs

One of the benefits of training TAs in the department is that the faculty and experienced TAs who get involved in the planning and facilitation of the teaching development program tend to become better teachers themselves. They become more reflective about their own teaching and can then share it with others.

The English Department at the University of Michigan has an elaborate training program that includes a faculty mentor for every four TAs. The small group works together for the first year, developing assignments, observing and discussing each others' classes, grading papers together, etc. The mentors who start out as good teachers quickly become even better, and some are among the top instructors at the university. I have observed the same phenomenon in the Mathematics Department. Most of those who have worked closely with the various training programs have changed the way they think about teaching and learning.

This change occurs most frequently when the mentors teach sections of the same class as the teaching assistants. The mentor then becomes a member of a working group in which members share teaching strategies. This also allows young instructors to observe and discuss the mentor's class. The project director of the New Wave calculus project at the University of Michigan didn't teach a section of the course for a year and indicated to me that he thought that he wasn't as helpful to others (and didn't learn as much) as when he was teaching a section.

Faculty in charge of TA training should consult the college's teaching and learning centers as a good resource for developing or improving a training program.

TRAINING AS AN ONGOING PROCESS

"When I went through TA training the first time I'm sure we must have talked about some of this stuff, but I had so much anxiety about teaching for the first time I didn't even know what questions to ask—so it was pretty much wasted on me. I'm glad I get another crack at learning about teaching after I've had some experience."

This quote is from an experienced TA in the math department who was going through the training program in order to teach the new calculus course. Many TA training programs in universities across the country use a one-shot approach, hitting the TAs with "everything they will ever need" before they teach. This would be like a football coach spending a week describing how to play football to a bunch of rookies: putting charts and examples on the chalkboard, describing each play and wishing them luck as they line up in the field to play against their first opponent. A football coach wouldn't do that, yet we do it to our teaching assistants all the time. Like football players, graduate students need instruction, practice, and feedback before playing and throughout the season.

New TAs are usually new graduate students, so their worlds are filled with new roles and anxieties about how they will fit in. We have found that in the initial training it is best to focus on helping them to prepare for the first few weeks of class. The more pertinent the training is to what the TA is to do, the more it gives the support the TAs need in order to gain some measure of confidence. The Mathematics Department at the University of Michigan spends a lot of time preparing for the first day since that first day can often make or break a course. New instructors practice teaching by presenting some of their first lessons to their peers and getting detailed help in preparing for their first teaching assignment. They get a chance to see other instructors in action in the classroom, and they get practice in facilitating cooperative learning, including setting up activities and using the results from group work.

One of the major goals of the training is getting instructors to think of teaching as coaching rather than performing. The training goes on throughout the semester, addressing other teaching issues as new instructors are ready to grapple with them and giving instructors feedback to improve their teaching. (This may include such things as help in giving feedback on students' homework, discussions on how to help students learn to write, and sharing strategies for helping students learn how to work effectively in groups, etc.) In addition, the course is laid out in detail so the instructors can put their major efforts into learning how to facilitate their students' learning.

Because training should be an ongoing process, training and feedback must be available in each course that TAs teach, helping them learn a variety of strategies to use in different situations. Currently, the Center for Instructional Development and Research at the University of Washington is in the process of conducting a study to better understand the developmental stages that TAs pass through in order to identify the appropriate training needed at different levels (Lambert and Tice, 1993).

Assistance With New Skills

Training and support must be available for both TAs and faculty whenever they start something new. Many TAs go through a fairly comprehensive training when they first start teaching but their responsibilities change over the years, and they are often left to figure out on their own how to do the more difficult assignments.

Most of the instructors in the New Wave calculus course at the University of Michigan found that changing the way they teach was a little unsettling. As they became skillful in using cooperative learning, many of their underlying assumptions about how students learn crumbled. The discussions about teaching and the support of their colleagues was essential for them as they developed new ways of thinking about teaching. One instructor who had not been initially sold on the idea of using cooperative learning, blurted out the following comment during one of our meetings:

> "I always thought that what it took for students to learn math was for me to explain a concept very clearly and work out an example step by step on the board. It is almost painful to find out how wrong I was. When I listen in on groups as they are trying to understand and work on an additional example, I find that most students have to go through a lot of muddle to clarify the material in their own terms before they really understand."

Expressing and discussing this new knowledge about how students learn mathematics helped all of the instructors of the course.

Midsemester Feedback

It is important for TAs to get midsemester feedback from both their students and the faculty member in charge of the course. In the English Department at the University of Michigan, the mentor visits the sections of new TAs three or four times during the semester in order to give feedback. As the TA gains experience, visits are more infrequent, but they continue for the first couple of years that a TA teaches.

CRLT has found a midsemester assessment process to be useful in helping individual TAs improve their teaching. The process uses small discussion groups to get feedback from students. It is used to help individual instructors gather data at midsemester on how students perceive their experience in the class, and it gives them assistance in interpreting and responding to the data. This often leads the instructor to make adjustments halfway through the term that make a difference for those students giving the feedback. (For more details on the process see Clark and Bekey, 1979.)

CRLT has found midsemester feedback invaluable in helping departments improve large courses and training programs for TAs. All of the TAs teaching sections of a large course go through the process and receive confidential feedback from their students. In addition, the data from across all sections are summarized to show the patterns of responses and general feedback about the course as a whole. We have used a similar process to get feedback from TAs on their experience in teaching the course and on the training they received. Feedback from TAs teaching sections of a course coupled with a summary of the students' perceptions has resulted in major changes in some large courses and TA training programs at the University of Michigan.

Mixing TA Development with Faculty Development

The results of including faculty in our training for the calculus course have been overwhelmingly positive. Typical faculty comments include:

> "For the first time in twenty years I love to teach again. Students are really learning, and they seem to be happy to be in class! I am even trying cooperative learning in my graduate class!" (This comment was made by an instructor who found the training

program essential in helping him facilitate cooperative learning activities.)

"You just don't know how interesting it is to watch videotapes of other faculty teaching the same thing I am trying to teach. Teaching has been so private this just hasn't happened before."

"I found out that I am not the best teacher in the department. I have learned a lot from talking to and watching the TAs who are teaching this course."

"In the past there were very few faculty and teaching assistants with whom I could discuss teaching. Now teaching seems to be a common conversation around the department."

Comments such as these, as well as seeing first-hand how some "seasoned" faculty struggle as they change their teaching, have convinced me that we are shortsighted if we don't find ways to include faculty along with graduate students in departmental teaching development programs. At the University of Michigan we have found that including a teaching development program with course and curriculum revisions has made a big difference in undergraduate education.

TEACHING AND LEARNING CENTERS AND CENTRAL TRAINING PROGRAMS

Teaching and learning centers can be an important resource for TA training. Staff in centers typically have a solid background in the literature on teaching and learning and a wealth of experience in working with faculty and teaching assistants. In addition, they have planned and conducted workshops and training programs.

Lambert and Tice (1993) describe 28 of the best university-wide training programs in the country. Many of the centralized programs featured share responsibility for TA development with faculty in the disciplines. And some of the universities have departmentally based training with the teaching and learning centers working as a support to those programs (e.g., Cornell, Harvard, the University of Washington).

It is my belief that teaching and learning centers can make the biggest difference as catalysts for good training programs across the campus and as partners and/or consultants to departmentally based programs. Centers can: (1) help design training; (2) provide training for faculty and staff who are developing and facilitating the departmental training; (3) assist with the collection of assessment data; (4) provide opportunities for TA coordinators from across disciplines to discuss and exchange ideas about TA training; and (5) provide resources to departments.

Additional training programs that we found to be important are optional university-wide TA workshops to complement those in departments, consultation services for individual TAs, and the development and facilitation of programs for international TAs (ITAs) that require expertise beyond what departmental personnel can provide. (It is important, however, for ITAs to also receive training within the departments with special effort to socialize them into the departmental networks.)

Many universities across the country provide most of the training of their TAs through central training programs. Some are very good, and they are certainly better for TAs than no support. However, it is very difficult for a central training program to focus on the specific tasks that the TA will be required to do. When departmental training is not available, TAs have to find out independently what is expected of them within the specific departments and courses that they teach. (Sadly, in my experience, some of them never find out.) The biggest problem with central TA training programs is that they take the responsibility of preparing graduate students to teach away from departments (where it can make the biggest difference in undergraduate education and in preparing graduate students for a lifetime of teaching). At the University of Michigan, those TAs who seem to gain the most from the central training programs are those from departments that send a faculty member to the programs and subsequently help the TAs build on and relate what they have learned to their responsibilities within the department.

I strongly agree with the view of Lambert and Tice (1993, p. 17) who say that: "On most campuses, even those with the most comprehensive, sophisticated, and effective centralized programming, the reality is that the quality of the graduate teaching assistantship experience depends directly on how willing faculty in the disciplines are to commit themselves as mentors and guides."

AUTHOR

Beverly Black is a member of the staff for the Center for Research on Learning and Teaching (CRLT) at the University of Michigan. Since joining CRLT in 1973, she has worked with a variety of programs in faculty and TA development. In 1983, Black started concentrating on the development and implementation of training programs for graduate teaching assistants.

REFERENCES

Clark, J., & Bekey, J. (1979). Use of small groups in instructional evaluation. *POD Quarterly, 1.*

Lambert, L.M., & Tice, S.L. (Eds.). (1993). *Preparing graduate students to teach: A guide to programs that improve undergraduate education and develop tomorrow's faculty.* Washington, D.C.: American Association for Higher Education.

Nyquist, J.D., Abbott, R.D., & Wulff, D.H. (1989). The challenge of TA training in the 1990s. In J.D. Nyquist, R.D. Abbott, and D.H. Wulff (Eds.), *New Directions for Teaching and Learning: No. 39. Teaching assistant training in the 1990s.* San Francisco, CA: Jossey-Bass.

Staton, A.Q., & Darling, A.L. (1989). Socialization of teaching assistants. In J.D. Nyquist, R.D. Abbott, and D.H. Wulff (Eds.), *New Directions for Teaching and Learning: No. 39. Teaching assistant training in the 1990s.* San Francisco, CA: Jossey-Bass.

SEVEN

FITTING PROGRAMS TO INSTITUTIONAL CULTURES: THE FOUNDING AND EVOLUTION OF THE UNIVERSITY TEACHING CENTER

Susan A. Ambrose

The success of any faculty development program in improving teaching depends in large part on how well it is integrated into the institution. This integration naturally takes time as the program evolves, but there are critical prerequisites which, we discovered through our experience, can help to enhance the program's formation and its performance within the institution. Initial positioning of the program strategically within the institution takes careful thought and a lot of planning. This chapter describes the establishment of one faculty development center and identifies tenets which are important for the successful creation and maintenance of any faculty development program.

I discuss the founding and development of a center because it is important to understand the conditions under which successful programs have been created and maintained. Although we often see the "finished product," like a beautiful theorem, poem, or sculpture, what we really learn from is the process of how it was created.

I use the narrative approach for several reasons. I was a graduate student in the Department of History when the University Teaching Center began at Carnegie Mellon. I witnessed the birth and participated in the development of the Center, first as a graduate student, then as associate director (1986), co-director (1988) and currently, director (1991). So, it is natural for me to recount the unfolding of events which lead to the creation and success of our faculty development program. I also use the narrative approach because, as an extended example, it shows the many forces which shaped our program in a context that readers can compare to their own institutions. Finally, we all learn from stories, despite the fact that, or maybe because, "no one's stories are quite like anyone else's..." (Coles, 1989, p. 11), and so I offer this story as just one example.

Overview: The University Teaching Center in Context

Let me begin with a brief overview of the institution because the nature of an institution (its mission, size, organizational structure, faculty characteristics) greatly influences the creation and maintenance of a faculty development program. Carnegie Mellon (CMU) is a private research university with approximately 4400 undergraduate students, 2700 graduate students and a faculty of 547. It is small enough to be amenable to change. The university is organized around seven colleges which include 27 departments, and the deans and department heads know each other and senior administrators well. CMU is an institution that, within a relatively short period of time, grew in reputation and status from a small, regional technical institution to a research university with a national reputation.

Like many faculty development programs, the role of the University Teaching Center (UTC) at Carnegie Mellon (established in 1982) is to organize and conduct programs to improve the quality of instruction at the university. The Center helps both faculty members and graduate students to improve their teaching practices by introducing them to theories of teaching and learning, providing opportunities for reflection, encouraging practice, and providing feedback. The UTC offers public forums to discuss and explore issues related to teaching and learning along with private consultations on course design, implementation, and evaluation. Individual consultations are the principal activity of the Center and are strictly confidential. Whenever possible, the Center facilitates discussions of teaching and learning across departments and colleges both to address common concerns and to help transfer and adapt promising strategies to a variety of contexts. The Center always aims to respond to the continually changing educational needs of the campus community. In any given semester, at least 32 percent of the CMU faculty interact in some way with the UTC, and this percentage has remained consistent since 1986, although the individuals involved with the Center change.

We attribute this success to the careful attention we paid to important building blocks in the early phases of conceptualization of and planning for the Center. While the details may vary from campus to campus, there are vital components necessary for the success of any faculty development program. I introduce these key factors for success, which we have learned through the years, as tenets in the rest of the chapter.

THE FOUNDING OF A CENTER

Tenet 1: Recognize the Importance of Getting Buy-In from the Constituencies Necessary for Success at Your Institution

The impetus for the faculty development program at CMU was neither external motivation (e.g. legislative pressure for improvement) nor market driven (e.g. part of the TQM movement or an attempt to "catch up" with competitors). Rather, it was internally motivated by President Richard Cyert who was concerned with the increasing number of complaints about the quality of education at the university. He was alerted to the situation by faculty course evaluations administered each semester for every course on campus (published in a pamphlet and available on-line) and complaints which he heard during his open office hours and the student luncheons which he sponsored periodically. Because the impetus was internally-driven, we had the luxury of time on our side—time to get "buy-in" from the deans, department heads, and the faculty, which is vital to the success of any program. In our case, both time and the size of the institution made it relatively easy to establish and maintain contact with each of the 7 deans and 27 department heads.

In order to determine how to proceed, Cyert turned to a long-time faculty member who had joined CMU's History Department in 1954 and knew the University well. Professor Ted Fenton had successfully accomplished all that CMU asked of its faculty: he had received a large number of research grants, published widely, consulted both nationally and internationally, and won the University's most prestigious teaching award. His "insider" track and accomplishments would be important in building the credibility of both the idea and the Center.

Tenet 2: Clearly Define What You Mean by "Faculty Development"

As part of the solution to the student-identified problems, President Cyert narrowed the broad definition of professional development for faculty from support to help faculty improve the performance of all of their professional responsibilities to support to help faculty improve their teaching and thus positively impact student learning. The president was not concerned with the research or publishing activities of the faculty because many had already proven themselves in these realms. The Center's mandate, then, was broad but focused solely on the educational mission of the university, and while we use the term faculty development in our work (and in this paper), we really mean both faculty and instructional development; we try to promote faculty growth by helping faculty members to acquire knowledge, skills, sensitivities, and techniques related to teaching and learning, and we try to improve student learning by helping faculty members to prepare effective courses and learning materials (Gaff, 1975).

Tenet 3: "Listen" to all Perspectives—Administrators, Faculty Members, Graduate Students, Undergraduate Students—in Determining Issues to Address and Priorities to Set for a Faculty Development Program

In order to determine where to begin and to get buy-in from the various constituencies up front (Tenet 1), Fenton spent a semester interviewing all of the senior academic administrators, all 7 of the deans, all 27 department heads, about a dozen influential senior faculty members, about a dozen junior faculty, and a sampling of graduate and undergraduate students. He asked each group to identify needs based on their experiences in courses and to provide suggestions to help us respond to those needs. From these discussions we distilled a number of guiding principles specifically tailored to our institution but applicable to many others.

✦ Develop a culture of teaching which parallels the culture of research so that teaching is viewed as scholarly.

✦ Keep responsibility for improving and promoting the importance of effective teaching where it belongs—in departments.

✦ Enlist the active support of key administrators and key faculty so that the notion of a center and the importance of improving teaching has validity and status.

✦ Make sure that the center is not identified as a place for "pedagogical cripples," but rather a place where faculty interested in issues related to teaching and learning and/or concerned about their teaching can go.

+ Finance core endeavors with hard money to indicate that this is not a fad but a serious attempt to provide continuous support for teaching in a rapidly changing educational environment (e.g. demographically, technologically).

+ Don't build an empire.

+ Start slow to build credibility and trust—undertake a new project or two each year while maintaining successful ones.

Tenet 4: Understand and be Sensitive to the Culture and Nature of Your Institution in Creating and Implementing Your Program

One of the messages that came across loud and clear in our discussions was the importance of understanding the institution and what is or would be acceptable to those within it. For example, like many colleges and universities, power at CMU lies within departments; consequently, we needed to recognize that responsibility for effective teaching remains with department heads who would promote and encourage use of the UTC. So, we sought input and advice from department heads about what issues we should address and how we might address them. Also, since faculty at CMU suggested during the initial interviews that "empire-building" was not necessary for success, the notion of the center had to be consistent with that: keep the staff small, be innovative and creative, and utilize faculty expertise and talent. Both Cyert and Fenton understood the institution well; Cyert knew that only an "insider" could pull off the creation of a faculty development center, and Fenton knew who and what was important in building credibility.

Tenet 5: Clearly Define Your Goals

Out of these discussions, we also determined that the goals of the UTC were three-fold. While we would not talk with faculty in these terms, we knew that we needed to:

+ Develop a culture of teaching to encourage respect for teaching so that people value it as much as they value research (because attitudes and perceptions influence behavior, we needed to influence attitudes and perceptions).

+ Provide pedagogical "development" to those new PhDs who were trained as researchers, not as teachers.

+ Provide the opportunity for pedagogical "renewal" to those experienced faculty who learned a lot over the years, often through "trial and error," but who, for example, were interested in exploring different strategies and techniques or were interested in understanding the principles underlying some of the things they successfully did.

ORGANIZATIONAL FRAMEWORKS TO CONSIDER

Once we defined the goals of the UTC, but without realizing it at the time, we carefully considered each of the four organizational frameworks which Bolman and Deal (1984) developed and Rice (1991) outlines as imperative for every faculty development professional to consider.

Tenet 6: Strategically Place the Program Within Your Organization

The "structural" frame, described as the formal elements of organizations, includes "functions of, and lines of authority for, positions and the formal rules and procedures that prescribe how members of organizations are to function" (Rice, 1991, p. 90). In our case, the Director of the UTC reported directly to the provost, with once-a-year updates to the president. Because of the reporting structure, the faculty knew that the staff of the center had a direct line to the administration. Importantly, the provost and president also understood and respected the importance of confidentiality and thus never asked us to disclose or discuss individuals with whom we were working. Finally, the president provided hard money for the Center to indicate its importance and longevity—we have never had to devote time and energy to seeking money to keep the Center afloat.

Tenet 7: Continually Focus on Identifying and Meeting the Needs of Your Constituencies

The second of Bolman and Deal's frameworks, the "human resources" frame, reminds us that "organizations are inhabited by people and that organizations function better when one attends to the needs of people" (Rice 1991, p. 90). We have always tried to identify needs and respond to those needs, whether that means creating workshops for adjunct Architecture faculty who are practicing professionals teaching for the first time, helping the engineering college to implement their new first year undergraduate curriculum, or training undergraduate lab assistants. It is faculty interests and needs which help us to identify new programs and initiatives of the Center. Thus, with justification, faculty feel ownership of the programs.

Tenet 8: Know Which Individuals are Important on Your Campus in Building a Power Base and Foster Those Relationships

The third frame, the "political frame," focuses on "power, the formation of coalitions, and the dynamics involved in the distribution of scarce resources" (Rice, 1991, p. 91). As mentioned earlier, it has always been important at CMU to garner the support of deans and department heads from whom faculty take their cues. It is equally important at our institution to get buy-in from "key faculty" to whom others look for cues, and our best example of this was the creation of an advisory committee which includes, for example, a Nobel laureate, the only tenured woman in the School of Computer Science, a recently named department head, and faculty members who are well-known and respected by colleagues from across the university. We needed to build these coalitions so that others could help us to leverage scarce university resources and provide visibility for the center in order to promote our work. It also helped that the president and provost seized every opportunity to stress the importance of undergraduate education and to praise the work of the center in enhancing teaching at the university.

Tenet 9: Be Sure That Your Program is Consistent With the Larger Culture at Your Institution

The final frame is the "symbolic frame" which encourages one to pay attention to "the elements of organizational cultures, typically values, traditions, and symbols, especially as those define meaning within the culture" (Rice, 1991, p. 91). While it is difficult to identify a few values, traditions, and symbols to represent complex institutions like colleges and universities, it is important nevertheless because people take cues from them. Our university subscribes to a research culture, and the majority of faculty come from other research institutions where they were socialized and prepared as researchers but not as teachers. We respond [in part] to this socialization of our population by framing the individual consultation process within the basic research process with which faculty are comfortable—collecting, analyzing, interpreting, and translating data (discussed later in this chapter). Ours is a relatively small institution with little bureaucracy and a high value on efficiency. Not surprisingly, our center is small with two "faculty professionals," an administrative assistant, and a part-time video technician. We knew that our faculty would call a person, not a "center," and so we keep the staff small and make ourselves highly visible and accessible so that faculty get to know us as colleagues. Ours is an entrepreneurial culture which values calculated risk-taking and innovation, so we undertake a new project or two each year to determine what works well and what doesn't.

Space is also symbolic in our institution (as in most institutions), symbolic of status and legitimacy. The first suite of offices the UTC occupied were faculty offices in one of the academic buildings that houses engineering, humanities and social science departments, faculty offices, and classrooms. These quarters validated our faculty status and the perception that the center was founded by faculty for faculty. From the beginning, we presented ourselves as colleagues who were interested in supporting others' attempts to improve their teaching. The professional staff of the center has always held faculty positions in their departments (History and now Psychology) as well, and maintain their teaching responsibilities, albeit reduced as the years go on (currently one course per year). Individual campuses all have values, traditions and rituals which, if used strategically, can lend credence to a faculty development program.

Tenet 10: Identify a Model for Change to Which Your Faculty Can Relate

Once we determined where to place the program within the university, how to generate faculty ownership, who our power base was and how to win their support, and how the culture and nature of the university would impact our work, we chose a model for developing and changing teaching behavior which permeates everything we do. The model consists of exposing faculty to theory, providing modeling, encouraging practice, and then providing specific, frequent and prescriptive feedback (Bennett, Joyce & Showers, 1987; Levinson-Rose and Menges, 1981). We expose faculty to theories related to teaching and learning, especially those which come out of the field of cognitive psychology because of CMU's strength in that area and subsequently the rest of the university's respect for this field of study (notice that this is part of the culture of the institution, Tenet 4). We provide modeling, when possible, by showing faculty what colleagues have done or are doing. For example, when we discuss course planning which results in effective syllabi, we offer several examples from different domains. When we discuss effective lecturing, we show videotapes of several lecturers at our institution. When we're working one-on-one with faculty colleagues, we suggest that they talk with or visit the classrooms, labs, or studios of colleagues who are doing similar things, often across domains. As we use this model, we talk with faculty about the importance of exposure, modeling, practice, and feedback in learning any type of new skill or body of information, and so this model is consistent with how people learn.

THE FIRST PROGRAMS

After about a year of planning, we were ready to launch some programs. If it seems as if the pre-planning stage was long and drawn out, it was, and it should be if one wants to create a program which becomes an accepted and integral part of the institution.

Tenet 11: Start Slow and With the Least Threatened Group on Your Campus

We began in the 1982–83 academic year by creating programs for the least threatened group on campus, graduate student teaching assistants. It appeared that all of the groups Fenton interviewed agreed that the center should begin by working with teaching assistants and, because some faculty showed signs of feeling threatened, we agreed that this was the place to begin. We created a series of workshops to prepare graduate students to effectively fulfill their teaching responsibilities.

Tenet 12: Involve Key People in Planning and Implementing the Program Who Then Become Your "Allies" and "Marketers"

In the process of creating the workshops for graduate student teaching assistants, we both consulted faculty about what we should include in the workshops and involved them in running the actual workshops. We also instituted a one-day orientation for incoming faculty. That orientation has now grown to three half-days (voluntary) and draws between 50–60% of the incoming faculty (both new PhDs and experienced teachers) each year. As with the TA workshops, we asked veteran faculty members to help us plan and conduct the sessions. For both of these programs, we invited "key" faculty on campus to participate (a suggestion which came out of the initial interviews). We defined "key" as faculty who were well-known and respected in research and in securing grants but who were also "closet pedagogues," very strong teachers with an interest in teaching. These were the people who eventually suggested that we offer similar development opportunities to faculty in the form of workshops or seminars (some of these people also later became members of our advisory committee).

Tenet 13: Be Patient and Persistent

Responding to the suggestion from those faculty members who participated in the TA workshops and Incoming Faculty Orientation, we began to offer a faculty luncheon seminar series each semester. We advertised the luncheon series as a forum for faculty members to hear and learn from colleagues across the campus. We facilitated some of the discussions ourselves and asked faculty colleagues to facilitate others. We polled the faculty to determine what topics would interest them, and began with those topics. As a result of continuous polling, we have always varied themes between very general pedagogical issues which transcend domain, such as planning courses, lecturing effectively, and monitoring students' learning, to issues more specific to certain domains, such as teaching studio and lab courses. We also capitalize on faculty research, for example, with a series on understanding experts' problem-solving skills in order to teach them, and we capitalize on faculty teaching experience with a series which examines how and why faculty use collaboration in their teaching.

In addition to creating and implementing these programs, we initiated discussions early on about the need to better prepare the "faculty of the future." We offered to help departments or colleges create programs which went beyond TA training to provide graduate students with the opportunity to discuss and reflect on theories about teaching and learning and the opportunity to practice techniques and create teaching materials.

Tenet 14: Create a Reputation of Credibility and Trustworthiness Which Can Facilitate One-on-One Consultations

Conducting TA workshops, incoming faculty orientation, and faculty luncheon seminars gave us enough exposure in the first few years to build our credibility with the faculty and foster a sense of trust which eventually lead to what we consider the principal activity of the Center: consulting with individual faculty members on issues related to effective instruction.

THE HEART OF THE PROGRAM: INDIVIDUAL CONSULTATION

Tenet 15: Offer a Smorgasbord of Support Services, but be Sure that the Opportunity for Individual Consultation is a Part of any Program to Improve Teaching

Today, we consult with faculty on a variety of issues, including such things as designing or revising courses, clarifying objectives, developing learning experiences to achieve stated objectives, exploring new instructional techniques, and improving presentation skills.

If a faculty member would like feedback on a course, the center staff uses Nyquist and Wulff's (1988) "research perspective," a method with which our research faculty are quite comfortable. In brief, we collect data from a variety of sources including interviewing the instructor, students, and TAs, analyzing previous student feedback, examining syllabi and other course materials, and observing or videotaping the class over three or four sessions. We then analyze and interpret the data to find patterns and inconsistencies and identify strengths and weaknesses of the course and the teaching style. Finally, we translate the information into recommendations for specific strategies to modify the course or classroom behavior. If faculty are not interested in the entire process, we use the component(s) which faculty chose. We believe that this is the most important service we offer because it enables us to customize our discussions, feedback, and suggestions to individual faculty, taking into account faculty personalities, specific domains, and types of courses. We are able to determine problem areas, suggest creative solutions, observe the faculty member experimenting with some of the recommendations, and provide further feedback to close the loop. While we often find ourselves working with a faculty member concerned about an individual course, we find that the "lessons learned" almost always carry over into other courses the individual teaches.

Tenet 16: Anticipate Success

One of the unexpected advantages which faculty members quickly identified early on was that the UTC provided the only forum on campus for them to meet colleagues from outside their departments. Adding to this delightful interaction was the epiphany on the part of the faculty that colleagues from different departments *actually* have things in common when it comes to teaching. Because of the small size of the institution, faculty at CMU often identify more strongly with other scholars in their fields than with colleagues in their own institution (Fenton, 1991).

Consequently, getting faculty to talk with each other, across departments, about issues related to teaching and learning is a definite change in the culture of our institution.

INTEGRATION

The University Teaching Center, after twelve years of existence, is now fully integrated into the institution and has had a marked effect on the culture of the university. This integration and changed culture is evident in several ways:

✦ Even with a change of administrations in 1991, the center has flourished. President Robert Mehrabian continues to support, both financially and in public forums, the work of the center. In July of 1991, the new president created the position of Vice Provost for Education as the primary academic officer responsible for increasing leadership and innovation in undergraduate education.

✦ Until two years ago, the UTC offered the only forum on campus which brought faculty members from different disciplines together for discussions related to teaching and learning. Because of the success of this model, this now happens regularly through not only the UTC but also through a series of Educational Research and Development Seminars and the Center for the Design of Educational Computing.

✦ In June of 1993 the University Teaching Center moved into a new suite of very nice offices in a prime location on campus. This move symbolized to the campus community the ever-increasing importance of teaching at Carnegie Mellon.

✦ In May 1994, Carnegie Mellon created the Center for Innovation in Learning (CIL) as a site for educational research and development in order to encourage and facilitate innovative, efficient, and effective teaching and learning at Carnegie Mellon. While closely tied to the UTC, the CIL's main emphasis will complement UTC activities by conducting educational research linked to major disciplines, with a primary focus on CMU courses in which the UTC can assist instructors and with broad potential applications.

✦ Each semester an increasing number of faculty members, including senior faculty members, use the Center, often on the recommendations of their colleagues. An increasing number also opt for the individual consultations, including classroom observations and student interviews.

While there are many approaches to improving the quality of teaching and learning on college campuses, many different models of faculty development programs, and many different campus cultures which influence the previous two, I am confident that the general tenets for successful faculty development programs outlined here hold true for large state universities, small liberal arts colleges, and community colleges as well.

AUTHOR

Susan A. Ambrose is Director of the University Teaching Center and Lecturer in the Department of History at Carnegie Mellon University. She received her doctorate in American history (1986) from Carnegie Mellon and is co-author with Cliff Davidson of *The New Professor's Handbook: A Guide to Teaching and Research in Engineering and Science.* Ambrose has designed and conducted seminars for faculty and administrators throughout the United States and Canada.

REFERENCES

Bennett, B., Joyce, B., & Showers, B. (1987). Synthesis of research on staff development: A future study and a state-of-the-art analysis. *Educational Leadership,* 45: 77–87.

Bolman, L., & Deal, T. (1984). *Modern approaches to understanding and managing organizations.* San Francisco, CA: Jossey-Bass.

Coles, R. (1989). *The call of stories: Teaching and the moral imagination.* Boston, MA: Houghton Mifflin.

Fenton, E. (1991). *Developing a culture of teaching in a small research university.* Pittsburgh, PA: University Teaching Center.

Gaff, J.G. (1975). *Toward faculty renewal.* San Francisco, CA: Jossey-Bass.

Levinson-Rose, J.L., & Menges, R.J. (1981). Improving college teaching: A critical review of research. *Review of Educational Research,* 51: 403–434.

Nyquist, J.D., & Wulff, D.H. (1988). Consultation using a research perspective. In K. G. Lewis (Ed.), *Face to face: A sourcebook of individual consultation techniques for faculty instructional developers.* Stillwater, OK: New Forums Press.

Rice, D.R. (1991). What every faculty development professional needs to know about higher education. *To Improve the Academy,* 10: 89–96.

EIGHT

LOW-COST OR NO-COST INSTRUCTIONAL DEVELOPMENT ACTIVITIES

Ronald D. Simpson and William K. Jackson

It might seem paradoxical that individuals responsible for a large, comprehensive, university-based instructional development program (Simpson and Jackson, 1990) with a budget of several hundred thousand dollars would write about inexpensive ways to improve teaching. However, we believe that even the most costly of our programs at the University of Georgia (UGA) is inexpensive when examined using any cost-to-benefit measure. Faculty support is crucial to the success of any instructional development program, and this support can be maintained only if there is the perception that funds allocated to the program are being used wisely.

This chapter focuses on approaches to teaching improvement that we have implemented at no cost or very little cost. We first describe activities designed for individuals and then discuss activities for groups of faculty members. Inexpensive in terms of absolute as well as relative measures, these approaches can be used in even the most resource-limited environments. Activities such as those discussed here are especially important during times of tight budgets. During these times a few dollars, administered centrally, can stimulate innovation and renewal in spite of even the most limited departmental resources.

ACTIVITIES FOR INDIVIDUALS

Individual Consultation

Most experienced instructional development practitioners agree that one-on-one consultations with individuals provide the best opportunities for improving teaching (Lewis, 1988). Faculty members who are having

91

difficulty with their teaching should be able to receive confidential one-on-one consultation through their institution's instructional development office. In addition, the availability of individual assistance is an important management tool for academic administrators responsible for addressing the teaching deficiencies of their faculty members.

Although individual consultations with faculty members do not require any direct allocation of funds, these activities can consume substantial amounts of staff time. The key to an effective, low-cost program of individual consultation is the use of volunteer peer consultants whenever possible. As a well-established instructional development program, the University of Georgia's Office of Instructional Development (OID) has access to a corps of faculty members who are especially skillful at certain aspects of their teaching. Once the professional staff has diagnosed the problem, help is sought from the faculty member best suited to address the problem needing attention.

In this model, the instructional development office serves a facilitating role. Faculty are encouraged to support and assist their colleagues, and most one-on-one consultations can be provided with no direct allocation of funds and limited staff time. Commitments of large amounts of staff time are reserved for complex cases needing intensive professional assistance.

Mentoring

Mentoring programs have become regular components of many faculty development efforts (Wunsch, 1994). While an individual consultation is likely to be a short-term effort to address a specific instructional problem, a mentoring relationship is more likely to be long-term and address the mentee's development in a more holistic way. (See the chapter by Sorcinelli.) Like individual consultations, mentoring programs can be established at virtually no cost except for the staff time needed to administer them.

At the University of Georgia, mentoring relationships are established through our Teaching Improvement Program (TIPs). This program matches junior faculty members, typically in their first or second year on the faculty, with senior faculty members who serve as their mentors in a teaching improvement activity (Diehl and Simpson, 1989).

The mentor and mentee visit each others' classes and engage in ongoing discussions about teaching. In many cases the mentors report learning as much as the mentees. Some of the mentor-mentee relationships established in the TIPs activity end after one quarter; others continue indefinitely. The only cost for this program is the staff time needed to recruit potential mentors, publicize the program to potential mentees, and match the mentors and mentees based on teaching areas and course schedules. At UGA this program is also available to teaching assistants.

Handbooks

A number of outstanding handbooks for college teachers are currently available (Brookfield, 1990; Davis, 1993; McKeachie, 1994). At UGA, we place McKeachie's *Teaching Tips* in the hands of every new faculty member. For many, this is their first exposure to the literature on college teaching. Although most do not read the handbook cover-to-cover, it is a ready reference for them when they have to address an instructional problem or question, and many report using the helpful tips found in the McKeachie volume. Although the unit cost of a commercially distributed handbook is typically about twenty dollars, a locally produced handbook tailored to the individual institution can be produced for much less. We use both approaches. We purchase *Teaching Tips* for each of our new faculty members, and we prepare an institutional handbook for our teaching assistants. These are both relatively low-cost means of placing effective teaching tools in the hands of large numbers of instructors.

Mini-Grants

We have found that small amounts of money can sometimes contribute to significant improvement in teaching. For example, at our institution funding for travel to present research papers is more readily available than funding for travel to a teaching conference or seminar. However, a small grant to partially fund travel to such a conference or seminar will frequently be matched by departmental sources. The same is true for purchases of software or other instructional materials. An instructional mini-grant of a few hundred dollars can, therefore, serve as leverage to attracting departmental support for an instructional activity. In addition, these grants can serve as seed money to lay the foundation for future institutional or externally supported grants for instructional innovation. Recipients of these mini-grants can also be called upon to disseminate the results of their activities in a newsletter article or at a teaching seminar or workshop.

At UGA, instructional mini-grants range from $100 to $500, with the most common being about $250. A letter describing the need to be addressed is the only application that is required. Requests are considered on a rolling basis, and mini-grant awards are made throughout the year. Requests are reviewed by the instructional development staff using the potential for improving teaching as the principal criterion in funding decisions. In contrast, other OID grants that result in awards of several thousand dollars require substantial applications, are awarded only one time each year, and then only after extensive peer review by a panel of faculty and staff members.

ACTIVITIES FOR GROUPS

Colloquium for New Faculty

Organizing a one- or two-day activity for new faculty members is an outstanding way to introduce new members to the academic and social community. With very little cost, a comprehensive overview of the institution and its resources can be provided. In addition, new arrivals appreciate the opportunity to meet key personnel within the administration and find out to whom they should direct questions. This is also a very effective way to provide the new faculty members with information about the instructional support that is available to them. New faculty members play an important role in maintaining or shifting the organizational culture (Boice, 1992), and an emphasis on instruction during a colloquium for new faculty will help promote instructional excellence as a major institutional objective.

Figure 1 is a generic model of a two-day colloquium showing some popular topics for the activity. While emphases will vary depending on the nature of the institution, we find that most new faculty members are anxious to learn about such things as the students, promotion and tenure policies, research opportunities, instructional support services, benefits, the library, and the computer center.

Follow-up Activities for New Faculty

As a follow-up to the beginning-of-the-year orientation, many institutions find that it is beneficial to bring the group back together at the end of the year. At the University of Georgia, all new faculty members are invited back to share with the chief academic officer (CAO) the "highs" and "lows" for the year. This event is structured so that the new faculty meet in small discussion groups led by senior faculty and, in turn, each discussion leader then reports to the full group in the presence of the CAO a summary of the discussions. This format protects the

FIGURE 1

A General Model of a Two-Day Colloquium for New Faculty

First Day

8:30 am	Registration
9:00 am	Welcome and Opening Remarks Vice President for Academic Affairs
9:15 am	History of The University A Professor of History
10:00 am	Coffee break
10:30 am	Legal Issues in Higher Education Vice President for Legal Affairs
12:00	Luncheon in the Banquet Area Remarks by President of University
2:30 pm	Getting off to a Good Start: Departmental Procedures and Expectations A panel of department heads
3:45 pm	Reception Hosted by the Area Chamber of Commerce

Second Day

8:45 am	Coffee available
9:00 am	Instructional and Faculty Development Opportunities Instructional Development staff
10:00 am	Coffee break
10:30 am	Research Support Services Office of the Vice President for Research
12:00	Lunch at The State Botanical Garden
1:15 pm	Bus tour of campus, including visits to the Main Library and University Computing and Networking Services
3:15 pm	Graduate Faculty Status, Promotion and Tenure Panel of faculty and administrators
6:00 pm	Faculty Reception at the home of the President

anonymity of the younger and/or newer faculty members, allowing for even more honest feedback.

There are other formats that can be used throughout the year. New faculty can be polled and asked to suggest workshop or seminar topics. Social functions around holidays can also be used as a way of getting the new people back together periodically and sustaining the *esprit de corps* that emerged at the fall colloquium. These strategies can be used to share important information with new faculty while also building up morale and nurturing a sense of community.

Noon Seminars

Perhaps the lowest cost intervention is the noon seminar. During the noon hour many faculty members and teaching assistants have open schedules and are available to bring a bag lunch, if desired, and listen to an interesting topic presented by one of their peers. "Faculty teaching faculty" is a wonderful concept and requires no money and little time to sponsor. From experience we have learned that most faculty members are pleased to be asked to share some area of their expertise. We have also found that topics that are specific and offer something concrete, practical, or immediately usable draw the best attendance. For instance topics like "using humor in the classroom," "how to construct a good multiple choice exam," "dealing with academic dishonesty," "planning for retirement," "using e-mail to communicate with students" are more popular than broader, more abstract topics like "planning a new curriculum" or "developing a teaching philosophy."

One way to help plan good noon seminars is to establish a faculty committee to suggest topics. Also, e-mail can be used to elicit ideas and remind people of dates and locations of future presentations. Many important topics central to teaching can be learned by faculty members over time in this painless and inexpensive way.

Special Interest Groups

On every campus there are topics of special interest that can provide the focus for meeting and learning together. Two such groups on our campus are the Large Class Interest Group (LCIG) and Interactive Learning Systems on Campus (ILSOC). Both groups are led by faculty members, but administrative support and year-to-year coordination is furnished by the Office of Instructional Development.

With these and other groups, most of the effort comes in scheduling and distributing announcements. Once the group is in place, lively discussion ensues and those with common interests enjoy sharing ideas. Often with our LCIG no specific program is necessary. Informing people ahead of time with directions like "at the next meeting we're going to discuss ways of dealing with academic honesty in large classes, so please bring suggestions you have" is usually enough grist for a lively meeting. With ILSOC, each meeting usually consists of a presentation by someone in the group followed by discussion. Often with these meetings the location is important as special equipment is needed.

Special interest groups can be formed around almost a limitless number of interesting topics. Some groups run their course in a year or two, and some last much longer. This is an additional method of disseminating information and providing support to faculty members in a way that requires no funding at all.

Activities for Teaching Assistants

If faculty development can be viewed as a career-span activity, then it must begin in graduate school. Teaching assistants are the professors of the future. (See the chapter by Black, this volume.) An almost endless number of low-cost programs can be offered for TAs, starting with a one- or two-day workshop in the fall. Short courses or seminars on college teaching can be taught either in the academic department or from a central office.

Special services for international students are important. Some institutions now require a test of spoken English and then require subsequent training in language or teaching based on the readiness level of the individual.

Two group activities that have been successful in our office are the TA Advisory Committee and the GTA Mentoring Program. The TA Advisory Committee is comprised of TAs from most departments on campus. They meet once a quarter with a program coordinator and share needs, suggestions, and ideas concerning their roles as TAs and the nature of the support they are receiving in the departments. From these sessions emerges a pool of good ideas for the university to consider. The TA Mentoring Program selects 10 to 12 outstanding, often award-winning, TAs to participate in an intensive year-long program. The Mentors meet for an afternoon or morning before school starts. Here they get acquainted and help the coordinator set the agenda for the year. Meetings occur at least once a month, and guest speakers are invited to talk about topics important to teaching. Sometimes discussions are held around a predetermined topic. In effect, this program is designed to equip senior-level TAs with information and skills so that they, in turn, can assist less experienced TAs. In this manner they receive training on how to be a mentor to other graduate students in their departments. One TA recently established an evening seminar series on teaching in his department which not only attracted large numbers of graduate students but also faculty members.

Special Courses on Teaching

Courses that deal with the fundamentals of college teaching are an excellent option for those who wish to learn more about teaching. These courses can offer credit and be taken by graduate students, instructors, or faculty members.

One of the authors taught a course at another university during the noon hour every summer. Often faculty members would take the course and bring along one or two of their doctoral students.

A weekly study group with four or five members provides an excellent vehicle for a course on teaching. The instructor of this course at our university allows participants to have input on the contents that are covered, and those who enroll agree to read materials and do "homework" assignments prior to meeting as a group.

Publications and Materials

With desktop publishing capabilities, instructional materials, brochures, and newsletters can be published for minimal cost. For instance, a few years ago our office was faced with the dilemma of whether or not we could continue our quarterly newsletter. The cost for one issue had exceeded $1,200 and we began to question the efficiency and benefit of this expenditure. An enterprising staff member with excellent computer skills figured out how to internally publish the same batch of 2,500 newsletters for less than $200.

There are many other kinds of materials that can be housed as references for interested teachers or can be written and distributed campuswide. Topics such as "the first day of class," "writing good tests," "leading discussions," and "evaluating teaching effectiveness" are popular with faculty members and TAs and can be produced locally at a low cost. With the abundance of sources of good information and the many ways of distribution available, it is becoming easier to supply these resources at low costs.

ADDITIONAL ACTIVITIES

An older and wiser colleague of ours, speaking on the management of educational budgets, once said, "It's not our job to save money, but to spend it wisely." In these tight financial times we all have to stretch our dollars by spending them wisely. One principle associated with good management is to start with good values and important goals and then do good work that is consistent with one's beliefs and intentions.

If something is important, there is often a way to make it happen, at least on a small scale. Money does not have to be the ultimate barrier. A good example is the faculty renewal program that began over ten years ago on our campus. A small group of faculty convened over lunch to discuss the topic of "burnout." From this meeting emerged a committee that planned a low cost, on-campus "renewal conference" that ran successfully for three years. The planning committee then suggested a national conference which was held three times over a six-year span. The participant fees paid for all the expenses of the conference and left a little behind to plan the next one. These conferences came to fruition through the hard work of a small group of dedicated people, but they did not cost any person or unit money out-of-pocket.

The Office of Instructional Development is advised by a large committee comprised of faculty and staff. Among other things, this enthusiastic group helps referee instructional grant proposals, selects TA award recipients, and plans all noon seminars for the academic year. While these efforts require a lot of energy and good will, they demonstrate that if good people want to do good things, they will find ways to make them happen.

Another strategy that can serve as a springboard to mobilizing financial support from an institution's central administration is to acquire external funding to initiate pilot programs. The Lilly Teaching Fellows program on our campus was funded for three years by the Lilly Endowment of Indianapolis. The program was so successful that our central administration was pleased to keep it going with institutional funds. The same thing happened with the Senior Teaching Fellows program. After three years of funding from the U.S. Department of Education (FIPSE), this successful program was funded from instructional dollars. Both programs, now in their 11th and 7th years, respectively, are points of pride for the university. Impact studies show that for every dollar invested by the university, many additional dollars of benefit accrue. A much more extensive discussion of ways to build institutional support for teaching improvement is found elsewhere in this volume. (See the chapter by Ambrose.)

It is our belief that being smart, paying close attention to the needs of faculty and TAs, and working hard to find a way to make things happen are investments that lead to outcomes which are not easily measured by dollars spent. But as institutions continue to pay more attention to instruction, and as the value of what we do in this arena increases, a foundation is built that eventually pays dividends far beyond what was originally imagined.

Providing instructional and faculty development is much like putting money in the bank. The interest earned compounds daily, and before long the benefits that have accumulated exceed the small, early investments many times over.

AUTHORS

Ronald D. Simpson is Professor of Higher Education and Science Education and Director of the Office of Instructional Development at the University of Georgia. Prior to this position, he was a professor of science education and head of the department of mathematics and science education at North Carolina State University. He holds degrees from the University of Tennessee and the University of Georgia.

William K. Jackson is Associate Director, Office of Instructional Development at the University of Georgia. He holds B.S. and M.S. degrees in physics and an Ed.D in educational administration (higher education). In 1968, he began his career as a physics instructor at Presbyterian College and served in a variety of administrative roles there before joining the University of Georgia.

REFERENCES

Boice, R. (1992). *The new faculty member: Supporting and fostering professional development.* San Francisco, CA: Jossey-Bass.

Brookfield, S.D. (1990). *The skillful teacher: On technique, trust, and responsiveness in the classroom.* San Francisco, CA: Jossey-Bass.

Davis, B.G. (1993). *Tools for teaching.* San Francisco, CA: Jossey-Bass.

Diehl, P.F., & Simpson, R.D. (1989). Investing in junior faculty: The teaching improvement program (TIPs). *Innovative Higher Education, 13*(2), 147–157.

Lewis, K.G. (Ed.). (1988). *Face to face: A sourcebook of individual consultation techniques for faculty/instructional developers.* Stillwater, OK: New Forums Press.

McKeachie, W.J. (1994). *Teaching tips: Strategies, research, and theory for college and university teachers,* 9th ed. Lexington, MA: D.C. Heath.

Simpson, R.D., & Jackson, W.K. (1990). A multidimensional approach to faculty vitality: The University of Georgia. In J. H. Schuster, D.W. Wheeler and Associates, *Enhancing faculty careers: Strategies for development and renewal* (pp. 167–187). San Francisco, CA: Jossey-Bass.

Wunsch, M.A. (Ed.). (1994). *Mentoring revisited: Making an impact on individuals and institutions.* San Francisco, CA: Jossey-Bass.

NINE

CAPITALIZING ON DIVERSITY IN THE CLASSROOM

Judy A. Greene

Teaching college students to live successfully in a multiethnic, multi-cultural, and global society requires that we reach beyond traditional ways of instruction. Until now, the focus in teaching for many faculty has been the discovery and transmission of knowledge—a discrete set of facts, concepts, and assumptions within the context of the disciplines. We have remained loyal to an academic culture which values individuality, competition, and cognitive acquisition of knowledge. Moreover, some have assumed that knowledge is objective, logical, analytical in nature, and that the content of our disciplines must be "covered." Yet, in spite of the best efforts of many faculty to provide more inclusive curricula, one need only read the *Chronicle of Higher Education* to know that incidents of racial prejudice, gay bashing, and other forms of discrimination still occur on our campuses and in our classrooms.

"Diversity" has always been a part of our experience. Even when students were all white Anglo-American men, diversity was present. Then and now, people differ not only by race and gender but by social and economic class, religious preference, sexual orientation, political views, family structures, physical abilities, and age.

All these various identities are woven together in a complex web which has a profound impact on our lives and contributes to the formation of individual and collective perspectives and experiences (Collins, 1990; Andersen and Collins, 1992). All people—faculty, students, administrators, maintenance personnel alike—bring this rich collection of experiences with them into the academy. So, I use the term "diversity" to simplify an extremely complex set of variables which refer to *all* of the identities in an individual.

103

DEMOGRAPHIC CHANGE

Our diversity provides a rich array of life experiences to draw upon as we attempt to create community in our classrooms. Yet, an incoming freshman (who is a white male) said to me recently, "What's the big deal? We're all Americans aren't we?" If one of the goals of education is to provide students with the skills to be productive, fully functioning members of our society and the larger world community, we must first identify our different backgrounds and perspectives precisely for the purpose of learning *how* to know what we *need* to know.

In the 1950s white men made up approximately 94% of the college population and remained in the majority into the early 1970s. The faces of students in our classrooms today are vastly different. The majority (55%) of students in higher education in the U.S. today are now women. People of color (African American, Hispanic, Native American, and Asian/Pacific Islanders) are enrolling in predominately white colleges in increasing numbers and now comprise nearly 17% (1 in 6) of all students. One-third of our undergraduates are aged 25 or older. And there is an increase in the number of students planning to transfer from 2-year to 4-year schools (American Council on Education, 1988; Cagg, 1993; Institute for Research on Higher Education, 1993). In addition to the demographics, there are changes in student expectations of a college education, differences in learning support needs, and in the ways they take in, process, construct, and make meaningful connections with new knowledge (Belenky and others, 1986; Anderson and Adams, 1992; Schroeder, 1993; and Fried, 1993).

EFFECT ON FACULTY PRACTICES

The impact of these changes on faculty is equally dramatic. Major shifts in curricula and in course materials must take place. Faculty must learn about the diverse student body in their classes and the different groups represented among them. Beyond that, faculty are challenged to learn about bias in their materials as well as biased actions (such as racism, sexism, homophobia) in their teaching practices, including the legal and ethical implications of racism, sexual harassment, and hate speech. Faculty are confronting their own unconscious learnings about others as well as their own groups (Adams, 1992; Border and Chism, 1992; Bowser and others, 1993). Traditional methods of teaching and managing the academic enterprise are being challenged more often and with increasing hostility. Teaching practices that seemed to work well in the past no longer generate predictable or desirable outcomes. The kind of discourse and interaction desired with students often seems impossible to achieve (Gudykunst, 1991; Schroeder, 1993; Fried, 1994).

In short, it's a time when the thought of raising controversial issues in the classroom brings to the forefront all our fears and heightens our already fragile sense of adequacy. Weinstein and Obear (1992, pp. 41-42) surveyed an interdisciplinary group of colleagues asking, "What makes you nervous about raising issues of racism in your classroom?" The concerns they found faculty shared were dominated by personal fears. Among others, they included: 1) Confronting my own social and cultural identity conflicts, 2) Having to confront or being confronted with my own bias, 3) Responding to biased comments, 4) Doubts and ambivalence about my own competency, 5) Need for learner approval, 6) Handling intense emotions and losing control. These fears are no less present in our students and are blocks to learning for all of us.

We avoid uncomfortable topics and associate with people with whom we are willing to discuss "certain" topics. We believe there is always a technical fix or solution such as laws, policies, procedures, teaching techniques (Weissglass, 1994). Yet there are signs of progress, as evidenced by the development of inclusive curricula and courses, in which the voices and perspectives of marginalized groups are now closer to the center of our thinking.

At the same time, there is much work remaining to develop truly diverse learning communities. We can no longer leave the work of creating appreciation for diversity or of bias reduction solely to special campus units or programs such as: affirmative action, crisis intervention units, student affairs, graduation requirements in multicultural courses, or women's and ethnic studies faculty and their courses. We need to work collaboratively and join with these colleagues to find additional ways to raise difficult issues in our classrooms.

VALUING DIVERSITY

Valuing diversity means acknowledging that diversity and oppression exist and affect our lives. Diversity is not about lowering standards; it is about creating ways for all students to meet the standards of academic excellence. Building on diversity helps us to experience the rich mix of students, intellects, and experiences both in our classrooms and among our colleagues.

Learning to teach students to build appreciation for the complexity that exists within each of us, our groups, and among all people, may lead faculty to a feeling of hopelessness to effect change. However, faculty who value diversity and use it and the emotions around it as a part of the teaching and learning "process" (regardless of discipline), will produce a positive change in students that increases the breadth and depth of their learning. It will also build respect and understanding of others' views and experiences (Astin, 1993).

There are many paths to building a place where discussion of difficult or uncomfortable topics can take place. One such path is to lead our students to value the "process" of interaction as much as the content of our disciplines. To do so, we need to go beyond content and intellectual pursuits and "scientific" evidence to include the affective side of learning (values, attitudes, emotions). The result will be an increase in the possibility that students will make connections in meaningful ways and use those connections to think and act more rationally.

Among the classroom structures which value and promote diversity are those which give voice to peoples who have been marginalized and left out of "mainstream" curricula, materials, and interactions. Students need to be able to see and hear themselves in our course content. They need to know that their questions, comments, and perspectives will be heard with respect and attention in the classroom. They need to know that the teacher will treat them equitably, will stand up for each of them, and will not make (nor tolerate others to make) homophobic, racist, sexist, or anti-semitic remarks and other oppressive comments or assumptions in the classroom. Students need to be able to build trust among themselves and with teachers in ways which make the classroom a safe place to take risks and therefore to learn. Students need to be able to risk expressing themselves as they explore new information and new ways of seeing themselves and others and how they all fit into the world.

CREATING THE RIGHT ENVIRONMENT

Ground rules are essential to avoid the pitfalls that faculty may have encountered in their previous teaching experiences. Whether instructing a large class lecture/discussion or using small group learning projects, ground rules provide a framework for increasing meaningful interaction.

When used and honored, ground rules provide the safety-net within which students are more willing to examine their thinking, actions, and values. Cannon (1990); Weinstein and Obear(1992); and Palmer(1993) have suggested useful ground rules which can be adapted to any classroom situation, as well as for faculty discussion groups.

Conflict creates potential for both creative as well as destructive forces. To understand conflict as an important human process is to begin to learn how to use it constructively. Because human communication is complex, conflict in some form is inevitable, whether it is between two people or between nations. Classrooms are made up of individuals whose goals, values and perspectives may be different and may not agree with those of their classmates or the teacher. In truth, there are many benefits to conflict: 1) It encourages creative ideas, 2) It can lead to clarification of facts, feelings, and ideas, and 3) It can create positive energy. A certain amount of tension is considered necessary for motivation and learning; excessive tension can be channeled to new solutions and new relationships which serve to reduce or diffuse tension. Conflict also challenges our assumptions and experiences of power, for problem solving requires a balance of power among the problem solvers (Bailey, 1983).

When people with diverse backgrounds and perspectives interact with each other and their course materials, strong intellectual and emotional responses may occur. An environment that recognizes the effects of gender and culture in the formation of our points of view helps students to discuss "relevant personal experiences and reactions to the textual material....The issue becomes particularly acute in the presence of culturally encapsulated Anglo-Americans who, because of the dominance of their perspective in the United States, often do not realize that their values, perceptions, and behavior are shaped by Anglo-American culture: They simply see themselves as "normal," and others as "culturally diverse" (Fried, 1994, p. 123). Responding to differences in and among students in new ways will mean bringing who we are (our personal selves) to what we do (facilitate learning). As we work to become more conscious of our own biases through self-reflection and self-examination, we will begin to identify how our own perspectives influence our reactions to and interactions with students.

We need to develop attitudes in which we think well of all students. Often our fears and frustrations lead us to participate in "student bashing." A helpful model, which also forms part of the theoretical foundation for many antibias courses and workshops, is to adopt an attitude which is based on the idea that all people are born innocent, intelligent, cooperative, creative, joyous, competent, and caring. No infant is prejudiced or full of hate or is anxious to grow up to be racist or sexist. In the process of growing up people get hurt and take in powerful conscious and unconscious messages about themselves and others. (For example: "I'm not very smart." "Light skin is better than dark skin." "Conflict means I get beaten up." "Southerners are racist." "Jews are pushy.") These messages form something like a recording inside each of us. Each time we experience hurt we learn a new message and begin to develop protective layers (similar to the layers of an onion) of attitudes and behaviors in an attempt to avoid future pain. Even when our thoughts and experiences refute our "records," they still exist and influence our behavior in unconscious automatic ways (Jackins, 1978; Brown and Mazza, 1992; Weinstein and Obear, 1992). Since guilt is often the "glue" that holds our prejudices in place, being able to see the impact of these early learnings on our current attitudes and behaviors, however uncomfortable, is the first step in identifying the "recordings" we have internalized about ourselves and others.

LISTENING TO LEARN

Listening is critical for learning and for creating a climate for learning. When we are practicing helpful, attentive listening, we push aside our own thoughts as much as is possible (given our "records") and pay attention to trying to figure out what the speaker is experiencing. That means: 1) not breaking in with your own "stuff"; 2) looking delighted and welcoming of the information you hear; and 3) wearing a facial expression that shows the person he or she has your complete attention. It also means withholding advice, analyzing, asking questions, criticizing or judging what others have said (Jackins, 1978; Brown and Mazza, 1992). For a classroom environment in which we desire a different kind of interaction, we must teach students this kind of listening.

When students come to understand the difference between being heard and getting agreement or approval, they will also be able to understand the differences between advocacy (position-taking and position-holding) and coalition building (moving together in the same direction with common goals and interests) (Brown and Mazza, 1992). The result will be the discovery of solutions in which everyone's interests are met, increased cooperation, and an increased sense of being part of a community in which learning moves forward.

Empowering students in these ways increases the likelihood that they will come to see differences and disagreement as ways to learn new information and perspectives and build a climate which goes beyond "permitting" or "allowing," to one which *invites* differences and disagreements within a context where all people are well thought of, validated, and treated with respect.

In a major study designed to determine how multicultural education and institutional practices and policies affect students' experiences with their environments, Astin (1993, pp.46-48) found that "faculty who emphasize diversity issues in their teaching and research are likely to be found in institutions which also emphasize diversity and multiculturalism in their admissions and hiring policies....The strongest positive effects are on two outcomes: cultural awareness and commitment to promoting racial understanding....The faculty's focus on diversity issues contributes to these outcomes over and above the contribution of the overall institutional emphasis. Emphasizing diversity either as a matter of institutional policy or in faculty research and teaching, as well as providing students with curricular and extracurricular opportunities to confront racial and multicultural issues, are all associated with widespread beneficial effects on a student's cognitive and affective development."

WELCOMING DIVERSITY

There are numerous courses and workshops designed specifically for prejudice reduction and cultural awareness that are being offered on many campuses. One such model currently being used effectively on over 100 campuses is the "Welcoming Diversity" model developed and refined over the last 20 years by Cherie Brown, Executive Director of the National Coalition Building Institute (NCBI). Offered at the University of Delaware for the past two years, the NCBI model for "Welcoming Diversity" is led by faculty, administrators, staff and students and has included over 400 (so far) participants from all segments of the campus community.

The NCBI model provides a framework for thinking about ways to include explicit instruction for creating an appreciation for diversity in and out of the classroom, and for the purpose of creating a classroom climate that is more inclusive and where more meaningful dialogues can take place. The features of the NCBI model include: Identifying the groups we belong to, identifying our "records" about our own and other's groups, building pride in our own groups (e.g., whites who feel less than good about their own groups are not very helpful in ending racism), and identifying the ways in which groups have been systematically mistreated. Additional key features are the sharing of individual personal experiences of mistreatment from oppression, and building skills for interrupting oppressive remarks (the symptoms of oppression) through the role playing of scenarios offered from the participants' experiences (Brown and Mazza, 1992).

By using peer trainers, the workshop promotes a greater sense of well-being on the campus and provides a rich local resource to faculty who wish to offer the model to their students, as well as to take advantage of the learning opportunity for themselves. The impact on my own campus is probably best illustrated through the voices of several faculty (with their permission) who have participated in the workshop and are now using the experience to enhance their teaching:

"Personally, I find myself more accepting of students' different perspectives. I now introduce the concept of diversity and its benefits on the first day of class and use some diversity exercises in my graduate [science] course. This leads to a discussion concerning respect for other's opinions and differences. It has been interesting for me as the students all came to agriculture from different roads. They thus had different views as we approached new problems" [Science professor].

"In general, students seem to think the opening class in which we do the mini-workshop is a great way to start the course. Everyone who has attended the full day workshop [optional assignment] returns to class singing its praises and insisting that everyone on campus should take part in it" [Education professor].

This professor reports that he has changed his way of teaching and interacting with students. As a result of providing the workshop experience, he has seen an increase in the quality of class discussions and students' cognitive achievements as they think more critically about the course content. Several students have gone well beyond the course requirements to seek new knowledge and to examine their own attitudes and beliefs about multicultural issues.

This same professor shares some of the quotes from his undergraduate education majors:

"It made me realize how sensitive we need to be as teachers."

"It is important for all teachers to know in depth about cultural diversity in their classrooms."

"It should be a requirement. Having cultural biases and stereotypes can really damage the learning potential of students from other cultures."

A different faculty member, one who teaches a design course, says: "[My participation in the workshop] has had a positive impact on my teaching, both general and specific. I am now more aware of the issues students deal with and I make my class safer for students. For example, we have an up front agreement to uphold the university policy statements on affirmative action and civility as one of our ground rules. I can see when conflicts are coming up and direct them in useful ways. Since I believe the classroom is a part of life, not something you do outside of life, I have developed exercises to encourage awareness and appreciation for diversity. In one of my courses much of the content comes from the personal experiences of students and their family backgrounds. It is important to use these exercises so that students will feel safe to contribute material from their own experience."

In each of these cases and others as well, the faculty focus on diversity and create ways of bringing it to their students. In doing so, faculty and students engage each other on a more meaningful and honest level of understanding. When the fear of discussing racism, sexism, homophobia, and anti-semitism is reduced, students and faculty find it easier, if not more comfortable, to get the information they need from one another to function more effectively as an integral member of the learning community.

AUTHOR

Judy A. Greene is the Director of the Center for Teaching Effectiveness at the University of Delaware. A specialist in faculty development and college teaching, Greene has designed and conducted over 200 seminars and workshops for faculty and administrators on a wide variety of topics in university teaching, including workshops on welcoming diversity and conflict resolution.

REFERENCES

Adams, M. (Ed.). (1992). *New Directions for Teaching and Learning: No. 52. Promoting diversity in college classrooms: Innovative responses for the curriculum, faculty, and institutions.* San Francisco, CA: Jossey-Bass.

American Council on Education. (1988). *One-third of a nation.* Washington, DC: ACE.

Andersen, M.L., & Collins, P.H. (Eds.). (1992). *Race, class, and gender: An anthology.* Belmont, CA: Wadsworth.

Anderson, J.A., & Adams, M. (1992). Acknowledging the learning styles of diverse student populations: Implications for instructional design. In L. L. B. Border and N.V.N. Chism (Eds.), *New Directions for Teaching and Learning: No. 49. Teaching for diversity.* San Francisco, CA: Jossey-Bass.

Astin, A.W. (1993). Diversity and multiculturalism on the campus: How are students affected? *Change, 25*(2): 44–49.

Bailey, J.G. (1983). *Development of a competency based instructional module for vocational leadership personnel: Managing selected interpersonal conflict.* Unpublished doctoral dissertation, Temple University, Philadelphia, PA.

Belenky, M.R., Clinchy, B.M., Goldberger, N.R., & Tarule, J.M. (1986). *Women's ways of knowing: The development of self, body, and mind.* New York, NY: Basic Books.

Border, L.L.B., & Chism, N.V.N. (Eds.). (1992). *New Directions for Teaching and Learning: No. 49. Teaching for diversity.* San Francisco, CA: Jossey-Bass.

Bowser, B.J., Auletta, G.S., & Jones, T. (1993). *Confronting diversity issues on campus.* Newbury Park, CA: Sage.

Brown, C.R., & Mazza, G.J. (1992). Peer training strategies for welcoming diversity. Unpublished manuscript. Washington, DC: The National Coalition Building Institute.

Cagg, M.C. (November 10, 1993). Enrollment: Ups and downs. *Chronicle of Higher Education,* p. A34.

Cannon, L.W. (1990). Fostering positive race, class, and gender dynamics in the classroom. *Women's Studies Quarterly, 18*(1,2): 126–134.

Collins, P.H. (1990). *Black feminist thought: Knowledge, consciousness, and the politics of empowerment.* London, EN: HarperCollins Academic.

Fried, J. (1993). Bridging emotion and intellect: Classroom diversity in process. *College Teaching, 41*(4): 123–128.

Gudykunst, W.B. (1991). *Bridging differences: Effective intergroup communication.* Newbury Park, CA: Sage.

Institute for Research on Higher Education at the University of Pennsylvania. (1993). The changing faces of the American college campus. *Change, 25*(4): 57–60.

Jackins, H. (1978). *The human side of human beings: Fundamentals of reevaluation counseling.* Seattle, WA: Rational Island Press.

Palmer, P.J. (1993). Good talk about good teaching: Improving teaching through conversation and community. *Change, 25*(6): 6–13.

Schroeder, C.C. (1993). New students—new learning styles. *Change, 25*(4): 24–26.

Weinstein, G., & Obear, K. (1992). Bias issues in the classroom: Encounters with the teaching self. In M. Adams (Ed.), *New Directions for Teaching and Learning: No. 52. Promoting diversity in college classrooms: Innovative responses for the curriculum, faculty, and institutions.* San Francisco, CA: Jossey-Bass.

Weissglass, J. (1994). How institutions resist change and what we can do about it. *Present Time, 26*(2): 7–9.

Ten

Instructional Development in Community Colleges

Emily C. (Rusty) Wadsworth

Instructional development in community colleges is a matter of beginning and sustaining a conversation about teaching. People who work in community colleges from faculty and administrators to secretaries and custodians are fiercely committed to the community college mission to serve the local community through providing opportunities for lifelong learning. This traditional community college focus on teaching and the concern for the learning of all students regardless of their entering level of preparation create an institutional climate in which faculty and instructional development are seen as integral to realizing the mission of the institution.

The service mission of community colleges is further strengthened by state-wide meetings and organizations. In Illinois, for example, the annual community college administrators conference includes many sessions on new technologies and programs designed to enhance the learning of various groups of students. Illinois community college faculty also meet annually for discussions about teaching. Moreover, teaching is celebrated with a Teacher of the Year Award presented at a dinner which brings together the award winners from all of the Illinois community colleges.

COMMUNITY COLLEGE CONTEXT FOR FACULTY DEVELOPMENT

Faculty in community colleges expect their teaching to be a significant part of evaluation for retention, promotion, and tenure. They expect that students will evaluate all or many of the classes they teach, that administrators will make classroom visits, and that they will be provided with professional development opportunities to improve their teaching. At many

115

community colleges, each semester begins with faculty workshops on some aspect of teaching. Faculty also are often required to attend an annual in-service day. Faculty advance on a salary schedule through taking graduate courses. Rarely are class sizes over 50 which makes class discussions, active learning, and cooperative learning seem as natural as lecturing.

SOME ISSUES FOR FACULTY DEVELOPMENT IN COMMUNITY COLLEGES

Although community college faculty are not expected to do research or to publish, they have significant demands on their time. Community college faculty carry heavy teaching loads—usually in the neighborhood of 15 semester hours per term—and provide considerable individual help to students. They serve on college committees and attend regular department and division meetings. Community college faculty most often are trained in their disciplines and typically have no greater knowledge of the research on teaching and learning than university faculty have. The lack of emphasis on publishing and research leads some faculty to an anti-intellectual attitude and a suspicion of those who do publish, give presentations, and participate in their professional associations. Because they have been teaching for many years, some faculty believe they are teaching and learning experts and are not persuaded by the research on teaching and learning. Even in community colleges some faculty teach using only the lecture method based on lecture notes they created many years ago.

WHAT WORKS IN COMMUNITY COLLEGE FACULTY DEVELOPMENT

Only occasionally do community colleges support teaching and learning centers staffed by professionals trained in the art and science of teaching. The dialogue about teaching and learning in community colleges can build on the strengths of those colleges by using the positive attitudes toward teaching to provide opportunities to enhance already expert teaching. These opportunities can easily be connected to the in-place reward system, and to workshop and institute days.

Community colleges are usually organized into broad divisions containing disciplinary departments; e.g., psychology, anthropology, economics, sociology might be found in a Social Sciences Division or computer aided drafting and auto mechanics might be found in a Technology Division. The divisions are generally headed by an administrator (associate dean or chair) who has responsibility for hiring, firing, and evaluating faculty. These decisions are based primarily on their teaching. An effective instructional development program can be created with minimal funds by working with the division heads to increase their instructional development skills and to persuade them to include teaching as an important part of regular meetings. (See the chapters by Gmelch, and Simpson and Jackson, this volume.)

Working with Division Heads to Improve Teaching Evaluation

The community college faculty development coordinator can work with division heads to improve their knowledge of and skill in evaluating teaching. Division heads are generally trained in one or more of the disciplines represented in their division. They may or may not have training in the evaluation of instruction, and yet they are required to evaluate faculty primarily on the basis of teaching. Although these evaluations are, of course, ultimately summative, they can be conducted in a formative manner, i.e., as part of a process which seeks to identify teaching strengths and weaknesses and which provides opportunities to share strengths and to work on weaknesses.

Teaching Analysis by Students (TABS)

During the probationary period for tenure track faculty, division heads are often required to conduct classroom visits. These classroom visits sometimes include Teaching Analysis by Students (Clinic to Improve University Teaching, 1974) or Small Group Instructional Diagnosis (Diamond, 1988) to identify teaching strengths and weaknesses. Both of these diagnostic instruments use variables derived from the literature on teaching and learning and, thus, provide concrete areas for discussion of teaching and teaching improvement.

At McHenry County College (MCC), all faculty are evaluated every four years. This year I have used Teaching Analysis by Students (TABS) for each of the Humanities faculty up for periodic evaluation. The results of these surveys have helped to ground our discussions of their teaching in the literature. Each of the faculty evaluated this year, some of whom have been teaching at the college for up to twenty-five years, has been eager to discuss why the students responded the way they did and to think about new ways to approach their classes in the fall.

The evaluation process includes an "Action Plan" in which the faculty member identifies projects to work on before the next periodic evaluation.

One faculty member, an English professor and a very holistic thinker, found that some of her students had difficulty following where the day's class was going and how it fit into the larger context of the course. In the fall she will begin providing a linear outline of the day's subject matter on an overhead or the chalkboard as a supplement to her usual holistic approach. Another faculty member, this one a philosophy professor, will work with a science teacher to develop paired science and philosophy courses. The college will provide support in working out the details of scheduling and advertising the paired courses.

Some of the TABS results have puzzled us. A faculty member who uses films, simulations, class discussion, and small group work received one of his lowest ratings on "Uses a variety of teaching techniques." We are both curious about what the students meant. Next year we will do the TABS and conferences earlier in the year. The faculty member will then have the opportunity to share the results with the class surveyed and to begin a conversation with the students about teaching and learning.

The student response to the TABS has had an unexpected additional benefit. Disgruntled students, usually those who want an "A" and have earned a "C," often appear in my office to complain about a teacher. Frequently, students from classes where the TABS has been administered have stopped by or phoned to share positive responses to particular class sessions or to offer concrete suggestions for ways that things might be done differently to enhance their learning.

Working with Division Heads to Promote Teaching Discussions

Stark and others (1990) suggest that faculty learn and perfect their craft by talking about teaching with other faculty. A community college faculty development coordinator can work with division heads to encourage them to capitalize on that research by devoting a significant portion of regular division meetings to discussions of teaching. For the last several years in the Humanities Division at McHenry County College, we have rotated convening our monthly meetings among the departments in the division. The convener's responsibility is to generate a brief business agenda and to provide a "program" centered around teaching. Over the last few years we have had in-depth discussions of such things as how to conduct class discussions on emotionally charged issues, concept mapping, grading, and attendance policies. In the coming year we will vary this pattern a bit by generating a list of teaching issues from a random sampling of our students as well as the Humanities faculty. At the end of the year we will again survey students for their responses to our solutions to the teaching issues.

Community colleges use many adjunct faculty who often have little or no teaching experience or knowledge. Especially in the occupational areas, the adjunct faculty are likely to be practitioners who have no knowledge of the most basic aspects of teaching such as syllabus construction or grading and attendance policies. The instructional development coordinator can conduct pre-term teaching seminars for all new adjunct faculty or encourage division heads to provide discipline-specific workshops.

New adjunct faculty, as well as full-time faculty, expect that their teaching will be evaluated with classroom visits by the division head as well as through student course evaluations. As a part of this process, the division head can administer a TABS about a third of the way into the semester. The results can be used to begin a dialogue about teaching which results in improved teaching skills.

Orienting New Faculty

Faculty development coordinators can volunteer to help plan the program for new faculty orientations and, thus, make sure that new faculty are initiated into the teaching culture of the institution. (See the chapter by Armour, this volume.) In addition to the all-college new faculty orientation at MCC, the English Department conducts a morning "norming" and teaching workshop for new faculty who will teach composition courses. The workshop is facilitated by veteran English Department faculty and is followed by lunch. This event provides an opportunity for all English Department faculty to get to know each other and for the adjunct faculty to feel a part of the institution.

Mentoring

Mentoring programs for new faculty are another good way to initiate the conversation about teaching. The programs need not be elaborate to be effective. They can be as simple as providing lunch money and a modest stipend for a senior faculty member to meet with a new faculty member several times during the term. (See the chapter by Sorcinelli, this volume.)

All expert teachers have some combination of passion for their disciplines and passion for sharing their love of subject with others through teaching. In some ways, faculty development at community colleges is faculty development at research universities turned on its head. The culture of research universities rewards the passion for one's discipline by insisting that faculty "publish or perish" often to the detriment of teaching. The community college culture rewards teaching often to the detriment of publishing. If, indeed, both passions are a requirement for master teaching, community college instructional development coordinators can do much to improve teaching at their institutions by providing opportunities for faculty to examine their disciplines in new ways and opportunities for faculty to share their disciplinary expertise with new audiences.

Curriculum Change

The instructional development coordinator might form teaching cadres around curriculum issues such as writing across the curriculum or curriculum transformation for cultural inclusiveness. Any project that asks faculty to examine their disciplines in new ways has the potential to create enthusiasm, intellectual excitement, and conversations about teaching. In writing across the curriculum, content faculty must identify and make clear the writing conventions of their disciplines. This process requires not only an examination of how information is presented but also what information should be included, what is considered evidence, how knowledge is generated in the discipline. Writing teachers working with content experts must re-examine their notion of the writing conventions traditionally taught in beginning level writing courses.

The current movement to expand the canon of the curriculum to include voices previously silenced requires close attention to what is considered knowledge in the discipline, who is authorized to generate knowledge, what questions are asked, how are the questions asked, of whom are the questions asked, how and to whom is the knowledge presented. At McHenry County College, seven (of 70) faculty are participating in the President's Teaching Fellows Program in which they are redesigning a course or portion of a course to begin to include some of the silenced voices—to transform their disciplines. In the redesigned courses many more students will see themselves reflected as people who are worthy of study and who generate knowledge, and, thus, will feel more motivated to learn the subject matter which now seems relevant to their lives. Faculty are experiencing renewed excitement about their courses as they view the subject matter from new perspectives. As an added and unexpected benefit of the Teaching Fellows Program, the participating faculty are developing a sense of camaraderie and trust. At the conclusion of their most recent workshop, these faculty decided they need feedback on what is happening in their classrooms and have asked for training in peer consultation. Of course, peer consultation is an excellent way to provide professional feedback to faculty in institutions that do not have teaching and learning centers.

Sharing Teaching Expertise

Instructional development coordinators can also provide opportunities for community college faculty to share their expertise with new audiences. They might invite faculty to participate as planners and presenters for celebratory occasions such as Women's History Month, Martin Luther King Day, or Hispanic History Month. Or, the faculty development coordinator might organize a series of presentations by faculty that are open to the public. Presenting on such occasions provides faculty with a reason to think about their discipline in a new light and to "star" in a different setting, both of which are energizing and intellectually stimulating.

Sheila Tobias (1992-1993 academic year) describes an experiment in which she asked humanities faculty to take a mini-science course, and science and engineering faculty to take a mini-humanities course. Because of the different approaches to knowledge, both groups had difficulty following the lectures and the reading assignments. In the academy, our passion for our disciplines often derives from the ease with which we learned in the discipline. The very structure of the discipline, the way in which it constructs knowledge, fits with our preferred way of viewing reality. Because of this fit with and competence in our disciplines, we often do not reveal the most basic structure of the discipline to the students.

For community college students, all of whom are taking first- and second-year courses, it is particularly important that the faculty initiate them into the conventions of the discipline. A variety of activities can invite faculty to confront the structures of their own disciplines. Once faculty see for themselves how their disciplines differ from each other, they are better equipped to translate the mysteries of the discipline to their students.

Team Teaching

Team teaching across disparate disciplines when both faculty are in the classroom is an effective method of translating the structure of one discipline to another. At the College of Lake County in Grayslake, Illinois, some science and philosophy courses are paired. The philosophical issues focus on scientific content, and the scientific content is subjected to philosophical analysis. As faculty work together to design the paired courses, they are forced to explain their disciplines to each other and to uncover differences in approaches to knowledge. These differences in the structure of the disciplines are made strikingly real when the faculty interact with each other during class sessions. Philosophy becomes more understandable for the scientifically-oriented student, and science becomes more understandable for the philosophically-oriented student.

The "across the curriculum" of the 1970s and 1980s for writing, critical thinking, and substance abuse prevention all have the same effect. The current feminist and multicultural critiques of the disciplines also ask faculty to examine the ways in which their disciplines construct knowledge. Finally, many occupational divisions of community colleges are participating in "Tech Prep," a nationwide, federally funded movement to engage the middle 50% of high school students in preparation for an occupation beginning with their first year in high school and continuing through an associate of applied science degree. The program trains high school faculty to teach theory through application. Community college instructional development coordinators can involve their faculty in redesigning communications and general education courses so that they, too, teach theory through application or use job related content to teach communications skills.

Providing Learning Opportunities

Many community colleges provide faculty with funds to take graduate courses and reward them with higher salaries for successfully completing a specified number of graduate credits. The instructional development coordinator can make a connection with a local university to provide on-campus graduate courses on basic teaching issues such as test construction and grading policies, or on more complex issues such as curriculum transformation. Faculty will take the courses because they are convenient, paid for, and will move them up on the salary scale. Oakton Community College in Des Plaines, Illinois, formed a teaching company of faculty to examine critical thinking as it related to their disciplines. Faculty studied theories of critical thinking and applied them to their teaching. They met weekly under the auspices of a local university that provided graduate credit for the experience. At McHenry

County College we are concerned about redesigning our courses so that they include knowledge about and by the diversity of peoples in the population. Last fall we offered an on-campus graduate course in multicultural college teaching. Faculty read and discussed the feminist and multicultural literatures. As the course project, they applied the theoretical literature to a course they were teaching.

Providing on-campus opportunities for earning graduate credit will become even easier in Illinois within the next five years when most of the community colleges and public universities in the state will be connected by distance learning networks. (See the chapter by Arreola, this volume.) Universities can then offer distance learning courses for faculty development of community college faculty. Already, Kentucky offers state-wide instructional development for community college faculty through teaching improvement institutes sponsored by the University of Kentucky.

Using Technology to Improve Teaching

New technologies such as distance learning and computer aided instruction also provide opportunities for instructional development consultants to engage faculty in learning new teaching techniques. Faculty at MCC who wish to teach on the distance learning network participate in a two-day workshop on using the technology to its best advantage. Faculty discover that they must be particularly conscious of including the distant site student in the class activities. In the regular classroom this translates into a sharper awareness of the responses of all students and a heightened concern for the inattentive student.

Staff development committees often have funds available for the circulation of print materials and for attendance at teaching institutes such as the Great Teachers Seminars. Faculty development coordinators can make sure that print materials such as *Teaching Excellence* are regularly distributed to faculty and can personally encourage individuals to apply to attend teaching institutes.

Recognizing Good Teaching

Like all human beings, community college faculty appreciate having their accomplishments noticed. Instructional development coordinators can be intentional about searching out faculty who are trying new ideas, presenting at conferences, and organizing special events. A note of congratulations or appreciation goes a long way to inspire faculty to continue to try new things. Instructional development coordinators can also encourage division heads and deans to write similar notes to the faculty in their area.

When people ask me what I do as the associate dean for humanities, I jokingly say that I hang out by the Xerox machine. Although I am joking, there is a lot of truth to the statement. In a community college where the emphasis is on teaching, the most effective way to improve teaching is to stimulate conversations about teaching. Hanging out by the Xerox machine provides the opportunity for me to inquire about the article that the faculty member is copying and how it will be used. Soon, several faculty members are gathered around engaged in a discussion about teaching.

AUTHOR

Emily C. (Rusty) Wadsworth is Associate Dean for Humanities, McHenry County College in Crystal Lake, Illinois. She is a former president of the Professional and Organizational Development Network in Higher Education. Wadsworth has published in faculty and instructional development, multicultural education, and curriculum infusion for substance abuse prevention.

REFERENCES

Clinic to Improve University Teaching. (1974). Teaching analysis by students. Amherst, MA: University of Massachusetts, Amherst.

Diamond, N.(1988). S.G.I.D. (Small Group Instructional Diagnosis): Tapping student perceptions of teaching. In E. Wadsworth, (Ed.), *Professional and organizational development in higher education: A handbook for new practitioners.* Stillwater, OK: The Professional and Organizational Development Network in Higher Education.

Stark, J., Lowther, M., Ryan, P., Bomotti, S., & Genthon, M. (1990). *Planning introductory college courses: Influences on college faculty.* Ann Arbor, MI: National Center for Research to Improve Postsecondary Teaching and Learning.

Tobias, S. (1992–1993). Disciplinary cultures and general education: What can we learn from our learners? In M. Svinicki (Ed.), *Teaching excellence: Toward the best in the academy.* Ames, IA: The Professional and Organizational Development Network in Higher Education.

ELEVEN

HOW MENTORING PROGRAMS CAN IMPROVE TEACHING

Mary Deane Sorcinelli

During the early years of a faculty appointment, the potential for both rewards and pressures is great. New faculty must unravel the organizational structures and values, expectations for performance and advancement, and the history and traditions of their new campus setting. At the same time, they must balance the complex and sometimes conflicting roles and responsibilities of teaching, research, and responsible citizenship. The ability of new faculty to navigate these early years is critical to their success in, and satisfaction with, an academic career.

A number of studies have focused on the work experiences, satisfactions, and concerns of new and junior faculty (Fink, 1984; Turner & Boice, 1987; Reynolds, 1988; Sorcinelli, 1988, 1992; Sorcinelli & Near, 1989; Boice, 1991, 1992b; Whitt, 1991; Olsen & Sorcinelli, 1992; Sorcinelli & Austin, 1992). Across these studies, there is remarkable agreement. The picture one gets is of junior faculty working all the time with fairly high anxiety, not knowing how much is enough, not being comfortable with teaching or seeking help with it from their colleagues. As a result, they may not teach very well and may not produce much useful scholarship.

Fortunately, research on new faculty not only has investigated satisfactions and stresses, but also has pointed to recommendations for enhancing professional development (Fink, 1984; Jarvis, 1991; Sorcinelli, 1988, 1992; Boice, 1992b; Sorcinelli & Austin, 1992). This chapter focuses on one initiative that offers a valuable contribution to new faculty development—mentoring opportunities for teaching development. The following discussion identifies new faculty stresses specifically related to teaching, highlights several models for mentoring programs that

125

respond to new faculty concerns about teaching, and shares lessons learned about mentoring as a strategy for improving teaching among new and junior faculty.

New Faculty Stress in Teaching

In exploring facets of teaching perceived by new faculty as most stressful, the following themes arise: time constraints, lack of collegial guidance and support, and inadequate feedback, recognition and reward.

Time Constraints

A predominant source of stress reported in nearly all studies of new faculty stems primarily from the press of finding enough time to get everything done (Fink, 1984; Turner & Boice, 1987; Sorcinelli, 1988; Whitt, 1991). Difficulties in managing new teaching responsibilities nearly always head the list of complaints. Fink (1984) interviewed new faculty and reported that they had difficulty juggling heavy teaching loads with pressures for publication. Similarly, Turner & Boice (1987) and Sorcinelli (1988) described stresses related to the demand to meet longer-term goals for research (e.g., writing several articles, getting a lab up and running, securing outside funding) versus the immediate and unpostponable demands of teaching. Newcomers indicated difficulties in preparing too many different classes, in teaching large lecture classes, in dealing with poorly prepared or unmotivated students, and in compensating for their own inadequate preparation for teaching.

Lack of Collegial Support

Studies reveal that some of the most salient first year concerns include feelings of loneliness, isolation, lack of social and intellectual stimulation, and insufficient support from senior faculty members (Fink, 1984; Turner & Boice, 1987; Sorcinelli, 1988; Whitt, 1991; Boice, 1992a). Fink (1984) first documented the need for more support by peers of new college teachers. When first-year faculty were asked for recommendations for their own institutions, two thirds said that they would have appreciated more assistance from fellow faculty members. Types of assistance most desired included support for teaching and more discussion of criteria used in assessing teaching effectiveness.

Turner & Boice (1987), Sorcinelli (1988, 1992), and Whitt (1991) found similar concerns. New faculty described a lack of collegial relations as the most surprising and disappointing aspect of their first year. While new faculty reported general conversations with colleagues, they were much less likely to have received concrete help with teaching (e.g., sharing syllabi, suggesting ways to deal with difficult students, visiting a classroom). Many expressed a desire for more frequent discussions about pedagogy with chairs and senior faculty.

Moreover, while mentoring of new faculty did occur in a few departments, it was not widespread. In several studies, women and minorities, in particular, described acute feelings of personal isolation, less contact with colleagues, and a desire to meet someone who could help them as new scholars and teachers (Boice, 1992b; Sorcinelli, 1992; Wunsch & Johnsrud, 1992; Wunsch, 1994).

Inadequate Feedback, Recognition, and Reward

Another factor that produces stress among new and junior faculty is that of inadequate feedback, recognition, and reward. Under this rubric, new faculty express considerable tension about such issues as unclear criteria for evaluating teaching, lack of helpful feedback on teaching, and inadequate university recognition, particularly for their contributions to undergraduate teaching and learning.

Several studies of first year faculty conclude that early formal evaluations are significant contributors to faculty stress (Turner & Boice, 1987; Sorcinelli, 1988, 1992; Whitt, 1991; Boice, 1991). The particular stress of teaching evaluations is worth special mention. In a two-year study of new faculty as teachers, Boice (1991) found that new faculty taught cautiously and defensively, so as to avoid public failures at teaching. He reported that new faculty "routinely worried aloud about criticisms of their teaching, especially the sort that would earn repeated listings in reports of tenure committees" (p. 171). Boice recommended that departments consider safeguarding new faculty from all formal evaluations of classroom performance for a year or two. New faculty themselves recommended more constructive feedback on teaching from chairs and senior colleagues, oriented to development rather than to evaluation.

MENTORING PROGRAMS THAT TAKE TEACHING SERIOUSLY

Studies on the early experiences of new faculty make it clear that institutions need to take action in order to shape a positive experience for newcomers and to increase the likelihood that they will enjoy long and successful careers in academe. Mentoring has become a popular part of plans and programs for new faculty (Boice, 1992a; Sorcinelli, List, &

Hill, 1992; Wunsch, 1994). The goals of mentoring programs vary. Some provide information on the institution, orienting new faculty to resources, services, and campus culture. Others provide support for career development and advancement, particularly around teaching and research. Still others focus on collegial communications and interactions in order to provide a more supportive environment for the newest members of the academic community. And some place emphasis on all three goals.

Revitalized emphasis on undergraduate teaching at many colleges and universities has heightened interest in mentoring programs for new faculty that are specifically aimed at improving teaching. The four model programs described below place a primary emphasis on teaching development. Two of the programs are in large state universities, University of Massachusetts, Amherst and Temple University, with major research expectations of faculty. One is in a small private college, Cardinal Stritch College, focused primarily on a teaching mission, and one, University College, University of Maryland System, has a special emphasis on part-time faculty. Across programs there are also interesting variations in the profile, selection, training, and compensation of mentors. But despite these differences, all of these programs succeed because they are able to both facilitate professional development in teaching and offset the afore-mentioned factors that new faculty view as stresses and liabilities to their careers. Put simply, these four programs find ways to help new teachers manage time for teaching, to discover collegiality in teaching across such variables as age, discipline, gender, and rank, and to garner recognition and rewards for good teaching.

The University of Massachusetts Teaching Fellows Program

The Teaching Fellows Program at the University of Massachusetts, Amherst was originally funded by the Lilly Endowment and has been fully sponsored by the University through its Center For Teaching since 1989 (Austin, 1992; Sorcinelli, List & Hill, 1992; Sorcinelli & Aitken, 1995). The purpose of the program is to provide support through which junior faculty members can develop their expertise as teachers as they also establish themselves as scholars and citizens of the university community. Each year, eight to ten junior faculty members are awarded a teaching fellowship for a one-year term. Fellows, who have been at the university between one and five years, are given release time from one course each semester to take part in a program which includes the following elements.

Individual projects and teaching consultation. Each fellow carries out a teaching-related project. Typically, fellows design a new course or redesign one that was previously taught. They also receive individual consultation on their teaching which includes classroom observation, videotape, feedback from students and self-assessment.

Teaching fellows seminar. Fellows meet every two weeks throughout the year. Subjects for discussion vary depending on the interests of fellows, but include topics on teaching (e.g., lecture, discussion, grading) and learning (e.g., student development, diversity in the classroom).

Senior faculty mentors. Each fellow selects or is matched with a mentor, typically a senior faculty member who is respected as an outstanding teacher and scholar. The mentor can come from the same or a different department and pairs often are mixed across gender, age, race or ethnicity. Mentors and fellows meet early on, at a potluck dinner hosted by the fellows, to set out goals for the year. For example, some pairs visit each other's classes, collect and review student feedback from those classes, meet regularly to talk about teaching and career-related issues, and attend campus-wide workshops sponsored by the Center For Teaching. Both current and former mentors and fellows are recognized at an annual "Celebration of Teaching" dinner attended by over two hundred faculty, administrators, and students. Finally, all mentors and fellows meet for a culminating teaching seminar near the close of the academic year. Each mentor receives a $200 stipend for the academic year.

The Temple University Senior Mentoring Service

The Senior Mentoring Service at Temple University in Philadelphia was established in 1990 through a grant from the federal Fund for the Improvement of Post-secondary Education (FIPSE) and is now funded by the institution. Rackin (1994) cites three key elements of the program: all the mentors are retired, the consultations between mentors and protégés are confidential, and all participants are volunteers who determine the scope of their mentoring activities.

The program offers every full-time junior faculty member in Temple University's College of Arts and Sciences the opportunity to work privately on teaching skills with a senior professor recently retired from the College faculty. Such professors are recognized for their teaching effectiveness, their demonstrated willingness to help younger colleagues, and their broad knowledge of the academic culture. Pairs determine their own mentoring goals and schedules, meeting approximately ninety minutes every two or three weeks during the academic year.

The mentors and their protégés typically review protégés' course plans, syllabi, writing assignments, and exams. Mentors often visit protégés' classes or review a videotape of those classes. They are likely to tackle a range of issues such as handling difficult students, grading procedures, and managing time spent on teaching.

In addition, the program provides competitive Grants in Aid of Teaching Effectiveness ($300-$1500 per award) for which all junior faculty participants are eligible. Participants are also invited to luncheon workshops on specific teaching issues sponsored by the Senior Mentoring Service throughout the academic year. Each mentor receives a $500.00 stipend per protégé (most mentors work with two protégés over the course of an academic year).

Cardinal Stritch College New Faculty Mentoring Program

Cardinal Stritch College in Milwaukee, Wisconsin has developed a comprehensive New Faculty Mentoring Program, offering a three-phase program for new faculty: a college orientation and welcome dinner, a first-semester teaming of each new faculty member with an experienced colleague for general orientation, and a second-semester program in which the mentor provides coaching in teaching (*Academic Leader,* 1990).

During the first semester, Phase I, the new faculty member meets with the mentor to talk about college facilities, resources, and culture. The pair also observes each other's classes. Before and after each observation, the pair discuss teaching and learning goals, strategies, and outcomes. New faculty are also observed by chairs and evaluated by their students.

In Phase II, the mentor serves primarily as a problem-solver. The mentor observes his or her mentee again, but the emphasis during the second semester is on coaching to improve instruction. The mentor and mentee review the chair's assessment of teaching, the students' ratings, and their own evaluation of instruction. Their goal is to synthesize the diverse sources of feedback and to develop specific strategies for improvement and innovation.

Following the first two phases, mentors and mentees can participate in a voluntary "Peer Coaching Program" in which they can receive continued feedback on their teaching effectiveness. Partners or teams choose to work with one another over a determined period of time (usually one academic year). Classroom visits, reviews, and informal meetings are scheduled according to interests and goals of the pairs. When pairs feel they have exhausted their ability to suggest new ideas, they can part ways.

A faculty coordinator receives one course release time each year to administer the program. Mentors receive one-half of an overload credit for mentoring newcomers who are full-time and one-fourth of an overload credit for mentoring part-time faculty.

The University of Maryland Peer Mentoring Program

The Peer Mentoring Program at the University of Maryland University College was initiated in 1985 and expanded in 1990 with support from the Fund for the Improvement of Postsecondary Education (FIPSE). The heart of the program is "a two-term mentoring program—one of the few in the country designed for part-time faculty—that rests on one-on-one consultations occurring in conjunction with peer visits" (Millis, 1994, p. 75). The two primary target groups are adjunct faculty new to UMUC and all faculty nominated for the Excellence in Teaching Award (see the chapter by Millis and Kaplan, this volume).

Adjunct faculty new to UMUC are introduced to the mentoring program during their application interviews. They are promised support that will include a visit by a teaching colleague in the same or related discipline. To connect these part-timers with mentors, the program coordinator uses a specially designed software that matches mentors with mentees and generates all of the correspondence associated with the peer classroom visits. He also makes certain that mentors are scheduled for follow-up visits with their mentees.

Each mentor and mentee receives a scheduling letter suggesting a date for classroom observation and a peer visit packet that provides an overview of the program, classroom visit guidelines, and additional resources for the mentee and mentor. Following classroom visits, visitors share their observations with the mentee and later with the program coordinator.

Mentors are selected and trained with care and are drawn from nominees for the Excellence in Teaching Award and from adjunct faculty who have exceptionally positive student evaluations. In addition, all mentors participate in an intensive, three-hour workshop that explores how to conduct peer observations of classroom teaching and provide constructive feedback. One unexpected but positive outcome is that mentees often become mentors themselves after completing the program.

Mentors are paid a stipend of $50 for an initial visit/consultation and $35 for a follow-up visit.

MENTORING FOR TEACHING DEVELOPMENT: LESSONS LEARNED

Based on the author's personal experience in directing a teaching fellows program with an embedded mentoring program and on the experiences of others (Boice, 1992b; Sorcinelli & Austin, 1992; Sorcinelli, List & Hill, 1992; Wunsch, 1994) there are some important lessons on mentoring junior faculty members for teaching development that can be shared.

First, mentors and mentees need not be a perfectly "matched set;" indeed, unmatched pairs work equally well. Administrators of several programs have found that mentors from related or different departments work at least as well as mentors from the same department as the new faculty member. Also, pairs that are mixed across age, gender, race, and ethnicity work as well as more homogeneous pairs, although some programs have focused on specific groups—women, part-time faculty, mid-career faculty (Luna & Cullen, 1992; Wunsch, 1994).

Second, every mentor needs to be a good teacher, but need not have won major awards for teaching excellence. Although a number of mentors are winners of distinguished teaching awards, most programs rely on other criteria as well. For example, some select faculty members who have general reputations as teachers and academic citizens (e.g., undergraduate chairs, teaching and undergraduate curriculum committee members). Others call for volunteers and draw some faculty members who are simply interested and deeply engaged in undergraduate education. In the final analysis, an enthusiasm for teaching and student learning, and an interest in developing a collegial and supportive relationship are more important than the backgrounds, disciplines, and formal teaching accolades received by the mentors.

Third, while formal rewards for mentoring can serve as incentives, intrinsic rewards are at least as important. (See the chapter by Austin & Baldwin, this volume.) Compensation for mentors can range widely, from no financial incentive, to minimal resource support (e.g., a gift of books, teaching materials, a plaque), to a monetary stipend (e.g., $50 to $1,000 compensation). On many campuses, however, mentors report reaping career benefits far beyond any offered compensation. For example, in the eight years we've administered a Teaching Fellows Program on our campus, not one senior faculty member has ever turned down a request to serve as a mentor. In fact, our mentors often forego the $200 annual stipend or they donate it to their mentee or our Center. What then is the payoff? In our interviews with mentors, they cite the importance of opportunities for collegiality, for having a broader impact than they would as a regular teacher, for enriching their own teaching, and for understanding students in new ways. Across campuses, mentors indicate that they not only give assistance but receive benefits significant to their own personal and professional growth.

Fourth, beyond modest stipends and resources, programs should not overlook the importance of expressing appreciation for mentors and mentees who make an extra effort to be successful in teaching. We have tried to make participation as a mentor and mentee an honor. Interviews with our mentoring pairs indicate that they are supported in their mentoring activities when they receive positive recognition from their colleagues, department chairs and deans. We distinguish mentors and fellows through publicity, correspondence with their chairs and deans, public recognition at our campus-wide workshops, and as guests at our "Celebration of Teaching" dinner. In doing so, we ensure that selection and involvement in the Teaching Fellows Program bring recognition and prestige. These kinds of incentives are informal yet effective.

Fifth, mentoring programs for teaching need to be approached in a flexible manner. While the program director can suggest ways in which mentors and mentees might choose to interact, the specifics of the relationships are best left to each pair. We do strongly encourage our mentors and fellows to meet regularly and send our mentors several "Have you called your fellow lately?" memos over the course of the semester. We also schedule opportunities for all fellows and mentors to gather together around teaching concerns (e.g., potluck dinner, end-of-year seminar, campus-wide workshops, "Celebration of Teaching" dinner). And because junior faculty often are reluctant to press for help, we ask our mentors to be proactive in providing support, both in and outside the classroom.

Sixth, both mentors and junior faculty members are well served by an orientation to the responsibilities and possibilities of the relationship. Mentors especially need to think broadly about what they can offer the mentees. For example, at our potluck dinner early in the semester, we describe the Teaching Fellows Program, outline the role of the mentors, suggest possible activities (e.g., class visits, videotaping, collecting feedback from students), and arrange for pairs to chat with each other about goals, activities, and schedules. We also suggest that a trained teaching consultant from our Center For Teaching work with the pair in looking at teaching. On several occasions, not only fellows but also their mentors have taken advantage of our teaching consultation service (class visits, videotaping, student feedback). On other campuses, mentors are given specific training in observing and giving constructive feedback on teaching (Millis, 1994).

Finally, it must be noted that mentoring programs for teaching development are time intensive and need a coordinator to plan, deliver, monitor, and evaluate mentoring activities. Programs that are successful find that a great deal of attention needs to go into publicizing the program, working with deans or chairs, selecting and training mentors, enlisting mentees, connecting mentors and mentees, coordinating activities and events, and intervening when problems arise. Rackin (1994) and Wunsch (1994) note that regardless of whether a program is loosely or tightly structured, brand new or established, or coordinated by a faculty development office, teaching center, school or college, someone must devote constant attention to addressing the personal, professional, and organizational concerns in keeping it functioning smoothly.

As noted throughout this chapter, the desire of new and junior faculty to find time for teaching, more extensive and collegial relationships with other faculty, and recognition for their instructional role has been well documented (Boice, 1992b; Sorcinelli & Austin, 1992; Wunsch, 1994). Mentoring programs, particularly those with a focus on teaching, address these concerns by offering structured processes through which new and junior faculty can learn teaching skills, develop collegial relationships around teaching interests, and find affirmation for their commitment to the teaching mission of our colleges and universities.

AUTHOR

Mary Deane Sorcinelli is Director of the Center for Teaching and associate adjunct faculty in the Department of Educational Policy, Research, and Administration at the University of Massachusetts, Amherst. She has written widely in the areas of academic career development, college teaching and learning, and teaching evaluation.

REFERENCES

Austin, A.E. (1992). Supporting junior faculty through a teaching fellows program. In M.D. Sorcinelli and A.E. Austin (Eds.), *New Directions for Teaching and Learning: No. 48. Developing new and junior faculty.* San Francisco, CA: Jossey-Bass.

Boice, R. (1991). New faculty as teachers. *Journal of Higher Education, 62*(2): 150-173.

Boice, R. (1992a). Lessons learned about mentoring. In M.D. Sorcinelli and A.E. Austin (Eds.), *New Directions for Teaching and Learning: No. 48. Developing new and junior faculty.* San Francisco, CA: Jossey-Bass.

Boice, R. (1992b). *The new faculty member.* San Francisco, CA: Jossey-Bass.

Fink, L.D. (1984). *New Directions for Teaching and Learning: No. 17. The first year of college teaching.* San Francisco, CA: Jossey-Bass.

Jarvis, D.K. (1991). *Junior faculty development: A handbook.* New York, NY: Modern Language Association.

Luna, G., & Cullen, D.L. (1992). Mentoring women and minorities: Applications to higher education. *Journal of Staff, Program and Organization Development, 10* (3): 133–139.

Mentoring gives new faculty warm welcome. *Academic Leader, (6),* 7: 1–2, 1990.

Millis, B.J. (1994). Forging the ties that bind: Peer mentoring part-time faculty. In M.A. Wunsch (Ed.), *New Directions for Teaching and Learning: No. 57. Mentoring Revisited: Making an impact on individuals and institutions.* San Francisco, CA: Jossey-Bass.

Olsen, D., & Sorcinelli, M.D. (1992). The pretenure years: A longitudinal perspective. In M.D. Sorcinelli and A.E. Austin (Eds.), *New Directions for Teaching and Learning: No. 48. Developing new and junior faculty.* San Francisco, CA: Jossey-Bass.

Rackin, D. (1994). *Senior mentoring service.* Philadelphia, PA: Temple University, College of Arts and Sciences.

Reynolds, A. (1988). Making and giving the grade: Experiences of beginning professors at a research university. Paper presented at American Educational Research Association, New Orleans, LA.

Sorcinelli, M.D. (1988). Satisfactions and concerns of new university teachers. *To Improve the Academy,* 7: 121–133.

Sorcinelli, M.D. (1992). *The career development of pretenure faculty: An institutional study.* Amherst, MA: University of Massachusetts, Center For Teaching.

Sorcinelli, M.D., & Aitken, N. (1995). Improving teaching: Academic leaders and faculty developers as partners. In A. Wright (Ed.), *Teaching improvement practices: Successful strategies for higher education.* Bolton, MA: Anker.

Sorcinelli, M.D., & Austin, A.E. (Eds.). (1992). *New Directions for Teaching and Learning, No. 48. Developing new and junior faculty.* San Francisco, CA: Jossey-Bass.

Sorcinelli, M.D., List, K., & Hill, D. (1992). Mentoring junior faculty: Some models. *Educational Forum, 3* (1): 57–68.

Sorcinelli, M.D., & Near, J. (1989). Relations between work and life away from work among university faculty. *Journal of Higher Education, 60*(1): 59–81.

Turner, J.L., & Boice, R. (1987). Starting at the beginning: Concerns and needs of new faculty. *To Improve the Academy, 6*: 41–55.

Whitt, E. (1991). Hit the ground running: Experiences of new faculty in a school of education. *Review of Higher Education, 14*(2): 177–197.

Wunsch, M.A. (Ed). (1994). *New Directions for Teaching and Learning: No. 57. Mentoring revisited: Making an impact on individuals and institutions.* San Francisco, CA: Jossey-Bass.

Wunsch, M.A., & Johnsrud, L.K. (1992). Breaking barriers: Mentoring junior faculty women for professional development and retention. *To Improve the Academy, 11*: 175–187.

Twelve

Enhancing Teaching Through Peer Classroom Observations

Barbara J. Millis and Barbara B. Kaplan

The classroom door is opening at last, sometimes on creaky hinges, at other times with an exuberant thrust. Negative forces such as the specter of state manipulation or parental backlashes have sometimes prompted these glimpses into the hallowed sanctions of academia. But more significantly, positive forces have motivated faculty to become more open about an issue that specifically concerns them—teaching. As Centra (1993) documents, recent studies indicate that interest and commitment to teaching are widespread and long-standing throughout the academy, including at research institutions. The broad circulation and acceptance of the Carnegie Foundation's special report authored by Boyer (1990), *Scholarship Reconsidered: Priorities of the Professoriate*, the teaching/learning-centered initiatives by professional associations, and the leadership of national organizations such as the American Association for Higher Education (AAHE) have made faculty far more willing to accept expanding explorations of what it means to teach effectively in a changing world.

The dramatic changes faced by today's faculty in higher education include (a) the nature of the student body, which is becoming more diverse (see the chapter by Greene, this volume), more non-traditional (part-time, older students are now a norm on many campuses, as the chapter by Wagschal and Wagschal in this volume points out), and more pragmatically workplace-oriented; (b) the impact of technology on both academia and the workplace (see the chapter by Arreola, this volume); and (c) the awareness of global interdependence and the need for responsive, cooperative efforts in all fields of endeavor.

The more teaching-centered climate encourages faculty to profess an interest in and a commitment to their classroom lives, and the increased

137

demands of the 1990s provide an immediate incentive to seek more
responsive teaching methods (see the individual chapters by Armour,
Pastore, and Wadsworth, this volume). These forces are prompting faculty to take advantage of the many services of faculty developers, but they
are also prompting them to turn to a source of concrete help and inspiration directly related to the academic disciplines to which most faculty
pledge fealty. Peers—faculty members who are knowledgeable in the discipline—can offer specific advice about a number of relevant issues, such
as course content; relationship of material covered to departmental or
discipline-specific curriculum guidelines and educational objectives;
course design; instructional delivery; the assessment of student learning;
and logistical/departmental issues such as availability to students and
grade distribution expectations. Peers often share similar professional
goals and similar experiences that can shape and inform collegial dialogues intended to strengthen teaching.

Of all the approaches to peer review, classroom observations are
probably the most effective. Peer classroom observations—when conducted in a collegial, supportive context by carefully selected and well-
trained faculty using a systematic model—can positively affect perceptions of teaching and learning outcomes and foster increased collegiality
(Millis, 1989). Such a program, now in its tenth year, exists at the University of Maryland University College (UMUC).

An Historical Overview of Faculty Development at UMUC

Effective teaching at UMUC has never been a covert activity. In fact,
it has been the mission of UMUC since its creation in 1972 as a separate
institution—dedicated to serving adult part-time students—within the
University of Maryland System, now expanded to eleven campuses.
Although most courses, offered primarily during evening and weekend
hours, are classroom-based, an increasing number use distance-delivery
formats such as instructional television or facilitated independent study
or semi-independent study. The faculty consists primarily of part-time
adjuncts, most of whom hold full-time jobs outside academia. Although
teaching is not their primary vocation, they value their academic experiences and are committed to their own growth as effective teachers.

To meet the professional needs of faculty in the statewide undergraduate programs, UMUC has nurtured an ongoing faculty development
program since the 1970s. The program consists of teaching-enhancing

initiatives, including (a) a yearly series of workshops; (b) new faculty orientations; (c) a Teaching Excellence Award program; (d) a 16-page teaching newsletter published once a semester; (e) Teaching Innovation
Grants; (f) one-on-one consultation; (g) a teaching portfolio initiative;
and (h) a nationally recognized Peer Visit Program.

THE PEER VISIT PROGRAM

The Peer Visit Program at UMUC was established in the mid-1980s
to provide newly-hired faculty with an opportunity to enter into meaningful dialogues within the context of how faculty teach a particular subject to a particular set of students. Classroom observations allow these
kinds of focused discussions with faculty peers.

At present, the Peer Visit Program includes visits for all new faculty,
for all those nominated for the Excellence in Teaching Award, and for
randomly selected experienced faculty who have not had a classroom
observation within the last five years. Whenever possible, a second visit is
scheduled in the subsequent semester so that peers can develop a more
genuine mentoring relationship. The follow-up visit also encourages
commitment to specific teaching enhancement strategies, such as establishing cooperative structured groups, because of the opportunity for
ongoing feedback. The emphasis is on formative evaluation, even though
many Teaching Excellence Award nominees choose to include peer visit
reviews in the teaching portfolios they prepare. Because the program is
predicated on the conviction that the peer observers benefit as much or
more as those they visit, the inclusion of these distinguished nominees is
a "plus" for UMUC's program: their inclusion also emphasizes the fact
that visits are not intended as remedies for the teaching-impaired.

UMUC's Peer Visit Program has been well received. Both visitors
and those visited have provided what might be considered in theater par-
lance "rave reviews." This positive feedback has come through three formal surveys, including one conducted by a university TQM committee
that spent thirteen months examining the program, and through informal discussions and letters. Faculty visited feel a positive connection to
faculty peers and to the institution because they are offered support and
encouragement. They find that the visits and the subsequent reflective
exchanges help them to, in the words of Brandt (1991), "Ask better questions, break out of fruitless routines, make unexpected connections, and
experiment with fresh ideas"(p. 3). Visitors, too, repeatedly comment on

the personal and professional value of the observations for them. Not unexpectedly, they enjoy meeting peers, and they benefit professionally from observing classes first-hand and from the collegial exchanges that precede and follow the visits. The Teaching Excellence Award nominees provide special learning opportunities, but because almost 80% of UMUC's newly recruited faculty are also experienced teachers, collegial exchanges occur with virtually every visit.

This emphasis on teaching enhancement eliminates many of the barriers that arise when peers contribute to promotion and tenure decisions. As Centra (1993) notes, "Teachers will not be as open to discussing weaknesses or seeking advice from people who will judge them" (p. 5). Besides the emphasis on formative evaluation, several other factors contribute to the success of UMUC's Peer Visit Program.

The Peer Visit Program at UMUC

Successful administration of UMUC's university-wide program involves many complex logistical and interpersonal variables. It begins with the peer visitors themselves, who are the key to the program's success. Although most peer visitors remain active in the program for years, new visitors are recruited and trained annually. This active recruitment not only provides a sufficiently large pool of visitors in a variety of disciplines, but it also provides a constant influx of new, trained faculty members bringing their own sometimes diverse, but always pedagogically sound, insights on teaching and learning into the program. As a result, a growing and enthusiastic cadre of peers is available to engage other faculty members in substantive discussions on teaching improvement. The ongoing recruitment of new members to this prestigious cadre also prevents the misconception that a small, select clique might be responsible for fostering quality teaching at UMUC. More importantly, it builds among the faculty active in the Peer Visit Program a sense of community and commitment to the institution and its goals.

The targeted recruits are those with exemplary teaching records, strong interpersonal skills, a genuine interest in others, and a high degree of commitment to UMUC and the teaching profession. Potential peer visitors are identified each summer from two sources: those faculty members nominated for the yearly teaching excellence awards and those who have received high overall ratings (4.75 or higher on a 5 point scale) on student evaluation instruments. The names of potential peer visitors are then rejected or approved by the academic administrators in their disciplines.

Training of Peer Visitors

The acceptable candidates are invited by letter to become peer visitors and to attend a training workshop. The peer visitation training workshop (held toward the beginning of each fall semester) conveys, through interactive exercises, detailed information about UMUC's unique program and about effective classroom observations in general. The format emphasizes how to conduct the visits and how to provide meaningful feedback. Participants receive a 32-page Peer Visit Packet, a handbook that gives an overview of the program, including premises and procedures. It explains the three-stage process that will focus each visit: pre-observation discussions of broad teaching and course goals and immediate class objectives, plus review of key course materials; in-class practices during the observation; and post-observation discussions and written feedback. Those wanting an in-depth view of UMUC's peer visit process should consult Millis (1992; 1994). The handbook also gives suggestions for making the visit as unthreatening and collegial as possible. It offers examples of good oral and written feedback. Because this handbook is shared later with the faculty members scheduled for peer classroom observations, it also includes three self-assessment instruments for those visited. Participants leave this training workshop with a clear understanding of the goals of the program and a set of strategies to employ when conducting peer reviews and providing constructive feedback.

With a cadre of trained visitors and a list of the faculty to be visited,the Faculty Development Coordinator schedules peer visits by using a custom-designed software program to match observers—by days and times available, sites willing to visit, and discipline—with those to be visited. The computerized program also generates scheduling notification letters and reports.

The Peer Visit Program is large: a pool of approximately 60–65 trained visitors conduct over 70 visits a semester. Every peer visitor is asked to complete a preference form (Appendix A) each semester, providing information on the days they are available to visit, the class sites they are able to visit, and the disciplines they feel qualified to review.

Each faculty member scheduled to be visited receives a copy of the Peer Visit Packet which contains a copy of the faculty-designed classroom visit form (Appendix B) that will be completed by the visitor. To foster both collegiality and credibility, they also receive a short biographical sketch of the visitor, emphasizing academic credentials and teaching viewpoints (Appendix C).

Visitors are asked to take the initiative in contacting the instructors they visit. Pre-visit conferences are essential. If they cannot be scheduled face-to-face because of time and distance constraints, visitors typically telephone. These pre-visit contacts are intended to acquaint visitor and instructor, to focus discussion on specific teaching issues, and to familiarize the visitor with the content and format of the course. During this pre-visit period the visitor receives copies of course materials, including the syllabus and handouts to be used the night of the visit. The visitor is able to assess these tools beforehand and then to reevaluate their appropriateness after the class visit.

Because students have been informed of these pending visits, the faculty members feel comfortable introducing the visitors and, if appropriate, inviting them to join discussions or activities. Some visitors, usually with the agreement of the faculty member, choose to chat with students during breaks to gain greater insights into the classroom dynamics. After the observation, which typically lasts one to three hours, visitors provide prompt oral feedback to the faculty member, preferably immediately after the class but no later than within three days of the visit.

Feedback From the Peer Visit

Each visitor, in addition to giving oral feedback, completes a written report, which is mailed to the faculty member through the Office of Faculty Development, preferably within two weeks. A copy is placed in the faculty member's confidential teaching file. The Coordinator writes a personal letter to accompany each written report. This letter highlights, in a positive way, the teaching strengths noted in the report and encourages the recipient to consider any suggested improvements. Sometimes the letter offers additional suggestions to strengthen teaching, such as attendance at appropriate upcoming workshops or review of specific materials such as UMUC's "Syllabus Construction Handbook." The message conveyed is a simple but important one: "UMUC is committed to the professional growth of its faculty. We value the collegial discussions you have begun with your visitor and encourage you to continue your investigation of good teaching strategies." This emphasis on teaching enhancement and future growth helps faculty see the peer visits as professional development opportunities. They come to view peer visits as part of the larger "package" of faculty development offerings.

Visitors too are thanked for their key role in the teaching improvement process. The Faculty Development Coordinator sends them a standardized thank-you letter notifying them that the paperwork has been generated to pay them the $50 stipend reimbursing them—albeit modestly—for their time and mileage. Frequently she appends a hand-written post-script offering a more personal note of thanks and feedback about the depth and quality of the written review.

FACTORS CONTRIBUTING TO SUCCESSFUL PEER ASSESSMENT PROGRAMS

From UMUC's experience with this ten-year, constantly evolving Peer Visit Program and from what is known about effective faculty development and administrative procedures, several recommendations may help other institutions develop effective peer classroom observation programs. Although focused on formative observations, many of the recommendations apply equally well to observations intended for summative purposes. They are deliberately broad. Thus, they may be relevant both on the macro-level, such as when a peer classroom observation program is established institution-wide, and on the micro-level, such as when two individuals agree to reciprocally visit one another's classes. In practice, many classroom observation programs are initiated at the departmental level. Lucas (1990), for example, recommends that chairs "create a climate of trust and support so that visiting one another's classrooms is acceptable and non-threatening" (p. 68). Significantly, Massey, Wilger, and Colbeck's (1994) ongoing research on departmental conditions that inhibit or promote an emphasis on undergraduate teaching suggest that supportive departments are relatively open to peer review of classes. These are the recommendations:

1. Classroom observations must be conducted in an atmosphere of trust and collegiality within the context of teaching enhancement. A positive climate of support, reasoned dialogue, and mutual professional goals underlie successful programs.

2. Teaching enhancement must be valued: even if the rewards remain intrinsic, the faculty involved must feel that there is a "pay-off" for their considerable investments in teaching improvement. Ideally, the institutional and departmental reward structures will encourage effective teaching, despite cynics who point out that words of commitment are less powerful than the realities of promotion and tenure.

3. Faculty must "buy into" the value of classroom observations to enhance their teaching. They must be convinced that the process

itself works and that classroom observations offer rich, reflective, qualitative experiences. Good practice—supported by systematic, yet creative administration—can offer these assurances.

a. Responsive, responsible administrators—buoyed by conscientious support staff—must be selected to provide the infrastructure and motivation to insure that the program thrives.

b. Individual arrangements or any broader announcements or literature regarding classroom observations must make crystal clear the objectives. Full disclosure is essential: there should be no hidden agendas.

c. Effective faculty leaders are essential. The "best and the brightest" should be involved—individuals with the respect of campus colleagues who are committed to teaching but who also excel in research and service.

d. Even the "best and brightest" must be given systematic training in two essential skills: conducting the observation in a systematic, research-oriented manner and providing effective feedback within the broad context of sound pedagogical practices. Workshops offer concrete, interactive ways to accomplish this training, but less formal methods can also be effective, such as one-on-one coaching or serious review of prepared materials such as the Peer Visit Packet used at UMUC.

e. Faculty must be coached to use a three-stage consultation model that includes pre- and post-observation discussions and to conduct at least two classroom visits to get a broader perspective and to provide feedback on agreed-upon-changes.

f. Faculty must be encouraged to agree on a viable instrument to focus the observations. Many faculty prefer the type of focused narrative used at UMUC because it offers a holistic view of classroom activities and climate without presupposing any particular pedagogical approach, such as lecture.

g. All observations must be placed in the broader context of teaching enhancement. They should ideally be part of an extended review of classroom performance which takes into account other available data such as course materials, particularly the syllabi and exams; classroom research data; and student evaluations collected over time. (See the chapter by Fink, this volume.)

These recommendations emphasize key factors in the successful adaptation of a peer observation program. Faculty will be more motivated to participate if visits are conducted using principles of good practice in a climate of trust and mutual respect where teaching enhancement is valued.

PEER VISIT PROGRAM ASSESSMENTS

Assessment efforts must take into account the fact that teaching is an enormously complex undertaking involving many variables. Just within a single classroom, for example, these variables would include the interrelated impacts of institutional climate; instructor discipline expertise, teaching experience, and motivation; student learning styles, academic preparation, and motivation; and the physical environment. Measuring the impact of any teaching intervention over time, however controlled, is extremely difficult. Wunsch's (1994) warnings about the methodological pitfalls inherent in research and assessment of mentoring programs apply equally well to classroom observation models.

As an example, UMUC undertook a major three-year FIPSE-sponsored research project which sought to measure the impact of peer classroom observations on student learning outcomes using a classical experimental/control group design. Despite heroic efforts, this study produced relatively negligible results. After all the numbers were crunched and all the chi's were squared, it appears that ongoing peer classroom observations do no harm and quite possibly do some good, but there is no overwhelming statistically significant evidence to support their efficacy (Millis, 1995). Such an experiment was well worth conducting, however, because it reinforces the need for less quantifiably based measures to document teaching improvement and student learning.

In the clamor for accountability, reasoned voices must become advocates for thoughtful qualitative measures and for even more innovative research paths. Greene (1994), for example, suggests that "Rather than maintaining the long-standing conflicts between the quantitative and the qualitative, the objective and the purportedly subjective, educational researchers might turn to metaphor and the imagination to the end of recasting old opposition and, perhaps, to link theory and experience together in new and dynamic ways" (p. 457). Such measures are far more appropriate indications of the value of the reflective, recursive processes that constitute true teaching enhancement. As Richardson (1994) reminds us, the reflective teacher-researcher—the practitioner who conducts inquiries in the line of everyday work for the purposes of improvement—is constantly mediating ideas, constructing meaning and knowledge, acting on informed practice, and evaluating the results. This is what one hopes will come from well-conducted, collegial classroom observations.

CONCLUSION

The power of reflective discussions to improve teaching should not be underestimated. Canning (1991), for example, in her collaborative work with faculty at the University of Northern Iowa discovered that "Teachers found that reflection was an intrapersonal experience leading to insight about themselves as actors in their worlds. It prompted changes in self-concept, changes in perception of an event or person(s), or plans for a change in some behavior" (p.21). Such classroom-based discussions between two peers committed to student learning can help create the academic culture that nurtures community and collegiality that Lovett (1993) finds many faculty in the 1990s desire. Schilling and Schilling (1993) note in their advocacy of student portfolios (see also the chapter by Annis and Jones, this volume), "We need more approaches that are creative to describe what faculty members do in the classroom. We need to be able to convey a story that is supported by credible evidence; we need to open the classroom door so that parents and citizens can 'see' for themselves what we teach students and how we do it." Like portfolios, classroom observations open dialogues and open doors.

AUTHORS

Barbara J. Millis is Assistant Dean for Faculty Development, University of Maryland University College. She frequently offers workshops at professional conferences and for various colleges and universities. Her publications include books on cooperative learning and accounting and articles on cooperative learning, classroom observations (she directed a FIPSE project on the topic), the teaching portfolio, adjunct faculty, mentoring, TQM, and syllabus construction.

Barbara Beigun Kaplan is Coordinator of Faculty Development, University of Maryland University College. She received her B.A. and M.A. from the University of Chicago and her Ph.D. from the University of Maryland at College Park. She has worked as a college teacher and administrator for ten years and is the author of two books in her professional field of history.

Appendix A
The University Of Maryland University College
Peer Visit Preference Form, Fall 1994

Name_____ Soc.Sec.# _____

Address _____
             Street

_____
             City   State   Zip code
Phone (W) (   ) _____ (H) (   ) _____

Discipline _____

Number of visits during semester: one____two____three____four____over four____

Discipline areas you prefer to visit (e.g. IFSM, HIST, BEHS, etc.)

Discipline areas you DO NOT want to visit (e.g. IFSM, HIST, BEHS,etc.)

I can/cannot visit the following sites (please check one box for each):

Site Name	Site Code#	Can visit	Cannot visit	Might consider
ABERDEEN PROVING GROUND	70	____	____	____
ALEXANDRIA, VA	63	____	____	____
ANDREWS AFB	41	____	____	____
ANNAPOLIS, MD	75	____	____	____
ANNE ARUNDEL COMM CO.	71	____	____	____
BOLLING AFB (DC)	42	____	____	____
COLLEGE PARK	40	____	____	____
COLUMBIA, MD	82	____	____	____
CRYSTAL CITY, VA	84	____	____	____
DC (downtown sites)	22,25	____	____	____
FORT BELVOIR (VA)	68	____	____	____
FORT MEADE (MD)	45	____	____	____
PATUXENT (St. Mary's Co.)	58	____	____	____
PG COMM. COLLEGE (Largo)	61	____	____	____
ST. CHAS. CTR. (Waldorf)	50	____	____	____
SHADY GROVE (Mont.Co.)	51	____	____	____
WALTER REED MED.CTR (DC)	65	____	____	____

Days I CAN perform visits:
     M____ Tu____ W____ Th____ F____ Sa____ Su____

Days I CANNOT perform visits:
     M____ Tu____ W____ Th____ F____ Sa____ Su____

Can you visit during the day?_____ Which days? _____

I will/will not attend the Peer Visit Workshop on Tues., Sept. 13 from 6:15-9:15. (circle one)

I am/am not a new peer visitor this semester. (circle one)

Please fold, fasten, and mail. Please remember to affix a stamp. Thanks!

APPENDIX B

Classroom Visit Instrument (Consolidated)

University of Maryland University College
Undergraduate Programs

Classroom Visit

Faculty Member: Course & Section:

Date: Length of Visit: Place: Visitor:

Number of Students Present:

Classroom: Note any inadequate aspects of the classroom (size, temperature, acoustics, lighting, etc.)

Instruction: Comment on the presentation of the material: points to be covered and their relevance to class session, knowledge of subject matter, organization of lecture, explanation of terms and concepts.

Instructor/Student Rapport: Comment on student involvement and interaction with the instructor: opportunities for students to ask questions, answers to questions, guidance of class discussion, openness to suggestions and ideas.

Style of Presentation: Comment on gestures, physical movement, pitch and tone of voice, eye contact with students, use of resources such as blackboard, audio-visual media, handouts and other materials, demonstrations, student presentations and group activities, and the integration of various elements of the class session.

Syllabus: Comment on the syllabus and other written materials provided by the instructor. (Please refer to the University College *Syllabus Construction Handbook.*)

General Comments: What part of the class seemed particularly to enhance the learning process? What specific suggestions can you give for improving this particular class?

APPENDIX C
Peer Visitor Information Sheet

Name:

Years at University College:

Degrees Received/Universities Attended:

Primary Teaching Discipline:

Other Teaching Area(s):

1. What about your own teaching philosophy would you like to share with other faculty?

2. What do you consider your greatest teaching strengths?

3. Tell us a little about your interests outside of the classroom? (i.e. hobbies, sports, etc.)

4. Other comments:

REFERENCES

Boyer, E. (1990). *Scholarship reconsidered: Priorities of the professoriate.* Princeton, NJ: Carnegie Foundation for the Advancement of Teaching.

Brandt, R. (March 1991). Overview: Time for reflection. *Educational Leadership,* 48(6): 3.

Canning, C. (March 1991). What teachers say about reflection. *Educational Leadership,* 48(6): 18–21.

Centra, J.A. (1993). *Reflective faculty evaluation: Enhancing teaching and determining faculty effectiveness.* San Francisco, CA: Jossey-Bass.

Greene, M. (1994). Epistemology and educational research: The influence of recent approaches to knowledge. In L. Darling-Hammond (Ed.), *Review of Research in Education,* 20: 423–464. Washington, DC: American Educational Research Association.

Lovett, C.M. (November 1993). Listening to the faculty grapevine. *AAHE Bulletin,* pp. 3–5.

Lucas, A. (1990). The department chair as change agent. In P. Seldin (Ed.), *How administrators can improve teaching: Moving from talk to action in higher education.* San Francisco, CA: Jossey-Bass.

Massy, W.F., Wilger, A.K., & Colbeck, C. (July/August 1994). Overcoming "hollowed" collegiality: Departmental cultures and teaching quality. *Change: The Magazine of Higher Learning,* pp. 11–20.

Millis, B.J. (1989). Colleagues helping colleagues: A peer observation program model. *The Journal of Staff, Program, and Organization Development* 7(1): 15–21.

Millis, B.J. (1992). Conducting effective peer classroom observations. In D.H. Wulff and J.D. Nyquist (Eds.), *To improve the academy: Resources for faculty, instructional, & organizational development..* Stillwater, OK: POD/New Forums Press.

Millis, B.J. (1994). Forging the ties that bind: Peer mentoring part-time faculty. In M.A. Wunsch (Ed.), *New Directions for Teaching and Learning: No. 57. Mentoring revisited: Making an impact on individuals and institutions.* San Francisco, CA: Jossey-Bass.

Millis, B.J. (1995). Supporting part-time adjunct faculty through a systematic peer consultation program. In K. Brinko (Ed.), *A sourcebook on instructional consultation*. Reston, VA: National Center for Postsecondary Teaching, Learning, and Assessment.

Richardson, V. (1994).Conducting research on practice. *Educational Researcher, 23*(5): 5–20.

Schilling, K.M., & Schilling, K.L. (March 23, 1993). Point of view: Professors must respond to calls for accountability. *Chronicle of Higher Education*, p. A40.

Wunsch, M.A. (1994).Developing mentoring programs: Major issues and themes. In M. A. Wunsch (Ed.), *New Directions for Teaching and Learning: No. 57. Mentoring revisited: Making an impact on individuals and institutions*. San Francisco, CA: Jossey-Bass.

THIRTEEN

THE DEPARTMENT CHAIR'S ROLE IN IMPROVING TEACHING

Walter H. Gmelch

Department chairs are busy. Endless meetings, stacks of paperwork, constant interruptions, and fragmented encounters on a multitude of topics set the pace of a sprinter running long distances. But, what is most important to the chairs, and to their faculty? Do all the memos, meetings, phone calls, drop-in visitors and confrontations produce the desired results?

Effective chairs influence the important activities, but what are these activities? Faculty manuals at colleges and universities provide a list of the chairs' duties and responsibilities including: organizing and supervising curriculum; distributing teaching research loads; supervising department funds; recommending promotions and salaries. But such a list represents fragmented activities without focus on the bottom line—teaching.

THE CHAIR'S MOST IMPORTANT ROLE

What roles are critical for department chairs to achieve important results? Four main roles emerge from the popular literature and converge with current research: the Faculty Developer, the Manager, the Leader and the Scholar (Gmelch & Miskin, 1993). Serving as a *manager*, the foremost role from the dean's perspective, is the fiduciary requirement of the position, but it is often the role least liked (McLaughlin, and others,1975). Chairs spend over half their week in these activities.

As *leaders* of their departments, the second chair role, chairs provide long term direction and vision for the department, solicit ideas to improve it, and plan and evaluate curriculum development. Chairs seem

153

to like this challenging role because of opportunities to help others develop professional skills and to influence the profession and the department.

In contrast to the managerial nature of the two previously mentioned roles, chairs also try to simultaneously retain their *academic* identity. Not surprising, they enjoy and feel most comfortable in this role (McLaughlin, and others, 1975) but express frustration in their inability to spend much time on their academic interests.

Finally, department chairs view their *faculty developer* role as their most important responsibility. This not only involves the tasks of recruiting, selecting, and evaluating faculty, but also provides the informal faculty leadership to enhance faculty teaching, morale, and professional development. Ironically, chairs feel least trained and prepared in this area.

If chairs do not believe this is their most important role, they need only pull out their budget and calculate the percentage of funds they spend on personnel. Most will find 85 to 90 percent of department budgets allocated to faculty and staff salaries. In truth, in personnel selection a chair has only three choices: 1) Hire triple-stars, those senior faculty who have already achieved success in teaching, scholarship, and service. However, they are expensive and may not fall within budgetary constraints. 2) Hire assistant professors and develop them into excellent teachers, scholars, and citizens. Unfortunately, this takes time, energy, and a plan of action. 3) If a chair cannot afford to hire triple-stars and doesn't have the time and resources to develop faculty, their third choice is—prayer! The choice is to hire superstars or to develop faculty.

Where do the chair's primary interests lie? In order to obtain a sense of choice, a chair might reflect for a moment on how to develop his or her faculty, then look at each individual and identify the most important strategy that could improve teaching throughout the department. Are the strategies in line with the reality of obtaining results? Some time and energies may have to be realigned to maximize the chair's role as faculty developer. This is also the time to engage a *leadership* role and produce a conducive climate for effective teaching to flourish and be rewarded.

CREATING A PRODUCTIVE TEACHING DEPARTMENT

Remember the management axiom: what you pay attention to, you reward. Thus, chairs might ask themselves where their current energies are directed. Although colleges and universities pay lip service to effective instruction, chairs typically pay more attention to faculty research productivity. How can more time and attention be spent on the department's teaching? This chapter examines several types of chair behaviors that can build and maintain a conducive environment for effective teaching. These behaviors—selecting, supporting, developing, recognizing, rewarding, and reinforcing—constitute a framework necessary to practice the chair's role as a faculty developer (See Figure 1).

FIGURE 1

Effective Teaching Molecule: Elements of Chair Behaviors

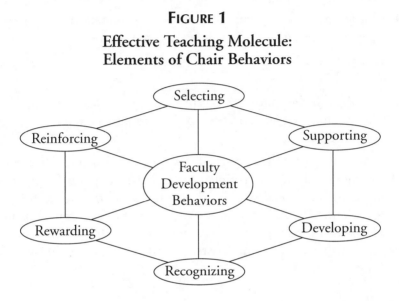

ELEMENTS OF CHAIR BEHAVIORS USED TO BUILD AND MAINTAIN TEACHING

Selecting

Deliberate and careful selection of new faculty affects the teaching and growth of a department more than any other decision a chair will make. Assuming faculty exercise little mobility in their professional career, the faculty recruited today will be on board for life. This is a million dollar decision, so it must be made wisely.

Analysis of the literature on faculty searches indicates there is no consensus on exactly how to conduct the most effective search. But simply placing an ad in *The Chronicle of Higher Education* isn't enough to attract the best teaching candidates. Recruiting requires a proactive, assertive, and positive approach, and any wait-and-see, passive strategy is insufficient

(Hynes, 1990). When searching for quality teachers in an applicant pool, these important organizing questions should be considered:

+ How much emphasis should be placed on effective teaching in the selection process?

+ Will there be an opportunity to observe the candidates teaching a class or lecturing to the institution's faculty and students?

+ Will teaching evaluations be requested by the selection committee, along with the customary evidence of scholarship?

+ Will the selection committee emphasize teaching over other faculty responsibilities?

+ Overall, will the candidate accept the position with the impression that teaching is a critical criterion for promotion, tenure and merit pay at the institution?

In our most recent faculty search, we requested that candidates submit evidence of effective teaching as part of their application process. A teaching portfolio would have been even more informative to our committee. (See the chapter by Zubizarreta, this volume). Afterwards many candidates mentioned that they were impressed with the covert message this sent to them about our priorities and our emphasis on effective instruction.

Supporting

While the findings in research on the effects of supporting behavior on employee performance is inconsistent, a chair can be assured that supporting has at least an indirect effect on faculty teaching performance. Supportive behavior contributes to higher performance when it increases confidence, lowers job stress, and increases cooperation (Yukl, 1994). Consider using two effective forms of supporting behaviors to increase cooperation and confidence and decrease stress: 1) modeling effective teaching and 2) filtering unnecessary faculty stress.

Adults learn better when they interact, and faculty teach better when they have an opportunity to observe effective teaching. Chairs can help faculty get together with a colleague for any number of opportunities to model effective teaching. For example, they can ask faculty to observe each other teach. They can then take notes and later discuss their observations and suggestions. The objective is to pick up ideas, techniques, and support from each other.

Another option is to have a faculty member join a colleague and observe a third teacher in action. The observers will then have a common basis for discussion and comparison of approaches (Magnan, 1989).

Third, when chairs or faculty members attend seminars, workshops, or conference presentations, they can keep a separate set of notes on teaching tips they observe. Once I attended a two week seminar on management development conducted by a host of highly effective presenters. During the seminar I kept two sets of notes: one on the content being covered, and the other on the effective teaching techniques I observed during the seminar. Upon returning to campus, I revised my class based on the techniques I picked up.

When asked the most important role a chair plays to support teaching faculty, one chair in our survey responded: be a stress filter for my faculty, keep the administrivia and aggravation out of the classroom. The stress-productivity research suggests that an optimum level of stress is required to maximize performance. Those faculty who are under-stimulated suffer from the trauma of routine: underchallenged, suffering from boredom, fatigue, frustration, and dissatisfaction with teaching. Such faculty literally "rustout" from teaching the same course year in and year out without variety, change, or stimulation to keep their motivation high. Their skills and/or knowledge have become obsolete. At the other extreme are faculty who have been teaching too hard for too long and find themselves "burned out." Here we find the ambitious, aggressive, and impatient faculty who have become exhausted from teaching too many classes, dissatisfied from not seeing the results, and despondent from loss of self-esteem in teaching (Gmelch, 1993).

In our study of stress and productivity, faculty reported higher stress from their teaching duties than for either scholarship or service (Gmelch, Lovrich & Wilke, 1984). Their teaching performance also resembled the stress and performance curve: With either too little stress (rustout) or too much stress (burnout), teaching performance declined and only at moderate levels of stress did faculty report excellence in teaching (Wilke, Gmelch & Lovrich, 1985).

Remember that stress, in the proper amounts, is not bad. Stress is much like your body's temperature; you must have it to say alive. The chair needs to apply treatment only when faculty temperatures run above or below normal. The treatment is to filter out excessive stress or light the fire under some faculty to ignite their teaching. Some of the following suggestions may help (Gmelch & Chan, 1994).

Stay alert for tips on teaching. Have faculty participate in special workshops or seminars on effective teaching, and make reading materials available such as books (e.g. Weimer's *Improving Your Classroom Teaching* or McKeachie's *Teaching Tips*), bulletins (e.g. *The Teaching Professor* , Magna Publications), or journals (*College Teaching*) on effective teaching.

Take risks to become an innovative teacher. Tell faculty to be bold and to take enough risks so that their teaching skills are challenged, but not so many that they are overwhelmed. Growth and productivity results from taking risks.

Avoid isolation in teaching. Under duress, many faculty begin to withdraw from spending time on teaching and from discussing teaching with colleagues. Isolation can draw them further into depression, so team the rusted out faculty with the teaching stars.

Overcome obsolescence through professional opportunities. In times of rapid change and advances in disciplines, faculty can become obsolete or dated in their professions. Encourage them to attend the numerous learned societies and professional associations so they can stay current with the latest thinking in the field.

Stretch for teaching success. Probably the most important relationship in effective teaching is the right tension between stress and success. One day I asked a premier consultant on effective teaching if he was as stressed now as he was when he first taught. His response: "No, but I am not as effective either." The right amount of stress spurs good teaching; it can motivate and provide energy.

Develop teaching associations. Often the isolation of teaching magnifies its difficulties. Some faculty have found that joining collegial groups interested in teaching encourages peer support. At our institution, an ad hoc group on effective teaching formed and functioned for several years as a catalyst and support group for those interested in honing their teaching skills.

Change the teaching scenery. The simple task of changing courses, roles, or geography can be beneficial to faculty. Chairs, for example, may enjoy the change in teaching assignment that accompanied the department chair position. Faculty can also benefit from visiting other campuses, meeting new colleagues, and taking a teaching sabbatical or exchange.

Faculty can—and should—engage in the above activities that help spark or maintain motivation. There are also some actions that chairs can take to prevent instructional burnout.

Allow faculty to say no to extra opportunities when overloaded. If a faculty member already has a full teaching load and she is asked to teach an extra course for extra pay, allow her to say no. Propose additional responsibilities as opportunities, not obligations.

Break larger classes into smaller modules. The thought of teaching a three credit course on a narrow subject for 45 hours over a semester is enough to burn anyone out before the semester even starts. Have faculty break the class into smaller, more manageable teaching modules and treat each module as a separate class with its own time line and set of requirements.

Help faculty find time for themselves, away from teaching. Experienced teachers often advocate the practice of blocking time for themselves, at least a few hours before class for preparation and reflection. One afternoon prior to class I put a note on my door "Please do not disturb—preparing for class." A couple of senior faculty commented that it appeared I wasn't accessible. But do we have to be constantly accessible? Won't classes be better if we are better prepared? Most people are better able to be attentive to others when they know they also have time to attend to their own concerns. The goal is quality access, not quantity.

Developing

Developing includes supportive behaviors such as coaching, training, mentoring, and counseling. As a rule, mentoring programs are misunderstood, inappropriately labeled, poorly developed, and not widely used. The chair should not accept total responsibility for coaching and mentoring all faculty in the department but should share responsibility with other competent and experienced department members. (See the chapter by Sorcinelli, this volume.) Although coaching and mentoring by senior faculty may occur informally, these activities should be formally established through designated mentors or mentor committees for each new faculty member. A chair can provide the following guidance.

Show concern for each faculty member's development. Most chairs spend little time on career counseling with faculty members because faculty are semi-autonomous and have few rungs in their career ladders. However, the basic principle of mentoring is to show genuine concern for the personal development and career progress of faculty. To that end, chairs should establish with each faculty member an annual individual development plan (see Gmelch & Miskin, 1993). The plan could end up in the form of a teaching portfolio at the end of the year, not necessarily for annual review purposes but for self-development and advancement (see Seldin, 1991).

Provide support for effective teaching development programs. Another way to promote skill development in teaching is to keep faculty informed about relevant workshop and seminar opportunities. The chair should encourage enrollment in workshops and seminars, and the department should cover the expenses. Some universities and colleges facilitate and encourage attendance by not only covering the expenses but by providing financial compensation in the form of a daily stipend for their attendance, or by rearranging faculty schedules to allow time away from daily duties.

Provide special opportunities for skill development. In addition to formal workshops, chairs and colleges can support the development of effective teaching in other ways. One approach is to provide special teaching projects and assignments. For example, allocating funds for summer teaching stipends to support course development or innovative teaching techniques not only improves teaching but elevates the visibility and importance of effective teaching on campus.

Promote faculty reputation. A department chair can promote the reputation of those who teach and encourage the refinement of teaching by letting students know about faculty members' achievements, expertise, and excellence in teaching. Trumpet faculty success.

Serve as a role model. Our studies of department chairs from community colleges and research universities showed that almost all maintained some teaching responsibility while serving as chair.[1] This is an opportunity to demonstrate a chair's prowess as a teacher. Others can be invited to attend, and the chair can offer his or her service as co-teacher or guest lecturer in the classes of other faculty.

Networking

Networking includes developing and maintaining contacts with other colleagues who are important sources of information and assistance on teaching, both inside and outside the university setting. Most networking involves people other than junior faculty or the department chair. Faculty can use networks to accomplish a variety of teaching objectives.

Faculty may welcome new ideas from external networks consisting of colleagues in other departments, universities, colleges, and professional associations as well as client and customer groups. Chairs can help get faculty involved in opportunities which they might not have access to. Recently three colleges at our university developed an interdisciplinary program to infuse TQM into our curriculum. The chairs from different disciplines were able to network with colleagues from different colleges to share and develop courses and to team teach the principles of TQM.

Faculty members' rate of tenure and promotion may, in fact, be related to their ability to network effectively. As Boice points out, faculty "...cannot flourish in isolation. Before they will feel comfortable and efficient, they must find social supports and intellectual stimulation" (1992, p. 43). This means relaxing the usual autonomy so often characteristic of faculty so that colleagues can assist each other in their teaching efforts. Boice found in his research that "Those new faculty who made teaching a collegial and sociable venture found that task of teaching easier and more rewarding" (1992, p. 80). The stark absence of collegial support and networking, such as co-teaching and mentoring, reinforces the need for the chair to facilitate faculty connectedness. (See the chapter by Hecht, this volume.) Clearly, we need to find ways to change the culture of solitary teaching to one that makes teaching a more public and collective activity.

The following suggestions can help a chair use networking to support effective teaching in the department.

Celebrate effective teaching by using ceremonies, meetings and social events. Talk with faculty, even informally, before, during, and after these events about the importance of teaching.

Provide opportunities to meet and introduce department colleagues to others interested in faculty development and effective teaching.

Demonstrate acceptance and positive regard for teaching.

Be accessible to provide social support and empathy when someone is anxious or upset about his or her teaching.

Be discreet about teaching problems that come to your attention.

Provide recognition for special accomplishments by faculty in your department. For example, send a letter or note congratulating people for positive comments you have heard about their teaching.

Facilitate opportunities to join groups supporting teaching. These groups or memberships for external networking may include professional associations, learned societies, or even workshops.

Introduce faculty to new technology that fosters networking, such as Internet or Bitnet.

Keep in contact with network members. Attend professional meetings and use them as an opportunity to make new contacts, renew old ones, and introduce your faculty into your networks.

Recognizing

Although recognition comes in many forms, the most common are praise and awards. Neither has to cost the department fiscal resources. It just means that the chair catches faculty doing things right and provides a verbal commendation, expression of appreciation, or gesture that acknowledges the faculty member's teaching accomplishments. Chairs need to be "out and about" to find out who is achieving success in their classrooms. When things are being done right, comment on the spot and follow up with a letter of commendation for their file (with a copy to the dean). Eventually a chair may wish to nominate the faculty member for a teaching excellence award.

Most praise is private, but it can be used in a public gathering, exhibition, or ceremony as well. The use of a news release on faculty teaching activities, departmental bulletin boards displaying acts of teaching, and yearly faculty excellence awards for teaching, not just scholarship, can be bestowed at the departmental level to ensure a culturally motivating environment to support teaching excellence (Gmelch, 1987).

Recognition should be based on the following questions: What should be recognized? When should it be done? Who should be recognized? What form of recognition should be used? Given these questions, the following guidelines may be helpful (Yukl, 1994):

+ Recognize a variety of teaching contributions and achievements.

+ Actively search for teaching contributions to recognize.

+ Recognize improvements in teaching.

+ Recognize commendable teaching efforts that may have failed.

+ Do not limit recognition to senior faculty; boost the morale of new and junior faculty as well.

+ Do not limit recognition to a few best teachers because other faculty may feel that recognition is not within their reach.

+ Provide specific recognition for unique achievements such as innovative teaching techniques.

✦ Provide timely recognition—once a year rituals will not motivate the masses.

✦ Use an appropriate form of recognition that is acceptable to faculty.

Rewarding

Reward is different than recognition in that it involves giving a tangible benefit to faculty for effective teaching performance, a significant teaching achievement, or teaching assistance provided to other faculty or teaching assistants. These rewards may be in the form of merit increases, promotions, or better teaching assignments.

The opportunities for rewarding faculty for teaching excellence may be limited on two accounts. First, chairs may not have the authority or resources to dispense tangible rewards, such as merit increases. Second, chairs may well have greater reward power over staff than with peers since faculty excellence awards are usually governed by faculty committees, formal policies, and reward systems in colleges or universities. But chairs should not miss an opportunity to nominate and promote their faculty colleagues. Even with limited reward power, the following guidelines should be considered to help the chair make the most effective and appropriate decisions to enhance effective teaching.

✦ Find out what rewards are attractive to faculty.

✦ Find out what rewards are available both within and outside the institution.

✦ Identify and evaluate the relevant aspects of effective teaching to be rewarded.

✦ Explain the criteria used to determine rewards.

✦ Distribute rewards in a fair way.

✦ Give rewards in a timely manner.

Reinforcing

How can chairs reinforce effective teaching in their departments? Where does one start? Although many faculty perform admirably as teachers, some have not maximized their capabilities. Lovett observes that "Most members of the professoriate are dedicated scholars and teachers.... But for many of them the fun seems to have gone out of their work" (1993, p. 3). Some faculty can improve their teaching without outside help, while others need added support and reinforcement.

Creswell and others (1990) propose a five-step process based largely on the consultative/collegial models found in instructional development. Four of the steps are listed here.

Gather background information. Before approaching faculty about their teaching problems, gather data about their performance beyond the formal student evaluations collected each semester and reported once a year. Consider the multiple sources outlined in teaching portfolios. For instance, visit with students, talk with senior faculty, and tap into the grapevine—staff, students, faculty, and other administrators. The chair's support staff may have especially helpful information from their contact with faculty and students.

Observe the performance. While faculty autonomy usually means the right to teach behind closed doors, most faculty manuals and administrative policies provide both the right and responsibility of chairs to directly observe teaching. With a troubled teacher, the chair's objective is to explore the potential problem so that it can be remedied. In cases where direct observation by the department chair is too threatening, a senior faculty mentor can observe the teaching and formally report directly back to the faculty member and chair.

Facilitate improvement and the practice of new skills. The chair and/or the faculty mentor may want to refer to books on teaching, workshops, or their own practical experience to help the faculty member develop a plan for improvement.

Monitor the progress and advocate the faculty member. Revert to step one and gather new information on the success of the new teaching method(s). It may take time to see progress but chairs have a moral obligation to their colleagues and an ethical commitment to their students to try to help struggling faculty improve their teaching.

In conclusion, faculty lead complex lives but they worry most and work hardest at teaching, scholarship, and collegiality. "Mastery of any one of the three is difficult, and mastery of all of them is miraculous" (Boice, 1992, p. 17). Nevertheless, success at any one of the three activities rarely comes in isolation from success in the other two. The role of the chair is to foster good teaching, good scholarship, and good collegiality, forging them into a productive and supportive department.

AUTHOR

Walter H. Gmelch is Professor and Chair of the Department of Educational Leadership and Counseling Psychology at Washington State University, where he also serves as Director of the Center for the Study of the Department Chair. An educator, management consultant, university administrator, and former business executive, Gmelch has conducted research, written extensively, and conducted workshops on the topics of leadership, team development, conflict, stress, and time management.

REFERENCES

Boice, R. (1992). *The new faculty member.* San Francisco, CA: Jossey-Bass.

Creswell, J.W., Wheeler, D.W., Seagren, A.T., Egly, N.J., & Beyer, K. D. (1990). *The academic chairperson's handbook.* Lincoln, NE: The University of Nebraska Press.

Gmelch, W.H., & Miskin, V.D. (1993). *Leadership skills for department chairs.* Bolton, MA: Anker.

Gmelch, W.H. (1993). *Coping with faculty stress.* Newbury Park, CA: Sage.

Gmelch, W.H. (1982). *Beyond stress to effective management.* New York, NY: John Wiley.

Gmelch, W.H., & Chan, W. (1994). *Thriving on stress for success.* Newbury Park, CA: Corwin.

Gmelch, W.H. (1987). What colleges and universities can do about faculty stress. In P. Seldin (Ed.), *Coping with faculty stress.* San Francisco, CA: Jossey-Bass.

Gmelch, W.H., Lovrich, N.P., & Wilke, P.K. (1984). Stress in academe: A national perspective. *Research in Higher Education, 20*(4), 477–490.

Hynes, W.J. (1990). Successful proactive recruiting strategies: Quest for the best. In J. Bennett and D. Figuli (Eds.), *Enhancing departmental leadership: The roles of the chairperson.* New York, NY: American Council on Education/Macmillan.

Lovett, C.M. (1993). Listening to the faculty grapevine. *AAHE Bulletin, 43*(3), 3–5.

Magnan, B. (1989). *147 practical tips for teaching professors.* Madison, WI: Magna.

McKeachie, W.J. (1986). *Teaching tips: A guidebook for the beginning college teacher,* (8th ed.). Lexington, MA: D. C. Heath.

McLaughlin, G.W., Montgomery, J.R., & Malpass, L.F. (1975). Selected characteristics, roles, goals, and satisfactions of department chairmen in state and land-grant institutions. *Research in Higher Education, 3,* 243–259.

Seldin, P. (1991). *The teaching portfolio: A practical guide to improved performance and promotion/tenure decisions.* Bolton, MA: Anker.

Weimer, M. (1993). *Improving your classroom teaching.* Newbury Park, CA: Sage.

Wilke, P.K., Gmelch, W.G., & Lovrich, N.P. (1985). Stress and productivity: Evidence of the inverted U-function. *Public Productivity Review, 9*(4), 342–356.

Yukl, G. A. (1994). *Leadership in organizations.* Englewood Cliffs, NJ: Prentice-Hall.

Endnote

[1] The Center for the Study of Department Chair (CSDC) at Washington State University has conducted three national studies (in 1990, 1992, and 1994) of department chairs at research and doctoral granting universities and community colleges. For further information contact the author at CSDC, Department of Educational Leadership and Counseling Psychology, Washington State University, Pullman, WA 99164-2136.

FOURTEEN

USING TEACHING PORTFOLIO STRATEGIES TO IMPROVE COURSE INSTRUCTION

John Zubizarreta

Teaching portfolios are used in over 500 colleges and universities in the United States and Canada as part of a determined program of faculty development and teaching improvement and often as a valid and effective method of evaluation for personnel decisions. That figure is climbing. Although some Canadian institutions implemented "dossiers" some time ago, it took longer for the portfolio to take firm root in American institutions. But the trend indicates clearly that portfolios rapidly are becoming the preferred tool for encouraging the kind of reflective analysis and attention to evidence of sound performance and student learning that result in improved teaching.

The portfolio idea is now well beyond the testing stage. Institutions as diverse in mission and size as Harvard University, University of Nevada-Reno, Wake Forest University (North Carolina), Valdosta State University (Georgia), Columbia College (South Carolina), and Miami-Dade Community College (Florida) routinely or experimentally use portfolios in vital ways to enhance the quality of instruction in their academic programs. Numerous turns on the portfolio's utility appear in Knapper (1978); Shore, et al. (1986); Bird (1989); Boyer (1990); Watkins (1990); Edgerton, Hutchings, and Quinlan (1991); O'Neil and Wright (1991); Seldin (1991, 1993); Lemm (1992); Urbach (1992); and Anderson (1993). The 1993 National Symposium on Improving Teaching Quality sponsored by Texas A & M University focused on the efficacy of portfolios for enhancement and assessment of teaching performance. The portfolio is here to stay.

For many faculty, the portfolio provides the necessary formal process and product to make sweeping changes in pedagogy or methodology. As an instrument that grows out of substantial reflection and analysis tied to hard evidential materials or "artifacts" of teaching, the document also offers teachers a revealing and credible system for valid assessment of performance. But considering its flexible, discipline-based format which respects and validates the individuality and integrity of teaching, the portfolio serves equally well as a catalyst for substantive improvement of the philosophy, strategies, materials, outcomes, evaluations, and goals of a single course. The focus of the teaching portfolio then shifts from profiling general accomplishment to close scrutiny of one course.

One of my own interests in the teaching portfolio project has taken the direction of using the portfolio for improvement of a particular course. As Director of the Honors Program at my institution, I have drafted my own portfolio for an honors course and served as a mentor to other honors faculty interested in identifying, documenting, and cultivating the distinctive nature of an honors class with special attention to improvement. Investment in such a project is totally voluntary, and faculty who have elected to write a portfolio with my collaboration have reaped benefits that extend beyond the honors arena. Such adaptation of a teaching portfolio has resulted in clearer, stronger missions for several honors courses and in significant enhancement of teaching in the program. The concept works in honors, and I have written another document on a tough course I teach for English majors. The results in both courses are comparable: better teaching; better learning.

THE COURSE PORTFOLIO AS PROCESS

The *course portfolio* modifies the basic purpose and components of a more comprehensive teaching portfolio by highlighting a professor's concentrated interest in improving a specific course. If a teacher's responsibilities include certain regularly scheduled classes, then the process character of a course portfolio offers the benefit of providing a concise, authentic record of performance which details progress and setbacks, success and disappointment in a framework of selective but honest, varied, and judicious information reexamined on a timely basis. The course portfolio may be used, of course, for evaluation of teaching, and a professor may submit to a personnel committee a package of such documents for a representative sample of achievement in variously assigned courses.

But the more comprehensive and diverse model of the teaching portfolio developed by Seldin (1991, 1993) may be better suited for such a purpose because it allows for compact presentation of abundant information and empirical evidence from a number of sources. The real advantage of a single course portfolio, and the strongest motive for writing one, is the ability of such a focused and cogent process document to improve the quality of instruction and learning in one class.

I continue to stress the notion that the course portfolio, just as its parent, the large scale teaching portfolio, is a *process* document because the conscientious teacher knows that improvement depends upon establishing a baseline of information and then progressing through stages of experimentation and development until enhancement of particular areas becomes evident through assessment. A valid and serviceable portfolio is not a one-time effort but rather a document that helps the careful instructor record levels of achievement in a concentrated manner. A course portfolio engages the faculty member in a process that periodically assesses the effectiveness of the various dimensions of a particular course. As a continual product of research and critical thinking, the course portfolio encourages both intellectual and practical revisions that set the stage for genuine improvement.

THE CONTENTS OF A COURSE PORTFOLIO

The course portfolio is an evidence-based narrative document in which a faculty member concisely organizes selected details of teaching effort in a chosen class, emphasizing the kind of reflective analysis that leads to viable conclusions about instructional performance and student outcomes. As a result, the portfolio provides the impetus for improvement of the course. In short, the portfolio reflects the same careful methodology of good research that results in creditable scholarship, helping to demonstrate that the teaching enterprise is not apart from the intellectual growth of faculty or from the professional imperatives of scholarly development. Writing a course portfolio reveals precisely how vigorous teaching and diligent scholarship are inseparable facets of the professoriate.

As opposed to about eight pages of abundant materials in the *teaching* portfolio, an effective *course* portfolio consists of about four pages that critically study selected information about a particular class. If the genuine purpose for engaging in the process of composing such a portfolio is improvement, then the teacher gains nothing from choosing only evidence of success. The outstanding instructor knows that risks are vital to development, and such ventures continually supply new areas for progress. If in the portfolio a professor articulates the charges of experimentation and growth in teaching a course, then inclusion of disappointing experiences or results is proof not of failure but of vigorous commitment to improvement through challenge. If an institution states as mission the same charges, then the teacher's course portfolio is compelling proof of the vitality of instruction at the classroom level and of commitment to teaching improvement and support at the institutional level.

Strategies for Improved Teaching of a Course

The portfolio leads to improvement of a specific course and to strengthened teaching by helping the faculty member to engage the following strategies:

1. Identify specific duties of a course and how such responsibilities fit into the professor's teaching load and other assignments

2. Articulate a teaching philosophy for a particular course

3. Describe, analyze, and evaluate course materials, methods, and outcomes

4. Examine course competencies and objectives

5. Study student and peer reviews and formulate an action plan for improvement

6. Posit specific teaching goals

7. Provide supportive documentation of performance

Such self-conscious planning results in sound assessment and better teaching, especially if the portfolio as process is revised regularly.

Table of Contents

In a comprehensive *teaching* portfolio, an instructor develops various categories that profile the general teaching enterprise by incorporating both narrative reflection and hard evidence (see chapter by Annis and Jones, this volume). In addition to special headings that distinguish the individual character of each portfolio's foundation in disciplinary differences and teaching styles, divisions include seminal statements on teaching responsibilities, philosophy, methods, singular strategies and initiatives, materials, student and peer ratings, student products, awards, and goals. A "Table of Contents" identifies the major headings of the portfolio, and if the purpose of the portfolio is improvement of teaching, the table will favor description, analysis, experimental efforts, diagnostic review, and goals.

With improvement of a particular course in mind, a professor composing a *course* portfolio will modify the table only slightly and add, perhaps, a discussion of abiding efforts to perfect the various dimensions of the course through professional development of teaching.

Table of Contents

1. Assigned Course Responsibility
2. Reflective Statement of Course Philosophy
3. Methods and Strategies
4. Description of Course Materials: Syllabi, Assignments, Handouts
5. Products: Evidence of Students' Progressive Learning in Course
6. Description and Analysis of Student and Peer Evaluations
7. Professional Development of Teaching: Conferences, Workshops, Revisions, and Experiments Related to Improvement of Course
8. Short and Long Term Course Goals
9. Appendices

Writing becomes the vehicle for action, the recorded starting point for real change. Regardless of purpose or signature items that individualize each portfolio according to varied teaching values, styles, and academic disciplines, the narrative body of the portfolio offers an opportunity for written reflection about what and how we teach but more importantly *why*, an essential critical activity that enhances the quality of teaching an assigned course.

Documenting Evidence

The course portfolio also includes a valuable appendix of materials that document and support the narrative, offering the hard copy information and evidence necessary for thorough and solid assessment for either evaluation or improvement. Although such documentation is indispensable for evaluation, I have found in my experience with portfolios that careful corroboration through painstaking records and collected materials generates prompt and effective improvement because the professor has immediate access to course documents, rating forms, and student products which become the positive groundwork for enhancement. For example, before I developed a portfolio for a new course assigned to me two years ago, the attention to products of student learning which is so vital to instructional effectiveness was missing from my estimation of my teaching in a course on literary history and theory. Because of the highly conceptual nature of the course content and the predominantly seminar-type discussions and projects, my early decision to use traditionally graded, objective and short-answer examinations had not worked well to test the extent of student learning. Yet student essays and classroom discourses were generally good, suggesting that learning was occurring, students were acquiring conceptual knowledge, but such gains were not showing up on the type of exams I was using. Test results often seemed disappointing, and student ratings and comments pinpointed exams as an area needing improvement.

In my course portfolio, after considerable reflection and analysis stemming from meticulous and documented observation of student performance in class exchanges, informal assignments, and research projects, I recorded my decision to shift course requirements to use take-home exams which could serve as student study guides for the only formal, closed-book test given near the end of the term. Encouraged to collaborate on the take-home assignments, students now cooperate to reinforce learning effectively without compromising standards. Along with such "learning exams," students keep their own portfolios of written entries in which they document their thinking about key issues and texts of the course, sharing their writing periodically throughout the term and using their entries to identify questions, discoveries, connections. The representative products collected in the appendix of my course portfolio currently certify that my efforts to improve the course have paid off handsomely. The take-home assignments and the students' portfolios have greatly increased students' success in the course, and I have all the evidence needed not just to authenticate progress for evaluation, but also to begin a detailed, factual process of yet further improvement in the class. And the course portfolio will continue to frame the process.

Gathering Information

In addition to balancing reflective narration and evidence in the appendix, a successful, well-rounded course portfolio gathers and studies information in three key areas:

1. Materials from oneself

2. Materials from others

3. Products of student learning

Shore, et al. (1986); Edgerton, Hutchings, and Quinlan (1991); O'Neil and Wright (1991); Seldin (1991, 1993); and Urbach (1992) offer numerous items that can be collected in the three areas, and one should consult such sources for ideas about what details to incorporate into a portfolio, remembering, however, that the document consists of selective and current information.

Once the process is initiated, instructors generally find that producing materials from oneself is easy because we write our own statements of responsibilities, philosophy, methodologies, and goals; similarly, syllabi, assignments, and other materials are readily at hand. Materials from others are trickier to produce because they are comprised, for example, of student and peer evaluations of a course, feedback that varies in availability and utility. The most difficult area to address is the products of student learning, a prerequisite component of authentic and rigorous assessment of what and how students genuinely learn in a course. Examinations, written reports, research projects, formative journals, published papers, presentations at conferences, records of course application to higher level achievements—such items can constitute compelling evidence of student learning in a course, but professors must be shrewd and deliberate in discovering ways of strengthening student performance in a manner that will produce excellent outcomes. The course portfolio supplies the teacher with a vehicle for gathering evidence of learning and for definite action to improve the impact of teaching on a specific student group.

In compiling information in all three areas, the professor interested in improvement will scrutinize the connections among philosophy, actual methods, course materials, student feedback, peer reviews, and outcomes of learning. Using the course portfolio to collect such vital details and recognizing the importance of coherence among the various dimensions of the instrument, the instructor becomes thoughtful and intentional about scrupulously examining student products and materials generated by self and others to verify the extent of actual learning in a course. The portfolio effectively becomes a baseline document in a focused process of improvement, setting the stage for novel strategies in the classroom and for future assessment. As new items are added in each of the three main areas, old ones are removed; as old goals are achieved, new ones are added, keeping the document current and relevant. The portfolio becomes a process of continual reflection and specific, decisive action concerning one's mastery of a course.

THE VALUE OF A MENTOR

In the existing, growing research on portfolios, one emphatic point bears repetition. Writing a portfolio in isolation does not produce quality work; collaboration with a mentor is essential. When a faculty member chooses to compose a course portfolio, the temptation to work privately is great because of the inherent tendency of teachers to protect the valuable autonomy of their classrooms (see the two chapters by Hecht and by Gmelch, this volume). Yet one of the most invigorating, rewarding, and crucial facets of the portfolio process is the collaborative effort between the instructor and the mentor who helps steer the direction of the document to meet the needs of improvement or assessment. Collaboration—especially if the mentor is a consultant inside or outside one's discipline—insures a fresh, critical perspective that encourages cohesion between narrative and appendix. However, a colleague who shares responsibility for teaching the same course at other times can be a boon to the instructor working to improve the course because of the power of collective experience. In mapping out objectives, competencies, and strategies in my course on literary theory, for instance, I consulted with two colleagues who teach the same subject both in my department and at another institution to help me flush out what I had been doing in my class that worked and what I could do to enrich student learning. The input substantially affected the reflective component of my course portfolio and served to steer my action plan for improvement.

Virtually all literature on portfolios urges faculty to enlist the creative, supportive help of a mentor. Such an advisor—especially if trained in developing portfolios—helps to uncover objective information that is readily discovered in a teacher's work. The mentor's primary role is to assist a colleague in improving instruction in actual ways with definite products of student learning, exactly the supportive scrutiny needed to strengthen a particular course. Collaboration, then, is a pivotal dimension of the portfolio which balances subjectivity in the narrative and connects the portfolio to objective criteria.

Edgerton, Hutchings, and Quinlan (1991, p. 51) agree that working with a consulting mentor is important in writing a portfolio. They note that since teaching "tends to be a private, solitary activity, collaboratively designed portfolios are an antidote to this isolation and a way to promote collegial exchange focused on the substance—the scholarship—of teaching." Seldin (1993, p. 4) stresses that mentors are indispensable because "portfolios prepared by the professor working alone do not include the collegial or supervisory support needed in a program of teaching improvement." Normally, collaboration on the development of a single course portfolio is voluntary and faculty driven, breaching the delicate boundaries of classroom autonomy and inviting open and supportive examination of teaching performance in a specific setting. Both mentors and teachers have only one real objective in such an enterprise—to enhance the quality of teaching and learning—and mentors keep faculty fixed exclusively on that specific aim.

One important way a mentor can help guide the development of a course portfolio for improvement is to be sure the document offers a coherent profile in which all parts support the whole. Gaps in connections among the various components of a portfolio signal areas that an instructor may examine more closely for opportunities to strengthen performance. For instance, suppose that a professor has stated high scholarly expectations as a key value in an upper-level course. Student evaluations seem to bolster the claim of uncompromising standards, and the brief comment of a peer who has visited one class appears supportive. Everything looks good in the reflective, narrative portion of the portfolio, but the trained, supportive inquiry of a mentor reveals that while descriptions of methodology corroborate intent, materials such as the syllabus, supportive handouts, or assignment sheets lack evidence of the stated philosophy. The mentor might suggest a clear focus on scholarship in the course materials by recommending bibliographies of secondary readings included in syllabi or written library assignments incorporated into weekly activities. The essential gain is that through collaboration all efforts toward improvement are grounded in clearly identified, specific areas discerned best by a mentor who is intent not on the critique of disciplinary content but on the process of teaching. Initiatives for development are therefore purposeful and precise for effective action.

Tips on Composing and Maintaining the Course Portfolio

Research on the efficacy of portfolios in enhancing the quality of teaching supports the claim that portfolios do help improve actual classroom performance. Based on the literature and on my own experience in adapting the concept to help strengthen particular courses, I offer the following tips that may help faculty initiate the process of a course portfolio and maintain the momentum of teaching improvement.

Identify the purpose of the portfolio. Primary motivation should be the improvement of a course, but the document may serve for evaluation. Purpose helps determine not only the content but the format of the portfolio.

Start writing. Far from coy, the exhortation is sincere. As a teacher of writing, I know that while sometimes in college classes the reverse seems true, writing and thinking go hand in hand. The presumed effective writing and cogent scholarship that go into a sound portfolio are the result of thoughtful inquiry and analysis, the seeds for real improvement in teaching. Develop a preliminary "Getting Started" form, compose a series of key questions or explicit issues, or list a number of areas that require attention based on previous experience. Such drafting begins a process that builds progressively and culminates in a rich, rewarding product.

Regardless of purpose, documentation and ample evidence in an appendix are crucial to successful implementation of action plans based on the research conducted in the portfolio process. Hard evidential support is the solid starting point for both meaningful improvement and positive assessment.

Begin a comprehensive and intentional effort to gather selective, honest data from as many diverse sources as possible but with fair representation in the three main areas of information from oneself, from others, and from products of student learning. Maintain good records. One of the advantages of writing a course portfolio that collects such details is that the professor is encouraged to act decisively to improve specific facets of a course and to authenticate development efforts with recorded evidence.

Date the portfolio. Although the advice seems elementary, a date helps to establish a baseline for improvement and for goals. Not insignificantly, a professor acquires a great sense of completion and satisfaction when a later draft clearly reveals substantive gains in a course.

Keep the portfolio complete but compact. Four pages should be adequate for cogent description, analysis, and conclusions necessary for lay-ing the foundation for enriching a course. As changes occur, both the narrative and the appendix are revised to account for new details and set new goals. If the professor has engaged in writing a comprehensive teaching portfolio of about eight pages for evaluation purposes, the course portfolio may be incorporated into the larger document as a brief demonstration of improvement efforts in a specific teaching assignment; thus, the teaching portfolio serves to profile a vigorous instructor committed both to valid, empirical assessment for career advancement and to determined growth in teaching proficiency.

Pay particular attention to student outcomes of learning in a course. Without the inclusion of such products, the capacity of the portfolio to prompt positive change is diminished. Good teaching must be connected to good outcomes. The bottom line on whether a professor's teaching has made a difference in student learning is the work produced by students. The impact of teaching on students' progress may be demonstrated by evidence such as course projects, field reports, successive essays in drafts, pre- and post-tests, presentations at conferences based on course work, publications of course papers, documentation of students' success in higher level courses or post-graduate careers. No extensive studies exist to prove that portfolios strengthen student outcomes in a course, but a portfolio raises a professor's awareness of the importance of products and of what kinds of outcomes to develop for more effective teaching and for a stronger course; such reflection and strategy can improve products as a consequence of the portfolio's processes of discovery, description, documentation, and planning.

Do not side step occasional disappointments in teaching or learning. Improvement depends upon risk and experimentation, and a course portfolio can provide a vehicle for change and development through continual inquiry and analysis. Good teachers take chances yet continue to maintain overall excellence because they know the value of change based on detailed assessment and experience. The course portfolio offers a tightly organized model for such growth.

Enlist the aid of a mentor. Collaboration provides a critical and supportive perspective that is important in delineating areas for development. The mentoring process is a pivotal dimension of the portfolio that counters subjectivity and links the portfolio to objective criteria that set the parameters for improvement.

Work closely with a department chair, faculty development advisor, instruction committee head, or other supervisor to ensure that the portfolio addresses the wider considerations of departmental and institutional teaching missions. A single course portfolio can be a powerful tool in the processes of program accreditation and faculty evaluation. The bonus, of course, is the value of the portfolio in strengthening individual instruction and thus curricular programs in general, a premium virtue in revaluing the integrity of teaching in the individual setting of a single course.

As we strengthen courses one by one, professors will be better poised to make a difference in shifting institutional priorities to reclaim the significance of teaching in the individual classroom. With its emphasis on reflective analysis, assessment of empirical evidence, and articulation of specific action plans, the course portfolio can be a forceful instrument in changing the culture of a profession that has grown to favor research over classroom teaching. Ironically, such a schism actually is a false dichotomy, for the vigorous professor knows that the intellectual development of faculty and the advancement of disciplinary knowledge are inseparably linked to effective teaching. The course portfolio begins the process of improvement by engaging a professor in the scholarship of teaching, a strategy of critical inquiry into teaching performance in a single course, a starting point for better teaching all around.

AUTHOR

John Zubizarreta is Professor of English and Director of Honors at Columbia College, South Carolina. He has been recognized for exemplary teaching by the American Association for Higher Education, the Methodist Board of Higher Education, and the South Carolina Commission of Higher Education. He was named CASE Professor of the Year in South Carolina for 1994. Zubizarreta has published variously on modern literature, pedagogy, collaborative scholarship, and teaching portfolios.

REFERENCES

Anderson, E. (1993). *Campus use of the teaching portfolio: Twenty-five profiles.* Washington, DC: American Association for Higher Education.

Bird, T. (1989). The schoolteacher's portfolio. In L. Darling-Hammond and J. Millman (Eds.), *Handbook on the evaluation of elementary and secondary schoolteachers.* Newbury Park, CA: Sage.

Boyer, E.L. (1990). *Scholarship revisited.* Princeton, NJ: Carnegie Foundation for the Advancement of Teaching.

Edgerton, R., Hutchings, P., & Quinlan, K. (1991). *The teaching portfolio: Capturing the scholarship in teaching.* Washington, DC: American Association for Higher Education.

Knapper, C.K. (1978). Evaluation and teaching: Beyond lip service. Paper presented at the International Conference on Improving University Teaching, Aachen, Germany.

Lemm, R. (Feb. 1992). The I ain't got no teaching portfolio blues. *The Point, 1*(2). Charlottetown, PEI: University of Prince Edward Island.

O'Neil, M.C., & Wright, W.A. (1991). *Recording teaching accomplishment: A Dalhousie guide to the teaching dossier.* Halifax, NS: Office of Instructional Development and Technology, Dalhousie University.

Seldin, P. (1991). *The teaching portfolio: A practical guide to improved performance and promotion/tenure decisions.* Bolton, MA: Anker.

Seldin, P., & Associates. (1993). *Successful use of teaching portfolios.* Bolton, MA: Anker.

Shore, B.M., et al. (1986). *The teaching dossier* (Revised ed.). Montreal, PQ: Canadian Association of University Teachers.

Urbach, F. (1992). Developing a teaching portfolio. *College Teaching* 40: 71–74.

Watkins, B.T. (May 16, 1990). New technique tested to evaluate college teaching. *The Chronicle of Higher Education*, A15–17.

FIFTEEN

STUDENT PORTFOLIOS: THEIR OBJECTIVES, DEVELOPMENT, AND USE

Linda Annis and Carolee Jones

Educators are increasingly faced with demands by many constituencies for more information about how effectively teachers in college are teaching and whether their students are learning enough of the "right" kinds of things.

Schilling and Schilling (1993) point out that educators have three clear choices about how to respond. We can choose not to respond or we can respond minimally. But these choices open the door for educational agendas to be set by those outside academe. A far better choice is to directly address the public's questions. Why? Because this approach is much more likely to lead to teaching improvement and gains in student learning.

One of the thorniest problems we have to face is how to describe exactly what we are doing in the classroom and to specify exactly what our students have learned. Until recently we have largely been unable to provide information other than vague comments such as, "Since I think it is important for my students to write well, I give a lot of essay tests." The authors have become increasingly committed to the concept of portfolios as a way to effectively address these concerns and have been extensively involved with their use.

VARIATIONS ON A THEME: THE RELATIONSHIP BETWEEN TEACHING AND STUDENT PORTFOLIOS

A portfolio can be defined as a multidimensional, documented collection of either a teacher's or student's work put together in an organized way and including a reflective discussion of the materials contained in the portfolio.

Most work to date has been done in the area of teaching portfolios. (See Zubizarreta, this volume.) Their use began in Canada in the early 1980s and has spread from being used in fewer than ten schools in the United States to more than an estimated 500 schools in the mid-1990s. This rapidly increasing interest in the use of portfolios was reflected in a large attendance at the first national conference on the use of teaching portfolios held in 1993.

As we travel across the country helping faculty prepare portfolios, we are struck by the parallels between uses of teaching portfolios for faculty and learning portfolios for students. The following chart demonstrates these striking parallel uses.

Use of Portfolios

Faculty Teaching Portfolios	*Student Portfolios*
✦ improvement in teaching performance	✦ improvement in learning performance
✦ promotion, tenure, and merit pay decisions	✦ course grades or certification
✦ search for a new job or position	✦ help in getting a first job
✦ leave as a teaching legacy for new faculty	✦ leave as models for future students
✦ teaching excellence awards	✦ student excellence awards and scholarships

---

The main difference in these uses results from whether you are approaching the teaching/learning process from the top-down perspective of the instructor or from the bottom-up view of the student. All uses share in common the need for *documentation* of accomplishments.

Portfolios allow both faculty and students to change their view of accountability and assessment. Preparing a portfolio contributes to reflection on one's efforts and identification of areas for improvement. It also empowers the people preparing it to judge their own performances.

One of the best ways faculty members can assist their students to prepare portfolios is by first preparing their own teaching portfolio (Murnane, 1993). Faculty members can share their own personal portfolio with their students as a model for how to proceed in developing their own student portfolios. Instructors can provide much useful information about the field of study, give detailed explanations about how they chose what work to include, explain why they do what they do in their teaching, and why they think what they do is important. Instructors thus actively model the process of portfolio preparation, and their students have the added benefit of having seen the instructors' choices in action as they teach. Models from other students who have prepared similar portfolios also can be very useful. Students can use these models as a source of ideas and examples for documentation and information to include in their personal portfolios.

DIFFERENT USES FOR STUDENT PORTFOLIOS

Once the faculty member has decided to use a portfolio assignment, the next step is determining the objective or purpose. There are three basic purposes for student portfolios, all of which provide a broader perspective of student performance than most traditional assessment methods. Depending on focus and need, a single portfolio may be used to evaluate individual student performance in a classroom or program, or a group of portfolios may be used to evaluate an entire program.

A particularly important purpose is to evaluate student performance in a classroom. In one college, students enrolled in a study techniques course are required to prepare student portfolios documenting their growth during the course in areas essential for successful learning such as selecting main ideas and motivation. A log analyzing the kinds of growth that have occurred and citing specific examples of documentation is also part of the portfolio.

A second purpose is to evaluate a student's performance for a specific purpose such as determining progress in a special program. The Department of Education at Eastern Washington University uses student portfolios for this purpose. After completing two-thirds of the Teacher Education program, each pre-service student prepares a portfolio which includes a statement of teaching philosophy, the theoretical base that supports the student's pedagogical practices, and evidence of successful preparatory experience in classroom, laboratory, and field settings. The portfolio, which is organized on a computer disk, is presented to a three-member interview committee of educators for review.

A third purpose is to evaluate an entire program or any of its components. In this case, all students' portfolios are synthesized and evaluated according to criteria selected for program evaluation. Use of community or collegial resources may be helpful in establishing benchmarks.

Whatever the designated purpose, students must be adequately prepared to develop their portfolios. Suggestions based on recent experiences are provided by Carolee Jones, one of the co-authors.

A Case in Point: One Professor's Experience

I think of teaching strategies in terms of whether they will be beneficial to my students. Little did I know that my decision to use a portfolio assignment in a communications course would have such exciting rewards for me as well.

After developing my personal teaching portfolio, I began to read about the use of portfolios as a nontraditional assessment tool for measuring student learning. Believing that a portfolio assignment could enhance learning outcomes in my communications course, I decided to include student portfolios as one method of assessing their achievement.

The following information is based on my experience and the feedback provided by students informally, as well as in a formal assessment at the end of the semester. The three components that provide the structure for this segment of the chapter are: planning, implementing, and evaluating the portfolio assignment.

Planning for a Portfolio Assignment

A significant step in developing the assignment was answering questions such as: What kind of portfolio would I expect? What would the objectives be? How should it be structured; or in fact, should it be structured? How would I evaluate and weight this activity? What could I use for examples since I didn't have any?

Once these decisions were made, I developed a written assignment sheet outlining major components of the project. Contents of the assignment sheet included a definition of a portfolio, rationale for the assignment, the suggested organization, and evaluation information. The specific evaluation sheet that would be used at the end of the semester was also included.

COMMUNICATIONS PORTFOLIO ASSIGNMENT

Definition

A portfolio is a collection and interpretation of your work that allows an employer, teacher, or other person to evaluate your abilities. It may be representative of work in a specific class or it may be prepared to let a potential employer know what you can do.

Rationale

In this class, we will prepare a portfolio as one of several methods that will be used to evaluate the development of your communication skills and to determine your final grade. Total point value for the portfolio is 50 points. The portfolio may include writing and other examples of communication from previous classes or work experiences, as well as examples from the assignments completed in this class.

A key component in the portfolio will be the development of a statement about your ability to communicate, what you felt you gained in this course, what you believe you need to do to continue your communication improvement program, and the ways you see your ability to communicate as a valuable asset to a potential employer.

Be sure to save this portfolio so that you may include some of your work in an employment portfolio in the future.

Your portfolio should include information of two types:

1. A well-written statement about your ability to communicate as described above. This may take several double-spaced pages.

2. An appendix of communication samples. These items should be identified by page numbers and referred to in the introductory statement.

Evaluation

Your portfolio will be due two weeks before the end of the semester to allow sufficient time for evaluation. It will be evaluated on the basis of the following factors:

✦ Organization. Is the content organized for easy reading? Is the organization logical? How effectively are the appendix and the introductory statement coordinated? Is the selection of items appropriate?

✦ Content. Is the content credible? What is the quality of the examples included?

✦ Presentation. Is the information correct—no spelling or other mechanical errors? Does it suggest a professional appearance?

✦ Overall effect. What impression is created by the portfolio?

Implementing a Portfolio Assignment

Because I determined that most students had never developed a student portfolio, my strategy was to gradually introduce and define the assignment during the first three weeks of the semester. The merit of various types of class activities that could be included in the portfolio was discussed.

During this time we also discussed the components of communication as they related to the students' chosen profession. This was a great opportunity to use partners and teams or group activities in researching specific career areas.

Since samples of a completed project were not initially available, we brainstormed a list of possible activities that could be included in a portfolio. Some of these are included below.

Possible Portfolio Content

Writing samples: term papers, letters, memos, abstracts, English compositions, executive summaries

Exams: national, essay

Independent study projects

✦ Various types of class exercises

Case study analyses

Computer exercises

Simulation exercises

Videotape of class activities such as oral presentations

Photographs of class work produced

✦ Products of research

✦ List of experiences not included in résumé

✦ Newspaper articles that document your achievement

✦ Programs from events in which you participated

✦ Job evaluations from previous/current employment

✦ List of career goals

✦ Teachers' evaluations/notes

✦ Letters of commendation, thanks, awards, honors

✦ Products from previous employment (with employer's permission)

A frequently asked question is: How long should the portfolio be? No requirements were set for my students because of the emphasis on reflecting their learning experience; however, portfolios submitted ranged in length from 10 to 50 pages.

The activity that most students found helpful was learning how to write an analytical report. After explaining the adaptations that could be made for the reflective essay, I wrote a contrived model paragraph to demonstrate one effective way for providing documentation. Based on the example provided, here is an excerpt from one student portfolio.

> My ability to write has never been one of my strengths. When I entered college, my writing generally indicated a lack of coherence and an inability to organize my thoughts carefully, as indicated on page 1 of my appendix. However, as you will see on pages 2 through 7, this was an area of improvement over the next three years. Evidence of my current writing ability is provided on page 8; and it includes comments about my ability to write coherently. I am proud of this accomplishment, which I believe demonstrates my ability to identify a problem and work diligently to solve it.

Approximately three weeks before the portfolio assignment was due, students were invited to submit an outline and sample paragraph from their reflective essay for my feedback. Few students took advantage of the opportunity. However, at the end of the course, students suggested that in the future a *required* outline and sample paragraph (which would earn a specific number of points) be submitted. Class time was provided before the specified due date so that students could critique each other's outlines and/or sample paragraphs.

About two weeks before the portfolios were due, we discussed the mechanical presentation of the portfolio and looked at some of the possible methods for binding the portfolio. Some students presented their portfolios in leather binders, while a few simply stapled pages together without a cover. Minimum requirements for binding will be identified on the assignment sheet in the future to eliminate poorly collated pages.

Evaluating the Portfolio

Once the students were more familiar with the portfolio concept, we had another brainstorming session about evaluating their portfolios. Organization, content, presentation, and overall effect were offered as potential criteria. A general evaluation form was developed based on input from that session.

PORTFOLIO EVALUATION

Your portfolio will earn a potential of 50 points. These 50 points are allocated as follows:

Organization (15 points)

Appropriate for individual's objective	1 2 3 4 5
Coordinated appendix and introductory statement	1 2 3 4 5
Coherent	1 2 3 4 5
TOTAL	_____

Content (15 points)

Selection of items included is appropriate	1 2 3 4 5
Examples demonstrate communication ability	1 2 3 4 5
Examples effectively support current competencies claimed by student	1 2 3 4 5
TOTAL	_____

Presentation (10 points)

Items are mechanically correct	1 2 3 4 5
Appearance is professional	1 2 3 4 5
TOTAL	_____

Overall Effect (10 points)

Impact on the evaluator	1 2 3 4 5
	6 7 8 9 10

TOTAL _____

After submitting their portfolios, I asked students to complete a formal assessment form seeking their reactions to the assignment. Two items that concerned students were the number of points assigned to the project and the number of points assigned to the overall effect.

Students thought the portfolio assignment should be worth more than 10% of the final grade based on the amount of time required to develop it. The second item concerned what they believed to be too much weight assigned to the "overall effect." Use of benchmark portfolios as samples would be helpful in validating the points assigned for overall impact. Another suggestion was to use student input prior to teacher evaluation. For instance, small groups or partners could use structured forms as guidelines to provide consistency in feedback form. An instructor may even wish to place a point value on their feedback.

IMPACT ON TEACHING AND LEARNING

The assignment challenged me to expand my concept of assessment and required me to re-evaluate the value and authenticity of activities I was including in the course. This assignment gave credibility to other course assignments because students continually looked for connections to their future work and for material to include in their portfolios. I also put additional time into evaluating student papers. Nevertheless, I found the activity exciting and invigorating, mainly because I was serving a new role—facilitating learning rather than pulling my students along with me. They interacted more with the subject matter, with each other, and with me.

The more the students saw the relationship between their course work and their career objectives, the more enthused they became about the portfolio. At the end of the semester, 74% of the students indicated that they found the assignment to be beneficial and 81% believed it was helpful in placing communications in perspective as they began to plan their job searches.

The preparation for this assignment included a great deal of preliminary reading, thinking, and anticipating problems and questions. I believe that the key factor in the success of this assignment was carefully introducing the concept in stages and guiding students through the process in a systematic way. The sense of achievement for students and teacher alike created especially positive attitudes about their achievement. Perhaps that is why I received the highest student evaluations I have ever received in a communications course.

To others considering using a portfolio assignment, I would urge that they: 1) determine the purpose of the portfolio; 2) plan a systematic method of presentation; 3) assist students in selecting appropriate items; 4) be sure students understand the purpose of the "reflective" essay; and 5) urge that students include sample work because it provides documentation for the statements made about their performance in the class.

The impact of portfolios on teaching and learning is very positive because it invigorates and energizes both students and teachers. And a portfolio assignment is a worthy assessment tool in determining student performance.

SUMMARY

In *Scholarship Reconsidered,* Boyer (1990) comments that in his travels across the country visiting colleges and universities, he has been impressed by the increased debate on campuses about issues of under-graduate education ranging from the core curriculum to the quality of campus life. In fact, he says, "Given these lively discussions, I'm begin-ning to believe that the 1990s may well come to be remembered as the decade of the undergraduate in American higher education" (p. xi).

It is our judgment that a student portfolio can make an important contribution to improving student learning and thus the quality of the undergraduate experience. We believe that the student portfolio concept is an idea whose time has come and that its use can make a significant difference so that the 1990s truly do become the decade of undergradu-ate education.

AUTHORS

Linda Annis is Professor of Educational Psychology at Ball State Univer-sity, where for five years she also served as Founding Director of the Cen-ter for Teaching and Learning. She has been involved extensively in the national and international teaching portfolio movement by actively pub-lishing and presenting on the concept and by mentoring faculty as they prepare portfolios.

Carolee Jones is Professor of Business Education and Office Administra-tion at Ball State University, and has received the Indiana Outstanding Business Educator Award. She has served as a consultant to the Center for Teaching and Learning at Ball State, has published on the use of stu-dent portfolios, and is currently researching the impact of their use on improving teaching and learning.

REFERENCES

Boyer, E. L. (1990). *Scholarship reconsidered: Priorities of the professoriate.* Princeton, NJ: The Carnegie Foundation for the Advancement of Teaching.

Murnane, Y. (1993). Portfolio use in higher education: A primer. *The Beacon: A guide to faculty development at St. Norbert College,* 8 (5): 1–3.

Schilling, K. M., & Schilling, K. L. (March 24, 1993). Professors must respond to calls for accountability. *The Chronicle of Higher Educa-tion,* p. A40.

SIXTEEN

EVALUATING YOUR OWN TEACHING

L. Dee Fink

Each year faculty members in institutions of higher education take on the task of teaching others. For the majority of faculty, this is the central task of a lifelong career.

Assuming that no one is perfect and therefore everyone has room for improvement, evaluation is the means by which we try to identify which aspects of our teaching are good and which need to be changed. The question then arises as to who should be doing this evaluation? My belief is that evaluation is an inherent part of good teaching; therefore, it is the individual teacher who should take primary responsibility for the evaluation.

In this chapter, I will offer a basic definition of evaluation, state a few reasons why one should invest time and effort in evaluation, describe five techniques for evaluation, and identify resources for helping us evaluate and improve our teaching.

A DEFINITION OF EVALUATION

Evaluating is in some ways like researching. In both tasks, you try to answer some important questions about an important topic. Key elements in both activities are identifying the right questions to ask and figuring out how to answer them.

What are the key questions in the evaluation of teaching? Basically they are: "How well am I doing? Which aspects of my teaching are good, and which need to be improved?" The first question attempts to provide a global assessment, while the second is analytical and diagnostic in character.

Before moving to the task of figuring out how to answer these questions, we should look at the reasons for taking time to evaluate.

Why Evaluate?

It takes a certain amount of time and effort to effectively evaluate our own teaching. Is this a wise use of time? I would argue that it is, for three reasons.

First, consider Figure 1.

Figure 1

The Effect of Evaluation on Our Teaching

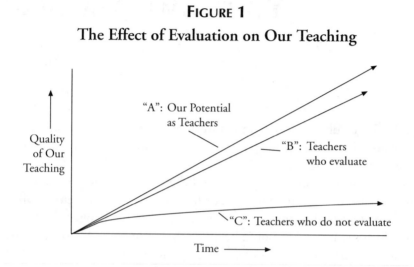

Regardless of how good or how poor we are as teachers, we all have the potential to get better (arrow "A"). Why, then, do some teachers continually improve and approach their potential (arrow "B") while others experience a modest improvement early in their careers and then seem to level off in quality or sometimes even decline? (arrow "C"). I would argue that the primary difference between those who do and those who do not improve, is that only the former gather information about their teaching and make an effort to improve some aspect of their instruction—every time they teach.

A second reason to evaluate is to document the quality of one's teaching for others. All career professionals have other people who need to know about the quality of their teaching. It may be the person's current department or institution head, or it may be a potential employer. But once a person teaches, she has a "track record," and others need and want to know how well she taught. The only way a teacher can provide that information is to gather it, and that means evaluation. Teaching portfolios are becoming a common way of communicating this information to others. As it turns out, putting a portfolio together also helps the teacher understand his or her own teaching better (see Zubizarreta, this volume).

Third, there is a very personal and human need to evaluate from which we derive mental and psychological satisfaction. It is one thing to do a good job and *think* that it went well; it is quite another, far more enjoyable experience, to have solid information and thereby *know* we did a good job. That knowledge, that certainty, is possible only if we do a thorough job of evaluation.

If evaluation is worth doing, how do we do it?

FIVE SOURCES OF INFORMATION

There are five basic sources of information that teachers can use to evaluate their teaching. All evaluation efforts use one or more of these basic sources, and each has a unique value as well as an inherent limitation.

In the following portion of this chapter, I will discuss the unique value, recommended frequency, limitation, and appropriate response to that limitation, for each of the sources of information.

Self-Monitoring

Self-monitoring is what people do semi-automatically and semi-consciously whenever they teach. Most of their mental activity is concerned with making the presentation or leading the discussion. But some portion of mental attention is concerned with: "How is it going? Are they with me? Am I losing them? Are they interested or bored?"

Unique value. One value of this source of information is that it is immediate and constant. You do not have to wait a week or a day or even an hour to get the results; it happens right away. Hence immediate adjustments are possible.

Another value is that this information is automatically created in terms that are meaningful to the teacher because it is the teacher who creates the information. It is the teacher, not someone else, who looks at the situation and says, "This is what is happening." While we don't always know why something is happening, or what to do about it if it is something we do not like, we do have our own sense of what is happening.

Frequency. Self-monitoring does and should happen all the time. We may only take a mental pause every few minutes to size up the situation. But in comparison with other sources of information, self-monitoring takes place continuously.

Limitation. The very strength of this source is also its weakness. Because the information is created by us for us, it is also subject to our own biases and misinterpretations. "I thought they looked interested," when in fact they weren't.

We all have blind spots and lack complete objectivity. This means that at times we are going to misread the responses of students to our teaching.

Appropriate response. What can be done about the subjectivity of self-monitoring? Combine it with an objective source of information.

Audiotape and Videotape Recordings

Modern technology has given us relatively inexpensive and easy access to audio and video recordings of what we do as teachers. We can put a small audio recorder on the teacher's desk or put a video recorder on the side of the classroom and let it run during a class session. Later, we can listen to or view the tape.

Special value. The value of this kind of information is that it gives us totally objective information. It tells us what we really said and really did, not what we thought we said or did. "How much time did I spend on this topic? How many times did I ask questions? How often did I move around?" These are questions the audio and video recordings can answer with complete accuracy and objectivity.

Frequency. I once had the experience of giving a workshop that was recorded. Listening to the recording later, I discovered to my surprise that I had some disruptive speech patterns of which I was completely unaware. And I am an experienced observer of teachers!

The lesson from this was that no matter how good we are at monitoring others, we can only devote a certain amount of our mental attention to monitoring our own teaching; hence we miss things.

As a result of my experience, I now try to do an audio recording at least once or twice in each full-semester course I teach. This gives me a chance to see if any speech problems are still there or if new ones have cropped up. If they have, the second recording tells me if I have gotten them under control.

Video recordings are useful once every year or two. While they involve more equipment and logistical planning, they also provide a more comprehensive picture of the teaching and learning going on in the class. What do we look like to others? As we grow older, we change, and we need to know what the continuously "new me" looks like to others.

Limitation. What could be more valuable than the "objective truth" of audio and video recordings? Unfortunately, the unavoidable problem with this information is that it is true but meaningless—by itself. The recordings can tell me if I spoke at the rate of 20 words per minute, or 60 words, but not whether the rate was appropriate for the students. The recordings can tell me whether I moved and gestured and smiled but can't reveal how those movements and facial expressions helped or hindered student learning.

Appropriate response. To determine the effect of my teaching behavior, rather than the behavior itself, I need to find another source of information.

Students' Test Results

Teachers almost always give students some form of graded exercise, whether it is an in-class test or an out-of-class project. Usually, though, the intent of the test is to assess the quality of student learning. We can also use this same information to assess the quality of our teaching.

Special value. The whole *raison d'être* of teaching is to help someone else learn. Assuming we can devise a test or graded exercise that effectively measures whether or not students are learning what we want them to learn, the test results basically tell us whether or not we are succeeding in our teaching effort. This is critical information for all teachers. Although the other sources of information identified here can partially address this question ("I *think* they are learning; the students *think* they are learning"), none address it so directly as test results: "I *know* they are learning because they responded with a high level of sophisticated knowledge and thinking to a challenging test."

Frequency. How often should we give tests? Many teachers follow the tradition of two mid-terms and a final. In my view this is inadequate feedback, both for the students and for the teacher. Weekly or even daily feedback is much more effective in letting students and the teacher know whether they are learning what they need to learn. If the teacher's goal is to help the students learn, this is important information for both parties. And remember: not all tests need to be graded and recorded.

Limitation. It might be hard to imagine that this information has a limitation. After all, this is what it's all about, right? Did they learn it or not?

The problem with this information is its lack of a causal connection: we don't know why they did or did not learn. Did they learn because of or in spite of our teaching? Some students work very hard in a course, not because the teacher inspires or motivates them, but because their major requires a good grade in the course. Even though the teacher is not effective, they work hard and learn the material on their own.

Appropriate response. If we need to know whether one's actions as a teacher are helpful or useless in promoting student learning, we need a different source of information, such as the students themselves.

Information from Students

As the intended beneficiaries of all teaching, students are in a unique position to help their teachers in the evaluation process.

Special value. If we want to know whether students find our explanations of a topic clear or our teaching stimulating, who could possibly answer these questions better than the students themselves? Of the five sources of information described here, students are the best source for understanding the immediate effects of our teaching; i.e., the process of teaching and learning.

This information can be obtained in two distinct ways: questionnaires and interviews, each with its own relative values.

Questionnaires

The most common method of obtaining student reactions to our teaching is to use a questionnaire. Lots of different questionnaires exist, but most ask similar kinds of questions: student characteristics (e.g., major, GPA, reasons for taking the course); the students' characterization of the teaching (e.g., clear, organized, interesting); amount learned; overall assessment of the course and/or teacher (e.g., compared to other courses, or other teachers, this one is…); and, sometimes, anticipated grade.

Special value. The special value of questionnaires is that they obtain responses from the whole class, and they allow for anonymous (and therefore probably more candid) responses.

Limitation. The limitation of questionnaires is that they can only ask a question once; i.e., they cannot probe for further clarification, and they can only ask questions that the writer anticipates as possibly important.

Questionnaires can be given at three different times: the beginning, middle, and end of a course. Some teachers use questionnaires at the beginning of a course to get information about the students; e.g., prior coursework or experience with the subject, preferred modes of teaching and learning, and special problems a student might have (e.g., dyslexia). Many use mid-term questionnaires to get an early warning of any existing problems so that changes can be made in time to benefit this set of students. The advantage of end-of-term questionnaires is that all of the learning activities have been completed; consequently students can respond meaningfully to questions about the overall effectiveness of the course.

Interviews

The other well-established way of finding out about student reactions is to talk with them. Either the teacher (if sufficient trust and rapport exist) or an outside person (if anonymity and objectivity are desired) can talk with students for 15-30 minutes about the course and the teacher. As an instructional consultant, I have often done this for other teachers, but I have also done it in some of my own courses. I try to get 6-8 students, preferably a random sample, and visit with them in a focused interview format immediately after class. I have some general topics I want to discuss, such as the quality of the learning thus far, reactions to the lectures, labs, tests, and so forth. But within these topics, I will probe for clarification and examples of perceived strength and weakness. I note when there is divergence of reactions and when most students seem to agree.

Special value. Students often identify unanticipated strengths and weaknesses, and the interviewer can probe and follow up on topics that need clarification.

Limitation. A professor can usually only interview a sub-set of the class rather than the whole. This leaves some uncertainty as to whether their reactions represent the whole class.

Frequency. I would probably only use a formal interview once or at most twice during a term. Of course, a teacher can informally ask students about the course many times, and directly or indirectly obtain a sense of their reaction to the course.

General limitation. Returning to the general issue of information from students, regardless of how such information is collected, one needs to remember that this is information from students. Although they know better than anyone what their own reactions are, they can also be biased and limited in their perspectives. They occasionally have negative feelings, often unconsciously, about women, people who are ethnically different from themselves, and international teachers. Perhaps more significantly, students usually do not have a full understanding of how a course might be taught, either in terms of pedagogy or content. Hence they can effectively address what is, but not what might be.

Appropriate response. As with the other limitations, the appropriate response here is to seek another kind of information. In this case, we need information from someone with a professional understanding of the possibilities of good teaching.

Outside Observer

In addition to the people directly involved in a course—the teacher and the students—valuable information can be obtained from the observations of a third party, someone who brings both an outsider's perspective and professional expertise to the task.

Special value. Part of the value of an outside observer is that they do not have a personal stake in the particular course; hence they are free to reach positive and negative conclusions without any cost to themselves. Also, as professionals, they can bring an expertise either in content and/or pedagogy that is likely to supplement that of both the teacher and the students.

A variety of kinds of observers exist: a peer colleague, a senior colleague, or an instructional specialist. *Peer colleagues*, e.g., two TAs or two junior professors, can visit each other's classes and share observations. Here the political risk is low, and each one can empathize with the situation and challenges facing the other. Interestingly, the people doing the observing in these exchanges often find that they learn as much as the people who get the feedback.

Senior colleagues can be of value because of their accumulated experience. Although one has to be selective and choose someone who is respected and with whom the political risk is low, experienced colleagues can offer ideas on alternative ways of dealing with particular topics, additional examples to illustrate the material, etc.

A third kind of outside observer, an *instructional consultant,* is available on many campuses. Instructional consultants may or may not be able to give feedback on the clarity and significance of the content material, but their expertise in teaching allows them to comment on presentation techniques, discussion procedures, and ideas for more active learning.

Frequency. Beginning TAs and beginning faculty members should consider inviting one or more outside observers to their classes at least once a semester for two or three years. They need to get perspectives on their teaching as soon as possible. After that, more experienced teachers would probably benefit from such feedback at least once every year or two. We change as teachers; as we do, we need all the feedback and fresh ideas we can find.

Limitations. Again, the strength of being an outsider is also its weakness. Outside observers can usually only visit one or two class sessions and therefore do not know what happens in the rest of the course.

Apart from this general problem, each kind of observer has his own limitation. The peer colleague may also have limited experience and perspectives; the senior colleague may be someone who makes departmental decisions about annual evaluations and tenure; and the instructional consultant may have limited knowledge of the subject matter.

Appropriate response. As with the other sources, the response to these limitation is to use a different source, either a different kind of outside observer or one of the other sources described above.

A COMPREHENSIVE EVALUATION SCENARIO

The thesis of this chapter is that a comprehensive plan of evaluation for improvement requires all five sources of information as each one offers information that none of the others does. How would this work out in practice?

To answer this question, I will describe a hypothetical professor who is not a perfect teacher and therefore has some yet-to-be identified weaknesses in his teaching. He wants to improve that teaching. What steps should he take to evaluate his teaching as a way of identifying those aspects that need changing?

The Case of Professor "X"

Professor "X" is a relatively young person, only two years into his tenure track position at University Wouldbegood. This fall he will be teaching a junior level course on international trade. He once attended a workshop on "evaluating your own teaching," so he knows what he should do.

On the first day of class, he keeps his eyes and ears open (self-monitoring) to see what sort of personality this year's class has. In addition, he asks students to fill out a short questionnaire about any business or international experience they have had, prior course work in related areas, and their expectations of the course. From this he discovers that his class has a wide range of backgrounds: some students have extensive international experience and others have none at all. Perhaps he can use the former as a resource for the latter.

A few weeks into the course, Professor "X" brings a small cassette recorder into class and makes an audio recording. After listening to it, he feels reasonably good about his presentation but notes there is little student participation. Class time consists mainly of "teacher-talk."

The weekly quizzes are turning out okay, but he had hoped that since they were upper division students the class would be "getting into it" a bit more.

After thinking about this awhile and talking to one of his departmental colleagues, he decides to call the university's instructional development program to request a class review. His colleague said these people actually make some good suggestions once in awhile.

The consultant, who has a doctorate in instructional communication, meets with the professor, visits his class twice, and then shares her observations with him. Her reaction is that the lectures seem good enough, but there is just too much of the same thing day after day: lecture, lecture, lecture. She suggests using some active learning strategies.

After hearing the reaction of the consultant, Professor "X" decides to use a mid-term questionnaire available from the instructional development program to see if the students feel the same way. The consultant helps him interpret the results, which indicate a degree of boredom with the steady diet of lectures. The consultant gives Professor "X" a handout on "enhanced lectures" that shows how to intersperse some active learning activities with shorter lecture segments. They also discuss some possible larger modifications for next semester.

On the end-of-semester course evaluation, Professor "X" adds some special questions about the changes he has made. The responses indicate that the students like the changes, and the overall results, while not yet outstanding, are appreciably higher than in previous terms.

The point of this scenario is to illustrate that a thorough evaluation of teaching can be effective in identifying important changes that can be made, and that such evaluation is much more extensive than simply looking at one comparative statistic on an end-of-semester questionnaire.

But how costly is a comprehensive evaluation plan in terms of the time required? The case study above is a composite of actual cases. Based on these cases, I would make the following estimate of the time required beyond what happens anyway in normal teaching:

Additional Time (hours)

Self-monitoring	0	(did automatically anyway)
Initial questionnaire	1	(writing, interpreting)
Audio recording	1	(reviewing afterwards)
Weekly quizzes	0	(did anyway)
Visit with consultant	3	(met three times)
Mid-term questionnaire	1	(constructing, interpreting)
End-of-term questionnaire	<u>1</u>	(for added questions)
	7 hours	

The seven hours required for a comprehensive evaluation is an addition of about 5% to the total time required for teaching one three-credit hour course in one semester. This amounts to less than 1/2 hour per week for the whole term. It is a small but wise investment that informed Professor "X" of an important area of his teaching that needed improvement. This investment will pay big dividends in effectiveness and satisfaction in a major area of his professional life for many years.

SOURCES OF ASSISTANCE

Professors should not think that they have to go it alone when it comes to evaluating their teaching. There are available sources of assistance for at least two important activities: constructing or selecting a questionnaire, and figuring out how to make needed improvements.

Student Questionnaires

The first option for getting a questionnaire to use in class is to write it yourself. At institutions with instructional development programs, a consultant can help in this process. Custom-made questionnaires can focus on specific questions the professor has about his or her teaching. Or they can be open-ended, asking questions like: "How satisfied are you with what you are learning? What do you like most about the course? If you could change one thing about the course, what would it be?"

A second source is often the institution itself. Many institutions have questionnaires that are available, or required, for end-of-term use. These have the advantage of being ready-made, but they also frequently allow the professor to include additional questions.

The third option is to use a nationally available questionnaire. The two I recommend on our campus are the TABS for mid-term use and the IDEA system for end-of-term use. The TABS questionnaire was developed at the University of Massachusetts at Amherst and is based on 20 common problems in teaching. The recommended use is for the professor to assess the course in terms of these characteristics, and then to compare his or her assessment with student reactions. The IDEA system is available from the Center for Faculty Evaluation and Development at Kansas State University. Its central criterion for assessing effectiveness is whether or not students learned what the professor was trying to teach. It also includes a diagnostic section and national norms that incorporate class size and initial student interest.

Ideas for Improving

The primary thrust of this chapter is how to find out what one's strengths and weaknesses are as a teacher. But, having identified those, a professor still needs ideas and assistance to make the needed improvements. Four resources can be helpful with this: selected colleagues, books and journals, institutionally-based instructional development programs, and off-campus workshops.

The handiest resource is undoubtedly colleagues who are creative and effective in their own teaching. They are usually flattered by requests to visit their classes, review their course materials, and discuss their teaching strategies and philosophy. (See chapters by Sorcinelli; Millis and Kaplan; and Gmelch, this volume.)

A wide variety of reading material is available on teaching improvement practices. Some journals have articles on teaching specific subject matter; others focus more broadly on college-level teaching. One such journal, *College Teaching,* contains high quality articles that are relevant to essentially all subjects. As for books, three I often recommend to teachers are: *Teaching Tips* by Wilbert McKeachie; *Mastering the Techniques of Teaching* by Joseph Lowman; and *Active Learning* by Bonwell and Eison.

A third resource, available on many campuses, is an instructional development program. During the last two decades, more and more institutions have sponsored such programs as an appropriate investment in the single most costly and important factor in a university's quality: the faculty. The professional staff in these programs can offer selected reading material, share their own ideas, and provide classroom observations and feedback to faculty members. (See the chapters by Simpson and Jackson, and Wadsworth, this volume.)

Finally, a number of disciplinary associations, regional consortia, and entrepreneurial persons at various universities now offer workshops, often in the summer, for regional and national audiences of faculty members wanting to learn how to become better teachers. These range from a few days to a few weeks in length. They give participants a chance to hear new ideas, systematically study a wide range of issues and topics, and practice new possibilities in a low-risk setting with feedback from understanding and sympathetic peers.

CONCLUSIONS

Teachers in higher education owe it to themselves, to their students, and to their institutions to fulfill their responsibilities as effectively as possible. The thesis of this chapter is that the only way to improve one's teaching over time is to continuously monitor and evaluate that teaching, and to use the information obtained to make needed changes. The various techniques described here, especially when used together, can give us the deep personal and professional satisfaction of being able to say, after a single course or after a career of teaching, "I did my best, and it was good."

AUTHOR

L. Dee Fink is Director of the Instructional Development Program at the University of Oklahoma. He has worked extensively on how to evaluate college-level teaching and on ways to help TAs and faculty members improve their teaching.

REFERENCES

Bonwell, C.C., & Eison, J.A. (1991). *Active learning: Creating excitement in the classroom.* ASHE-ERIC Higher Education Report No. 1. Washington, DC: George Washington University.

IDEA Evaluation System: Information about it may be obtained from the Center for Faculty Evaluation and Development, 1615 Anderson Avenue, Kansas State University, Manhattan, KS 66502–1604. Phone: (800) 255–2757.

Lowman, J. (1984). *Mastering the techniques of teaching.* San Francisco, CA: Jossey-Bass.

McKeachie, W.J. (1994). *Teaching tips: Strategies, research, and theory for college and university teachers.* 9/e. Lexington, MA: D.C. Heath.

TABS Evaluation System: Information about it may be obtained from the Center for Teaching, University of Massachusetts at Amherst, 239 Whitmore, Amherst, MA 01003. Phone: (413) 545–1225.

SEVENTEEN

FACULTY COLLABORATION IN TEACHING

Roger G. Baldwin and Ann E. Austin

College professors are increasingly turning to collaborative strategies to address complex problems in the classroom as well as in the research laboratory. Team taught courses addressing topics such as medical ethics, environmental policy, and gender roles in American society are now common in all types of colleges and universities. This trend is part of a gradual transformation in faculty roles and practices in response to new understanding of effective teaching strategies, society's growing need for advanced learning, and the public's desire for quality improvements in education.

Several forces account for the increased interest in collaborative teaching. The increased segmentation of many academic fields and heightened faculty specialization can leave professors uneasy about introductory survey courses or courses focusing on broad themes. Similarly, growing dissatisfaction with single discipline approaches to complex social or technological problems like the American "underclass," child abuse, or genetic engineering call for instructional settings that pool the expertise and unique perspectives of teachers from different fields of study. The growing interest in collaborative learning strategies (Bruffee, 1987; Johnson and Johnson, 1975; Johnson, Johnson, and Smith, 1991; Johnson et al., 1981) coupled with a national debate on the quality of college teaching (Boyer, 1987; Kerr, 1994) have opened the doors of college classrooms to novel approaches to teaching and learning. Angelo (1994) argues "there's never been a more promising time than now" (p. 3) to improve undergraduate education. The steady advance of collaborative teaching is part of this larger reform movement.

Collaboration Defined

LaFauci and Richter (1970) define collaborative teaching as "an organizational device by which a number of persons work together in a concerted effort to perform related instructional activities and to achieve common educational goals" (p.1). In collaborative teaching, professors combine their instructional efforts to achieve goals they could not fulfill at all or as well by teaching independently. By including more than one instructor in a course, team teaching examines the course's subject matter from different perspectives and expands the amount of material a course can adequately cover. For faculty as well as students, the interchange of information and ideas possible in a team teaching arrangement can provide increased intellectual stimulation. Team teaching can reduce the sense of isolation that highly specialized academics sometimes experience, and it can enhance the sense of community and shared responsibility that exists in a department, school, or institution as a whole. (See the chapter by Pastore, this volume.)

Effective collaborative teaching requires a great deal of colleague communication to ensure careful course planning and implementation. Regular interaction among team members provides a natural vehicle for peer feedback on teaching performance and for discussion of strategies for instructional improvement. This dialogue can enhance both individual and group motivation to improve teaching quality. Likewise, the partnership or team provides a social support structure to promote improved teaching performance.

Forms of Collaboration in Teaching

Team or collaborative teaching is not a single instructional technique that is applied uniformly in different educational settings. Collaborative teaching varies on three key dimensions: (1) the roles faculty take and the relationships of faculty team members to each other; (2) whether the collaboration is interdisciplinary, multidisciplinary, or within a single discipline; and (3) whether the collaboration involves one course or a set of interrelated though independent courses (cluster courses) (Austin and Baldwin, 1991). Each of these variables alters the nature of the collaborative experience and presents potential collaborators with important choices as they build their instructional team.

Relationships of Faculty Team Members

Easterby-Smith and Olve (1984) classify teaching collaborations into five categories according to the degree of hierarchy vs. equality in the team and the degree of interaction among the team members. In a *star team*, one professor has primary responsibility for designing and leading a course and invites experts to meet with the class as specific topics are addressed. For instance, the professor in an introductory physics course might schedule specialists in nuclear physics, astrophysics, and applied physics to give lectures. In a *hierarchical team*, more senior members of a team plan the course and offer regular lectures, while the junior members (often teaching assistants) lead discussion groups and perform other instructional duties as assigned by the team leaders. This collaborative teaching model is quite common in higher education, especially in very large institutions, and involves a hierarchical relationship with differing levels of responsibility among the team members.

In the next three models, faculty members carry equal responsibility for a course but divide the duties in different ways. Members of a *specialist team* work closely together to design their course but "divide teaching duties according to individual expertise" (Austin and Baldwin, 1991, p. 37). For example, in an introductory psychology course, a developmentalist may lecture on adolescence while a psychobiologist would lecture on left brain-right brain research. Similarly, in a *generalist team*, members have equal responsibility for planning and executing a course. However, they divide their teaching assignments according to their schedules or other factors, not on the basis of individual expertise. Theoretically, in a generalist team, any member could teach any portion of a course. The *interactive team* differs from other types of teaching teams because all members share full responsibility for every aspect of a course and are present together at each class. This is the most truly collaborative form of team teaching. Interactive team members work together on course planning, preparing examinations, and grading. They also meet regularly to discuss their subject, their students, and the teaching process.

The Disciplinary Mix

Collaborative teaching teams also vary according to their mix of disciplines. A teaching team may involve only persons from one discipline. In this case, each instructor brings his or her special expertise within the discipline to the course. Multidisciplinary teams typically focus on broad topics such as homelessness or the meaning of race in American society.

Each member of the team, however, sheds light on the course topic from the distinct perspective of his or her particular field. Interdisciplinary team teaching requires faculty to transcend their individual disciplinary perspectives in order to shape a common understanding of a complex topic. According to Rinn and Weir (1984), interdisciplinary team teaching "is planned and taught as if knowledge were one and the disciplines had not yet been invented" (p.5). The emphasis in an interdisciplinary team "is not on the distinct disciplines, but on what light the disciplines in concert can shed on the topic or issue" (Austin and Baldwin, 1991, p. 38).

The disciplinary mix shapes the dynamics of a teaching team. The required level of communication, role definition, and course planning varies according to the extent to which team members share a common frame of reference and even a common professional vocabulary. Collaborating teachers need to be aware of a simple rule of thumb: as the disciplinary mix of instructional teams becomes more complex, the necessary amount of communication and coordination among team members grows as well.

The Course Mix

Teaching collaboration, of course, is not limited to the boundaries of an individual course. Faculty may also collaborate on a sequence or package of related courses that build on a central theme like the ecology of planet earth. The level of faculty interaction around "cluster courses" depends on the degree to which the courses are intended to complement one another and move students toward common educational goals. Faculty may meet to coordinate course goals and content but have little contact as they implement their plans. On the other hand, they may meet regularly as they teach their courses to be sure they are well synchronized and moving effectively toward shared goals.

The "Buddy" System

The "buddy" system, or master faculty program, is another productive form of teaching collaboration. Although not a type of team teaching, pairing faculty to support one another's classroom performance can greatly enhance teaching quality. In such arrangements, professors take turns observing each other's classes and then meet to exchange assessments and share ideas about effective teaching strategies. Like all forms of faculty collaboration, participants in the "buddy system" benefit according to how well they communicate and invest themselves in the shared effort. (See the chapter by Millis and Kaplan, this volume.)

KEY ISSUES FOR COLLABORATORS TO CONSIDER

Collaborative teaching holds much promise for higher education. Still, collaboration presents distinct challenges and potential pitfalls professors should be aware of before entering blindly into a team teaching arrangement.

First, collaboration alters the dynamics of course planning and management. A team taught course may require more time to design and implement than a course developed independently. Collaborating professors must schedule time for meetings to build a shared understanding of course goals and procedures as well as to respond to unanticipated problems that emerge as a course unfolds. Team teaching has the potential to be disjointed and uneven in quality if team members "do their own thing" rather than carefully coordinate their individual efforts.

Second, faculty autonomy is sacrificed in order to teach a collaborative course successfully. This loss of full control of a course is one of the experiences team teachers must learn to accept in order to collaborate effectively (Fuchs and Moore, 1988; LaFauci and Richter, 1970).

Third, it is difficult to evaluate individual performance in a collaborative teaching arrangement, a factor that discourages some faculty from sharing their classrooms with colleagues. When two or more persons are responsible for the same course, there can be much confusion about how to measure individual contributions, assess responsibility when problems occur, and distribute recognition appropriately. The lack of clear policies for regulating and rewarding collaborative teaching may inhibit faculty from taking the risks associated with any professional activity somewhat removed from the professional mainstream. Arbitrary schemes such as dividing course credit by the number of team teachers involved oversimplify the nature of team teaching by failing to acknowledge the extra effort that is required to ensure the success of a collaborative teaching initiative. We are convinced that clearly defined policies on the evaluation of collaborative teaching would encourage more faculty to experiment with team teaching arrangements.

Fourth, special types of teaching partnerships may pose distinctive challenges for collaborating faculty. Collaborations involving members of unequal status as well as collaborations including women or minorities each raise special issues that team members must be prepared to address. Ideally, collaborations involving junior and senior colleagues or professors and students offer substantial benefits for all parties. Junior partners can learn much about teaching from their more seasoned colleagues, and senior partners can profit from the energy, enthusiasm, and fresh perspectives of their younger teammates. (See the chapter by Sorcinelli, this volume.) On the other hand, there is always the potential for exploitation within teams involving partners of unequal status. Team members must be certain that lower status colleagues are not saddled with clerical work or other less desirable tasks simply because of their lower rank. Collaborative teaching is most successful when all partners function as full fledged members of the team and have the opportunity to contribute to all aspects of the teaching process.

Fifth, women and minority faculty also bring special circumstances to teaching collaborations. The research literature suggests that both women and minority academics have difficulties establishing professionally rewarding collaborative relationships (Frierson, 1990; Garza, 1988; Hood, 1985; Wong and Sanders, 1983). Evidence suggests, for example, that unmarried women professors are often excluded from male networks (Kaufman, 1978). Likewise, many black professors report feelings of isolation and lack of support from their colleagues (Finkelstein, 1984; Frierson, 1990; Moore and Wagstaff, 1974). Collaboration can be an ideal mechanism for integrating under-represented groups into the academic profession. As higher education seeks to attract more women and minorities to the faculty ranks, more affirmative efforts to engage these types of faculty into collaborative teaching activities may well bolster their work in the classroom and enhance their overall career development by strengthening their collegial support system.

Collaborative teaching is a multifaceted process. Among the factors that contribute to its success are the eagerness of participating faculty to engage in a stimulating, interactive experience and their willingness to share responsibility with colleagues. However, if faculty members are reluctant to devote the necessary time to their collaborative work or feel the need to be entirely autonomous, they may encounter disappointing results when they combine their efforts with others in one classroom or in a series of related courses. Teachers who collaborate successfully rise to the unique challenges and avoid the pitfalls that seem to characterize most forms of collaborative teaching.

ADVICE FROM VETERAN COLLABORATORS

The literature on collaboration coupled with research we have done with veteran collaborators has yielded valuable advice for anyone considering joint teaching with colleagues. We offer eight key recommendations.

1. **Know Your Potential Collaborators Well**

   Check out the person(s) carefully before beginning to collaborate. Or as one person suggested, "date awhile" before you enter a long-term relationship. You may want to visit one anothers' classes to get a feel for each other's teaching styles. Doing some short-term projects together, such as planning a campus seminar series or working together on a conference presentation, is a good way to get better acquainted before making a commitment to a whole term of joint teaching. It is important to know the other person's work style and standards. As one veteran collaborator suggested, ask yourself, "Is this someone I would want to spend some intense time with?"

2. **Clarify What Each Person Brings to the Collaborative Relationship**

   Do you complement each other both in terms of subject matter and teaching style? It is not necessary that each party bring something different or unique to a team. It is essential, however, that all parties be comfortable with the teaching arrangement that is worked out. To achieve this objective, you should sort out what you want from the collaboration and ask the other people involved what they expect from the relationship. Each team member should be able to answer "yes" to the question, "Is this a good fit?"

3. **Work Out the Details in Advance**

   To avoid misunderstandings and disappointments, basic ground rules for collaborative teaching should be set early. Questions about course design, division of lecturing duties, strategies to assess students, and grading standards should be decided before a course gets underway. If there is to be a team leader or some other kind of hierarchical arrangement, this should be determined before the group starts its work. Clear expectations for all team members should be defined early in a collaboration to avoid confusion and conflict.

4. **Solicit Feedback from Students**

   Students are some of the best judges of the success of collaborative teaching. Hence, they should be consulted as the work of a teaching team unfolds. Using classroom research techniques like one-minute papers or classroom assessment quality circles offer a means to monitor the progress of team teaching while there is still time to resolve structural or implementation problems (Cross and Angelo, 1988).

5. **Renegotiate Roles and Responsibilities Periodically**
   Only one thing about collaborative teaching is certain: something will not go according to plan. For this reason, it is important that team members periodically revisit and discuss the nature of their collaboration. How is it working? Are we adhering to our original plan? Are we communicating effectively? Is our work distributed well and fairly? Reassessing roles and responsibilities regularly permits needed fine tuning and prevents minor problems from becoming major sources of tension among team members.

6. **Cultivate a Spirit of Camaraderie**
   The machinery of collaborative teaching is lubricated by the spirit of friendship and good humor. Collaborations work best if the participants respect each others' work and enjoy one anothers' company. Team members should have fun as they work together. If team teaching fails to offer the rewards of intellectual stimulation and good colleagueship, team members will surely retreat to the security of their separate classrooms.

7. **Communicate to Others the Nature of the Collaborative Arrangement**
   Collaboration is perhaps the most misunderstood way to structure work in higher education. Collaborative learning techniques for students that once would have been labeled cheating are now hailed as highly effective instructional strategies. Similarly, there is still a great deal of confusion concerning how to credit professors who work together on a research project or in the classroom. It is quite common for some collaborators (especially those with established reputations) to receive more recognition than they deserve while more junior colleagues may get less credit than they are due. To ensure that faculty colleagues, administrators, and personnel committees fully comprehend teaching partnerships, team members should explain the nature of their team to outsiders. For example, written descriptions of team assignments and procedures accompanying syllabi and course evaluation materials could preclude unfounded assumptions about the amount of effort invested in collaborative teaching or arbitrary assignments of workload credit.

8. Junior Faculty Should be Cautious About Collaborative Teaching
Without question, less experienced faculty have much to gain from teaching with more seasoned colleagues. However, due to misconceptions about collaboration and the absence of clear guidelines for rewarding collaboration, teachers who have not yet established a solid professional reputation should enter team teaching arrangements cautiously. Junior faculty should be sure to do some teaching alone as a means to develop an independent professional identity. They should be certain to clarify with their partners what the professional benefits of the collaboration will be. Finally, they should consult with their department chair or dean concerning how their collaborative teaching will be evaluated and how their institution will credit the team teaching they do.

ADVICE FOR ADMINISTRATORS

Deans, department chairs, and other academic administrators have an important role to play in promoting collaboration in the classroom. College and university administrators can foster collaborative teaching by following these six recommendations.

1. **Establish Policies Supportive of Collaboration**
Many personnel policies in higher education assume that faculty work by themselves. Often these policies unintentionally discourage faculty from teaching or conducting research together. To reap the benefits of collaboration, institutions should draft workload, evaluation, and reward policies that recognize collaborative faculty work as legitimate contributions to the academic enterprise. Written guidelines for assessing individual contributions to team teaching would foster more collaborative work in the college classroom.

2. **Provide Adequate Resources and Time**
Faculty wishing to collaborate in the classroom need time, and often additional resources, to prepare for this distinctive form of teaching. Administrators must be ready to offer some extra support if they want to implement quality team teaching initiatives on their campuses. Released time for course planning, summer stipends for course design work, and small grants to develop course materials may be needed to get a teaching team off the ground.

3. **Create Opportunities for Cross-Departmental Collaboration**
   As the academic profession becomes more specialized, the barriers to many forms of collaborative teaching grow higher. At the same time, more issues confronting education today call for cross discipline responses. Deans and other senior academic administrators are strategically placed to lower some of these barriers. Facilitating the development of study groups, curriculum reform initiatives, and interdisciplinary centers can promote more collaborative teaching. Likewise, senior administrators are well positioned to give moral and financial support for cross discipline team teaching that may not be forthcoming from discipline-based academic departments.

4. **Recognize Collaborative Efforts Publicly**
   Administrators who value collaboration in the classroom can aid its development by recognizing group teaching efforts in public forums. Articles in newsletters, comments in faculty meetings, and addresses at new faculty orientation are appropriate opportunities to raise the visibility and status of collaborative teaching.

5. **Be Alert to Problems That Emerge When Faculty Teach Together**
   The current system for training college professors does not prepare professors for team teaching. Inevitably, problems emerge as colleagues with different attributes try to merge their ideas, values, and beliefs into one course or course sequence. Department chairs and deans have important roles to play in resolving such difficulties. Until team teaching becomes common practice in higher education, trouble-shooters will occasionally be needed to consult and help remove obstructions from the path of successful collaborative teaching.

6. **Model Collaborative Teaching**
   Perhaps the most powerful message administrators can send in support of collaborative teaching is nonverbal. When a department chair, for example, team teaches with a colleague in another department, he or she states clearly that collaborative teaching is a legitimate and valued professional activity.

CONCLUSION

We recommend that college professors give collaborative teaching a serious try. Many faculty are reluctant to teach with a colleague for fear that some personal deficiency or knowledge gap will be discovered. The benefits of collaborating with colleagues, however, substantially outweigh the liabilities. Active collaborators cite increases in creativity, quality, and satisfaction when they reflect on their collaborative experiences (Austin and Baldwin, 1991; Baldwin and Austin, 1992). Only by experimenting with some form of team teaching will faculty members be able to reap the rewards of teaching with colleagues.

AUTHORS

Roger G. Baldwin is Associate Professor and Coordinator of the Higher Education Program at the College of William and Mary. His publications focus on the faculty career development process, conditions in the academic workplace, and faculty collaboration. He is coauthor, with Ann E. Austin, of *Faculty Collaboration: Enhancing the Quality of Scholarship and Teaching.*

Ann E. Austin is Associate Professor and Coordinator of the Higher, Adult, and Lifelong Education Program at Michigan State University. Her research interests include improving college teaching, faculty careers and professional development, and colleges and universities as workplaces. Austin's publications include *Developing New and Junior Faculty* (co-edited with Mary Deane Sorcinelli) and *Faculty Collaboration: Enhancing the Quality of Scholarship and Teaching* (with Roger G. Baldwin).

REFERENCES

Angelo, T. A.(1994). From faculty development to academic development. *AAHE Bulletin* 46(10): 3–7.

Austin, A. E., & Baldwin, R. G.(1991). *Faculty collaboration: Enhancing the quality of scholarship and teaching.* ASHE-ERIC Higher Education Reports. Washington, DC: The George Washington University.

Baldwin, R. G., & Austin, A. E.(1992). Toward greater understanding of faculty collaboration: Metaphors, emerging theory, and collaborators' advice. Paper presented at the National Conference of the Association for the Study of Higher Education, Minneapolis, MN.

Boyer, E. L.(1987). *College: The undergraduate experience in America.* New York, NY: Harper and Row.

Bruffee, K. A.(1987). The art of collaborative learning. *Change* 19(2): 42–47.

Cross, K. P., & Angelo, T. A.(1988). *Classroom assessment techniques: A faculty handbook.* Ann Arbor, MI: National Center for Research to Improve Postsecondary Teaching and Learning.

Easterby-Smith, M., & Olve, N.(1984). Team teaching: Making management education more student-centered? *Management Education and Development* 15(3): 221–236.

Finkelstein, M. J.(1984). *The American academic profession: A synthesis of social science inquiry since World War II.* Columbus, OH: The Ohio State University Press.

Frierson, H. T.(1990).The situation of black educational researchers: Continuation of a crisis. *Educational Researcher* 19(2): 12–17.

Fuchs, G. E., & Moore, L. P.(1988). Collaboration for understanding and effectiveness. *Clearing House* 61(9): 410–413.

Garza, H.(1988). The "barriorization" of Hispanic faculty. *Educational Record* 69(1): 122–124.

Hood, J. C.(1985).The lone scholar myth. In M. F. Fox (Ed.), *Scholarly writing and publishing: Issues, problems, and solutions.* Boulder, CO: Westview Press.

Johnson, D. W., & Johnson, R. T.(1975). *Learning together and alone.* Englewood Cliffs, NJ: Prentice-Hall.

Johnson, D. W., Johnson, R. T., & Smith, K. A.(1991). *Active learning: Cooperation in the college classroom.* Edina, MN: Interaction Book Co.

Johnson, D. W., Maruyama, G., Johnson, R., Nelson, D., & Skon, L.(1981). Effects of cooperative, competitive, and individualistic goal structures on achievement: A meta-analysis. *Psychological Bulletin* 89(1): 47–62.

Kaufman, D. R.(1978). Associational ties in academe: Some male and female differences. *Sex Roles* 4(1): 9–21.

Kerr, C.(1994). *Troubled times for American higher education: The 1990s and beyond.* Albany, NY: State University of New York Press.

LaFauci, H. M., & Richter, P. E.(1970). *Team teaching at the college level.* New York, NY: Pergamon Press.

Moore, W., & Wagstaff, L.(1974). *Black educators in white colleges.* San Francisco, CA: Jossey-Bass.

Rinn, F. J., & Weir, S. B.(1984). Yea, team. *Improving College and University Teaching* 32(1): 5–10.

Wong, H. Y., & Sanders, J. M.(1983). Gender differences in the attainment of doctorates. *Sociological Perspectives* 26(1): 29–50.

EIGHTEEN

DISTANCE EDUCATION: THE EMERGENCE OF AMERICA'S VIRTUAL UNIVERSITY

Raoul A. Arreola

Educational outreach, or bringing instruction to the learner rather than having the learner come to the instruction, is an ancient concept in the history of education. In a very real sense, religious missionaries, stretching back into antiquity, have been involved in educational outreach—that is, bringing teaching and instruction to learners located far from some base or center of knowledge and learning. However, limitations in transportation and communications technology have historically made systematic education more cost-effective by creating centralized educational institutions where faculty and students could gather together. This situation is changing.

Today, with the growing availability of sophisticated telecommunications and computer technology, educational outreach efforts have begun to shift away from sending the teacher to a remotely located learner to sending simply the instruction. The use of telecommunication technology to deliver instruction has emerged as an important, and potentially revolutionary, force in education especially in the form of live, two-way video connections that can bring "virtual" classroom experiences into students' homes or workplaces (Jacobson, 1994). Variously referred to as distance education, distance learning, distance teaching, tele-learning and tele-teaching, the application of electronic telecommunications technology to the ancient concept of educational outreach has begun to change the face of higher education (Willis, 1993).

DISTANCE EDUCATION TODAY

At present, courses and degrees in over 125 fields are being offered by nearly 90 colleges and universities in more than 40 states via distance education (Kohl, 1993). The fields represented range from accounting to mathematics to psychology to voice communications. In addition, a number of distance degree consortia and networks have been established to meet a variety of special needs. Among them are: (1) the Electronic University Network (EUN), comprised of the California Institute of Integral Studies, Heriot-Watt University, and Rogers State College; (2) the International University Consortium (IUC), a consortium of colleges, universities, and educational communications agencies in the U.S. and Canada, formed by the University of Maryland University College and Maryland Public Television to develop and use media assisted course materials; (3) the Mind Extension University, a network that offers distance education programs provided by over 20 colleges and universities throughout the country through cable and satellite; (4) the National Technological University (NTU), a consortium of over 40 colleges and universities offering courses leading to master's degrees in engineering; and, (5) the National Universities Degree Consortium (NUDC), a consortium of nearly a dozen colleges and universities using the Mind Extension network to deliver courses.

Over 300,000 people are taking for-credit courses in these distance education programs, with some 30,000 enrolled in degree programs. Clearly, distance education is becoming a major, if not a revolutionary, force in higher education. Since electronic telecommunications technology plays such a large role in defining the dimensions and characteristics of distance education, it is important to examine the features of this technology.

THE TECHNOLOGY OF DISTANCE EDUCATION

The printing press, coupled with a reliable postal system, may reasonably be considered the first major technological advancement which enabled distance education, in the form of correspondence courses, to become a permanent if not widespread feature of the educational landscape. However, it has been the development and common availability of television, computers, and other forms of electronic telecommunication technology which have enabled distance education programs to really come into their own as legitimate and desirable alternatives to traditional classroom instruction.

In the traditional classroom, the technology available to the instructor ranges from blackboard and chalk, to handouts, to overhead, slide, and film projectors, videocassette players, and television monitors. All these forms of technology are intended to assist the instructor in conveying information to the learner. Since the student is in the same room with the instructor, there is an ease of verbal and nonverbal (visual) feedback between them. The key differences in communication technology between traditional classroom instruction and distance education instruction can be seen by examining the conditions of teaching in an extremely large lecture hall.

When a traditional classroom expands to a large lecture hall holding 500 to 1,000 students, we begin to experience some of the same conditions common to distance education courses taught via electronic telecommunication technology. That is, we experience difficulty in seeing or hearing students at the remote sites (back rows), and we must make special provisions to ensure that they can see and hear us. Handouts may be prepared in advance and made available to students as they come into the lecture hall; a powerful projector may be used to show slides or films; large projection television screens and numerous television monitors scattered throughout the lecture hall may be used to show video images; and a public address system, coupled with strategically placed microphones enable the students to hear the teacher. Since it is difficult to take many student questions in the large lecture hall, the presentation or lecture has to be carefully prepared to both anticipate and answer the most likely questions. If we wish to permit a few questions or other student feedback we may strategically place a few microphones in the aisles for students to use. In short, we must make special accommodations for the fact that our students are somewhat remote from us in the large lecture hall. Likewise, the technologies of distance education and techniques of distance teaching are intended to simply make it possible for the teacher and student to interact with one another even though they may be separated by long distances.

Electronic telecommunication technologies of various sorts have been available for distance education programs for some time. These include: (1) using the telephone in conference call configurations with groups of students at remote sites; (2) distributing audiotapes of lectures or presentations; (3) sending videotapes to students for individual or group viewing; and, (4) broadcasting television courses either by cable or satellite. Instructors offering courses live on television may provide a telephone call-in line so students may call in questions. However, all these forms of electronic communication have been hampered by the fact that the instructor could not see, and often could not hear, the students. Thus, a significant aspect of normal teacher-student interaction has been missing.

Interactive Video

Recent advances in computer and television technology have finally made possible the realization of an age-old dream: instantaneous two-way audio and video communication between individuals separated by long distances. Generally referred to as interactive video, two-way video (with two-way audio) has emerged as a revolutionary force in distance education. Just like the communication screen on the bridge of the starship "Enterprise" in the popular science fiction television and movie series *Star Trek*, this technology permits the distance education teacher to both see and hear students at remote sites. Generally, special classrooms, called "smart classrooms", are configured with cameras, microphones and television monitors which permit students to hear and see the instructor and likewise permit the instructor to see and hear the remote learners. When these "smart classrooms" are configured with facsimile machines and computers linked through a common network with the instructor, the entire range of normal student-instructor interaction becomes available. In fully configured systems of this type, the students at each of the remote locations can see and hear one another as well as the instructor.

LIMITATIONS AND CONCERNS

The ideal distance education configuration is a network of smart classrooms in which a large, wall-sized screen shows life-sized images of either the students or the teacher, and large images of any slides, graphics or other visuals used during instruction. In such smart classrooms the instructor can see and hear the students at the remote sites and the students at each remote site can see and hear the instructor as well as students at the other remote sites. Although some approximations of this ideal exist in a few distance education networks, the full realization of this ideal requires a breakthrough technology which uses compressed video but eliminates time delays, echoing, and lack of synchronization between picture and sound.

The best current example of this breakthrough technology is the Imagewall interactive video unit produced by the ImageTel Corporation of Louisville, Kentucky. The standard Imagewall unit has a 4 x 7 foot screen which projects life-sized images. Other units can project 8 x 16 foot images all the way up to movie theater-sized images. Special microphones are strategically placed, generally out of immediate view, and provide a natural speaking and hearing environment. Distance teaching using these units is comparable to teaching a class of students who are on the other side of a glass wall. The adjustments in instructional technique a teacher has to make are minimal—especially when coupled with new electronic blackboards (soft boards) which instantly transmit an electronically produced version of what the teacher is writing on the blackboard without the use of a separate video camera. Several college and university systems are exploring the installation of Imagewall technology for their distance education networks. However, at this writing no university system has such a network in place because this technology is relatively expensive to purchase and operate. But, as with most electronic technology, the cost of the Imagewall videoconferencing unit is expected to fall significantly over the next few years and to launch a true revolution in interactive video distance education.

However, most distance education programs make use of less expensive equipment with lesser capabilities and thus present the teacher with a number of limitations and special conditions not found in the traditional classroom. These special conditions require significant adjustments in instructional technique.

The major limitation of commonly used equipment in distance education programs is in the quality and characteristics of the sound. Ideally, students should be able to hear the teacher, and the teacher should be able to hear students ask questions or make responses to questions. Interestingly, even though well-established telephone technology would seem to make this an easy task to accomplish, it turns out to be expensive and difficult. To prevent echoes and other sound feedback problems, special microphones must be used that either (a) require students to press a button before they can talk or, (b) automatically "clips" off the first part of any sound or spoken word so as to prevent echoing. Either situation slows up and inhibits the type of free and easy verbal exchanges by students and teacher found in a traditional classroom setting. Although recent advances in audio technology have improved this situation, and have essentially eliminated it in the more expensive systems such as the Imagewall videoconferencing unit, it is still a common problem in many distance education telecommunication configurations.

A second problem is synchronization between sound and picture when interactive video systems are used. Depending upon the equipment and transmission technology used, there may be a delay of one-third to one-half of a second between when a student starts to ask a question and when the teacher hears it. In many cases, the teacher may see a student's lips move only after the sound is heard. In addition, the picture seen by the students may be jerky or show a trail of ghost images whenever the teacher moves quickly. In short, visual communication cues on which teachers depend can become confusing and inhibit student-teacher interaction.

Both the audio and video problems described above are a function of the cost of transmitting electronic signals over cable television lines, special telephone lines, or satellite systems. It is possible to have perfect synchronization between the video image and sound and to have full, normal audio communication by electronic means. We see this demonstrated every night on our television sets, especially on news programs where newscasters interview and have normal conversations with foreign leaders half a world away. However, the cost of transmitting the signals required to accomplish this are generally more than an educational institution is willing to pay. Modern distance education telecommunication equipment tries to get around this problem by "compressing" or squeezing the audio and video signals so they take up less space on the communications lines and thus cost less to transmit. Unfortunately, this requires the receiving site to decompress the signals before they can be used. The compression and decompression process takes time, albeit a fraction of a second, and contributes to the delay and synchronization problems noted above. Computer technology can be used to minimize this compression and decompression delay time to such an extent that it is not noticeable. But, as is always the case with computer technology, faster means more expensive. Video compression technology is so widespread that two terms related to it have come to be commonly used in discussing distance education: "compressed video" and "codec." Compressed video refers to the use of video compression technology to compress the signals and thus reduce the transmission costs. The electronic compression-decompression device that accomplishes this is referred to as a "codec." The codec can be the single most expensive piece of electronic hardware in a smart classroom. The simple fact of life is that the faster (and thus more expensive) codec you buy, the better and more natural your interactive video distance teaching and learning environment will be.

THE IMPACT ON TEACHER PREPARATION

Distance education by means of electronic telecommunications technology poses its own unique requirements both on the teacher and the remote learner. The conditions under which the teacher is asked to teach can vary considerably from the conventional classroom and thus the preparation required to teach effectively can also vary significantly. However, one overriding principle holds true for all forms of technology associated with distance education—planning and organization is of paramount importance.

Interestingly, the preparation to be an effective teacher in a distance education course is essentially the same as that required to be an effective teacher in a conventional classroom. That is, the teacher must (a) plan in advance what the student is to learn; (b) develop the materials and experiences the student should have to enable them to learn (e.g., slides, handouts, lecture, lab experiments); (c) present the materials and experiences at such a time and in such a way that learning is facilitated; and (d) systematically evaluate the degree to which students have learned.

However, because using electronic telecommunications technology to deliver education at a distance has a clearly identifiable cost, the need to carefully design, deliver and evaluate instruction is much more keenly felt. Using television cable lines, special telephone lines, computer networks, and satellite communication technology involves a specific hourly line charge. This fact places a responsibility on the teacher to even more carefully plan for, and use, every hour they are "on." Also, as noted earlier, since the most commonly used two-way interactive video technology results in somewhat slower communication between teacher and students than that experienced in a live classroom, an hour of distance teaching time may not provide the same amount of actual instructional time as an hour of conventional classroom time. Thus, planning and preparation are of utmost importance for effective distance teaching.

Another factor which influences teacher preparation is the limitation on student feedback imposed by the technology and the need to accommodate what may be an even wider than normal range of student differences. Distance education programs, by their nature, try to reach out to people who may not ordinarily appear in a conventional classroom. Students who enroll in distance education programs tend to be over 25 years old, employed, highly motivated, and have had some previous college experience. Their completion rate tends to exceed that of students enrolled in traditional, on-campus courses (Kohl, 1993). Since a single distance education course may be delivered simultaneously to adult learners in their homes, select groups of employees at a business site, and conventional students on another campus, the teacher needs to be aware of, and prepared to respond to, the different capabilities, needs, interests, and motivations of remote learners.

PREPARING TO TEACH USING DISTANCE EDUCATION TECHNOLOGY

Formal training of faculty involved in distance education courses using telecommunications technology is highly recommended. Most educational institutions offering large-scale distance education programs provide some form of training to their faculty. One of the best known of these training programs is the Teletraining Institute formed by Oklahoma State University, in association with Parker Consulting, Inc. Some key guidelines for effective distance teaching may be identified. Those who teach should:

✦ Become familiar with the equipment available. Practice with it until its use becomes comfortable and natural.

✦ Become familiar with the characteristics of the equipment being used by students at remote sites. If a large group of students are all watching on a single 19 inch television screen, their ability to see what the instructor is doing or showing them will be quite different from that of a group that is watching on a large projected television screen with numerous strategically placed 27 inch monitors. In any case, the instructor needs to constantly be aware of how his or her image or the image of the materials being used are seen by students (Lochte, 1993).

✦ Design the course and presentations according to the principles of instructional systems design. That is, clearly specify the learning objectives for each hour of the "broadcast," design the presentations to facilitate accomplishment of the learning objectives, and select and use the appropriate media for the objective being taught. A common error is to place too much written material on the screen. More than four or five lines of text on a screen cannot be read by most students, regardless of the size of the television set being used. The worst and most common error of this type is to transmit a video image of a full typewritten page such as the one you are reading now. Again, be aware of what the students are seeing.

✦ Prepare all materials in advance and have in mind precisely where in the instruction each will be used. Although an instructor may be able to use various forms of technology that permit free-hand drawing or writing, the resulting video image may not be as clear as a previously produced slide or transparency.

✦ Prepare all handouts in advance and make sure they have been mailed or otherwise distributed to remote learners before class.

✦ Pace the presentation to permit questions and comments from students. Since the technology may inhibit student interactions, the instructor may have to specifically call for questions or comments from a remote site and wait for a response. The converse can sometimes also be true. That is, students at one remote site may monopolize the system by asking all the questions. Since most distance education audio technology automatically shuts off the sound from all other sites when one site is talking, be prepared to guide the questioning or discussion to give all remote learners an equal opportunity to interact.

✦ Decide whether students should be in the smart classroom with the instructor during the broadcast. Many instructors feel they must have live students in the room in order to make their teaching effective. Others feel that having students in the same room where distance teaching is being carried out is a distraction. Determine which situation is most comfortable. Keep in mind, however, that students in the smart classroom with the teacher sometimes complain that they do not get as good a learning experience. This is because students compare their experience with a traditional classroom in which the instructor can give those present in the room undivided attention. In a smart classroom the instructor must operate various forms of telecommunications technology and must attend to questions, comments and problems from remote sites. As a consequence, students in the room with the instructor sometimes report feeling shortchanged.

One strategy to deal with the issue of students on campus taking a course being offered as part of a distance education program is to establish separate "distance teaching" and "distance learning" classrooms (Arreola & Brown, 1994). That is, a "distance teaching" room may be a smart classroom specifically designed to accommodate only the instructor with no students present. A "distance learning" classroom may be a smart classroom designed to be used exclusively by students receiving a course from some remote origination site. A distance learning classroom may have a large television projection screen as well as individual response terminals which enable each student to interact easily with the teacher at the remote origination site. In the event that students at the same origination site as the instructor must take the distance education course along with students at one or more remote sites, they can be placed in a "distance learning" classroom while the instructor teaches the course from a "distance teaching" classroom. A "distance teaching" classroom may be located in close physical proximity to a "distance learning" classroom at the origination site. In fact, they might be right next door to one another. However, when the teacher is teaching, all students, including the ones in the "distance learning" room next door, are "remote" students visible only on appropriate television monitors. This approach ensures that all students, including those on campus with the instructor, experience the same quality of instruction.

IMPLICATIONS AND QUESTIONS FOR THE FUTURE

Increasingly, statewide educational systems are linking their colleges and universities electronically to form interactive video networks. One example is the University of Tennessee System which has linked all its campuses and institutes via a statewide interactive video network called UT EDNET. The UT EDNET is routinely used to deliver courses and certain degree programs throughout Tennessee. Other public and private college systems in Tennessee often request access to UT EDNET to deliver their own distance education courses (Arreola & Brown, 1994). Another example is the Educational Network of Maine which links the University of Maine System campuses, the Technical College System, and the State Department of Education of Maine. Each of these organizations participates in offering courses and other programming throughout Maine (Connick, 1992).

In such interactive video networks, distance education courses may be taught by a faculty member on one campus to students located in smart classrooms on other campuses. Special degree programs are being offered to various business firms by delivering instruction via interactive video directly to the work site. The faculty teaching these courses may be teaching from smart classrooms on different campuses—even in different states.

Two-way interactive video instruction can be delivered to virtually any location in the country, or even the world. This development has profound implications and poses significant questions concerning the future of higher education.

Mission and Service Area

The issue as to what constitutes the service area of an educational institution takes on a different meaning given the availability of interactive video technology. The conventional geographical limits to an institution's service area no longer apply. The mission of an educational institution very often is a function of its traditional geographical location and the needs and characteristics of its population. This is especially true of land grant colleges. However, the ability to deliver instruction to sites far removed from an institution's immediate traditional geographical service area can have a significant effect on the definition of its "client base" and thus its mission. Already a number of institutions are offering courses and degrees to remote learners in states other than their own. One of the earliest and most successful of these is California State University, Chico, which offers a master's degree in computer science to students in a total of 15 states including Arkansas, California, Colorado, Connecticut, Idaho, Illinois, Iowa, Nevada, New Jersey, Oregon, Pennsylvania, Tennessee, Texas, Virginia, and Washington (Connick, 1992). Other universities have joined consortia, such as the National Technological University noted earlier, to offer courses and degrees in engineering throughout the country.

Teacher Productivity

The definition as to what constitutes teacher productivity changes considerably in a distance education setting. When a lecture, presentation, or even an entire course, is prerecorded, either on videotape or computer disk or both, and delivered repeatedly while the teacher is doing something else—or perhaps no longer employed or even alive, is the teacher still "producing"? Should teachers get residual payments when their prerecorded courses are offered again and again just as musicians do when their recordings are played?

Academic Issues

Distance education programs tend to severely exacerbate traditional academic issues such as accreditation, registration, tuition and fee-charges, residency requirements, course evaluation, faculty evaluation, and teaching load (Connick, 1992). For example, does a faculty member teleteaching a course simultaneously to five sites, each with 20 students, have the same teaching load as a faculty member teaching that same course to an on-campus class of 20 students? Is it a violation to have copyrighted audiovisual work, originally shown in class, broadcast via satellite and carried on local cable systems (Switzer & Switzer, 1994)?

Courses on Demand

Cable television systems are moving in the direction of having hundreds of channels with many of these channels offering movies on demand. That is, the viewer can request, at any time, a particular movie to be shown with an appropriate charge being made to the viewer's account. It is not too far a stretch to envision a catalog of prerecorded courses also available on demand from these same cable systems. Industry training programs have introduced the concept of "just-in-time-training" in which employees are taught a new technique or procedure just before they need to apply it on the job. Since high technology has had the effect on our economy of giving many jobs a rather short lifetime, there is a clear need for continuous, on-demand, training and education for the American work force. Distance education technology offers a way for traditional educational institutions to respond to this new reality.

The Virtual University

In the same way that a University College may exist within a traditional academic organization wherein courses are drawn from various departments and colleges to form a specialized degree program, virtual universities, made up of groupings of courses taught via telecommunication technology by faculty located throughout a state or even the country may form an electronic university college or a "virtual" university.

The relatively easy access to facsimile machines and computer networks have begun to enable people to work at sites other than a centralized office complex. Some individuals, with lap-top computers, cellular phones, modems, and facsimile machines in their brief cases carry their "offices" with them. This phenomenon has given rise to what is being called the "virtual" office. Couple this with the spread of world-wide computer networks, and we can see the emergence of a virtual community. Virtual communities have been defined as social aggregations that emerge when enough people carry on public discussions, with sufficient feelings, over an electronic network to form webs of personal relationships. Such virtual communities exist not so much in time and place as in the minds of the "residents" (Rheingold, 1993). In some cases "virtual" magnet schools have been created using faculty from universities as well as from high schools and corporate sponsors. Students attend these virtual schools by means of signing on to computer networks and electronic mail systems (Goodrich, 1993). Virtual classrooms enable students to communicate with the teacher and one another exclusively by electronic means (Kilian, 1994; Mizell & Carl, 1994). Similarly, anyone with access to a cable television system or satellite dish, a videocassette recorder, a telephone, and a computer with a modem is a potential student of a virtual university. Any teacher with access to appropriate telecommunications technology is a potential member of the faculty of a virtual university. With the coming wave of desktop videoconferencing equipment, the concept of a faculty member as a "free agent" teaching from home as a member of a virtual university offering courses and degrees across the country is an interesting one to contemplate.

Universal access to telecommunications technology is not a fantasy. The Goals 2000: Education America Act enacted by Congress, coupled with the Clinton administration's commitment to bring to every classroom in America, by the year 2000, a broadband telecommunication service of voice, data, and two-way video known as the National Information Infrastructure (NII), will significantly alter our concept of a school (MacDonald, 1994). The Peterson's Guide publication, *The Electronic University*, (Kohl, 1993) stands as a veritable course catalog for America's "virtual" university listing hundreds of distance education courses from nearly 100 colleges and universities. The precise impact of distance education as made possible by advances in computer and telecommunications technology is difficult to predict. It is interesting to consider the views on this matter of Michael H. Spindler, president and chief executive officer of Apple Computer:

"For students, learning will no longer be limited to the lecture hall; learning will take place where and when students want it to. And electronic agents will help them to access the world's knowledge and build their own personal databases. For faculty, technology will help to develop

customized courseware they can deliver electronically to their students."
(Spindler, p.11, 1994)

Microcomputer and telecommunication technologies have already had a significant, if not revolutionary, impact on higher education. The fact that many leaders of the industries developing these technologies share Mr. Spindler's view of the future, a future they have a direct hand in shaping, provides a loud wake-up call for American higher education.

AUTHOR

Raoul A. Arreola is Professor and Director of Educational Technology at the University of Tennessee at Memphis. He holds a Ph.D. in educational psychology and has held numerous faculty and administrative positions in that field with a special interest in educational research and measurement, statistics, faculty evaluation, and the use of technology in teaching.

REFERENCES

Arreola, R.A., & Brown, R.A. (1994). *UT Memphis distance education facilities and support services: A proposal.* Report by the Committee on Distance Education of the Health Sciences Library and Education Center. Memphis, TN: The University of Tennessee, Memphis.

Connick, G.P. (1992). Higher education at a distance. In P.S. Portway & C. Lane (Eds.), *A technical guide to teleconferencing & distance learning.* San Ramon, CA: Applied Business Telecommunications, pp. 269–277.

Goodrich, B. (1993). Creating a "virtual" magnet school. *T.H.E. Journal, 21*(10): 73–75.

Jacobson, R.L. (1994). Extending the reach of "virtual" classrooms. *The Chronicle of Higher Education,* A19–A23.

Kilian, C. (1994). 2005: A virtual classroom odyssey. *Educom Review,* 17–18.

Kohl, K. (Ed.). (1993). *The electronic university: A guide to distance learning.* Princeton, NJ: Peterson's Guides.

Lochte, R.H. (1993). *Interactive television and instruction.* Englewood Cliffs, NJ: Educational Technology Publications.

MacDonald, J.T. (1994). Goals 2000:Educate America Act. *T.H.E. Journal, 21*(10): 10.

Mizell, A.P., & Carl, D.R. (1994). Inter-institution cooperation in distance learning. *T.H.E. Journal, 21*(10): 91–93.

Rheingold, H. (1993). *The virtual community: Homesteading on the electronic frontier.* Reading, MA: Addison Wesley.

Spindler, M.H. (1994). Apple and higher education. *Educom Review,* 9–11.

Switzer, J.S., & Switzer, Jr., R.V. (1994). Copyright question: Using audiovisual work in a satellite-delivered program. *T.H.E. Journal, 21*(10): 76–79.

Willis, B. (1993). *Distance education: A practical guide.* Englewood Cliffs, NJ: Educational Technology Publications.

NINETEEN

TEACHING ADULT LEARNERS

Kathleen Wagschal and Peter H. Wagschal

The rapid and sustained growth of demand for adult higher education was first described by two pioneering figures in the adult education movement: Knowles (1978) and Cross (1981). While much has been written on the subject since that time, the factors creating and sustaining demand for adult higher education have not changed and were most succinctly described by Cross.

The present and anticipated growth of lifelong learning in the United States can be attributed to three influences. First are the demographic factors that result in larger numbers of adults in the population. A second influence is social change—the rising educational level of the populace, the changing roles of women, early retirement, civil rights, increased leisure time, changing life styles. The third pressure springs from technological change and the knowledge explosion. These three factors have only intensified their pressure on demand for adult higher education over the past thirteen years, and all indications are that they will continue to do so for the next several decades.

AGE DEMOGRAPHICS OF THE AMERICAN POPULATION

The most obvious ongoing change in the age distribution of the American population is the fact that its median age has increased so consistently over the past 150 years.

✦ The aging of the American population is caused, in large part, by the aging of the baby boomers who will go from being 29–47 years of age in 1993 to being 61–79 years of age in 2025.

✦ These overall age demographics are reflected in projections of higher education enrollment, which derive from statistics compiled by the National Center for Education Statistics:

"...college enrollment is projected to rise to 16.1 million by the year 2003, an increase of 14 percent" (NCES, 1993, p.12).

"The college enrollment of students 25 years old and over is expected to range between 6.1 million and 7.0 million by the year 2003" (NCES, 1993, p. 13).

SOCIAL CHANGE AND LIFELONG LEARNING

The second important factor driving the increase in adult higher education in America continues to be a variety of social changes which create an ever-growing demand for education at all stages of an adult's life. As noted by Cross (1981) and Knowles (1978), among many others, the major social factors contributing to this growing demand include:

✦ "Blended life plans." Instead of "getting" an education, then having a work life, and then retiring, Americans now mix education with work at several points in their adult lives.

✦ Americans change jobs and careers frequently in their adult lives, and many of these switches require higher education.

✦ There is a well-established research literature which demonstrates that the more education Americans have, the more they want, and the American population is increasingly well educated.

✦ A large variety of previously excluded groups—Hispanics, African-Americans, Asians, handicapped adults—have rising educational expectations and will need to be served by non-traditional approaches to higher education.

✦ More women than ever are entering both the workforce and institutions of higher education that are structured in a manner that will serve their needs for higher education.

✦ Job obsolescence. Technological and social changes create new jobs and eliminate old ones at an increasingly rapid rate. Higher education opportunities are required to enable workers to gain the new skills and knowledge needed for careers that did not exist in the past.

✦ Increased longevity. As the average American lives longer, the number of years spent as a productive member of a changing workforce increases. This longer productive lifespan, combined with job obsolescence, fuels the growth in demand for higher education opportunities among adults.

TECHNOLOGY

It goes without saying that technological changes—particularly in the realms of information and telecommunications technologies—produce increasing demand for higher education opportunities for the adult learner. Many of the mechanisms of this pressure have already been mentioned: job obsolescence, frequent career changes, creation of new jobs and careers. But the nature of technological change in the future is such that it will mandate more attention to adult higher education for two other significant reasons.

The Knowledge Explosion

As a variety of national and international commissions have made quite clear, knowledge has become the most significant coinage of the modern world. New knowledge in many of the most significant fields is emerging so rapidly that professionals are likely to find their knowledge outdated in five years or less unless they continue to receive formal education regarding the latest developments. In most of the areas where new career opportunities are emerging and significant new opportunities exist for the business community, there is no such thing as a "trained professional." Rather, there is a necessity for constant re-education of professionals to assure that what they know reflects the most recent advances in their fields—at all stages of their careers.

The Technologically Challenged Adult

Finally, as information and telecommunication technologies replace print and other forms of communication in the modern workplace, they leave a large group of working adults—particularly the baby boom generation—in dire need of skills and attitudes that they never acquired. Although the younger generations have been exposed to, and are comfortable with, a wide range of information technologies (e.g., through their familiarity as children with video games and educational software), the thirty-and-over population remains unfamiliar with and frightened by computer technologies. As interactive electronic devices literally invade all aspects of the world of work, America's adult population becomes an increasing liability without the kinds of higher education opportunities that can help it to overcome its reluctance to understand and use current technologies.

TEACHING THE ADULT LEARNER

As the population of adult learners seeking higher education opportunities continues to grow, more of America's colleges and universities are
finding themselves faced with the unique opportunities and challenges
posed by teaching new categories of students. The adult education literature is filled with cautionary tales regarding the differences between
teaching "adults" and 18-21-year-olds. We learn from authors that go as
far back as Knowles (1978) and Cross (1981) to later treatments like
those of Brookfield (1990) and Houle (1992) that the adult learners (i.e.,
25-years-of-age or older):

   Are very pragmatic and want instruction that is utilitarian, job-
   related, useful

✦ Learn best when their wealth of personal experience can be tied to
   the subject matter

✦ Respond better to dialogue than to lecture

   Bring a wealth of experience to the higher education classroom, and
   expect to contribute that learning to his or her classmates

   Find learning most meaningful when they can make a direct connection between their past experiences and their current concerns
   (Brookfield, 1989)

   Find the most significant learning experiences to be those in which
   they have to confront and work through some kind of challenge

   Are involved in higher education either for job-related reasons or to
   become better-informed people

✦ Often are motivated to engage in higher education as a result of major
   life transitions; e.g., job change, divorce, geographic dislocation

✦ Are more likely to be problem-centered than subject-centered in
   their approach to learning (Merriam and Caffarella, 1991)

   Are motivated to learn more by internal factors than by external forces

   Tend to be more self-directed in learning than do their younger
   counterparts

Our experience confirms these long-standing generalizations, but
there is far more to be said. What we have learned about teaching "adult
learners" comes from over a decade of teaching working adults whose age
typically ranged from the mid-20s to the mid-50s. Our experiential

knowledge of these students has been augmented recently through a research project sponsored by the National Center for Adult Learning which provided us with the opportunity to read over 1,600 journal entries written by adult learners at the end of each class session in a set of eight different courses taught by four different faculty members.

This rich "database" provides a wealth of clues regarding what does, and does not, work well with a variety of different types of adult learners. In providing the following suggestions, we are hopeful that the reader will keep in mind two fundamental principles that must frame any advice regarding the teaching of any group:

1. All generalizations are false.

2. "The Adult Learner" is an amalgamation of *many* groups. Putting aside, for a moment, the obvious differences among adults of different social, cultural, ethnic, and economic backgrounds, we continue to be amazed that the higher education community considers everyone over the age of 24 to be in the same group. Age differences are of monumental significance in American society, and our classroom experience with students in their 20s, 30s, 40s, 50s, 60s, and 70s reconfirms that fact.

Much of what we advise in the pages that follow applies primarily to the "traditional" adult learner: a person who is employed full-time and in the 25-50 age range.

Despite the assumption of some to the contrary, human development does not stop at the age of 25. The differences between adults in their late twenties and those in their early fifties are significant, and at least as striking as the differences between high school students and 25-year-olds. The "bottom line" of any discussion regarding teaching "the adult learner" is that one must be sensitive to the needs, interests, motivations, background, and world view of one's students, regardless of their age or circumstances.

GRADING PROCEDURES

The adult learner is typically over-concerned with grades. On the surface, this can be annoying. Often, adult learners will actually say, "Tell me what to do to get an 'A' and I will do it." An intrinsic passion for learning may not seem to be anywhere in sight. In many cases, adult students have been out of the classroom for a long time. Their confidence level is often very low. Younger students who just graduated from high school know the rules of the game. Their study skills are current; they know how to get an "A." The adult learner's anxieties can be alleviated if faculty members take the time to explain their expectations clearly. Doing this in writing helps to avoid confusion later. Once faculty members deal with the understandable anxiety of their students, they will be able to enjoy a group of extremely dedicated students whose passion about learning is very evident.

SET HIGH EXPECTATIONS AND LET STUDENTS KNOW THEY ARE HIGH

One of the most interesting revelations contained in the journals of our adult students was their belief that they had little control over their success or failure. Their early journal entries made it clear that they had a high level of anxiety over how difficult the class was going to be and over their inability to meet the challenge. After their first exam, even those students who received an "A" attributed their success to luck or to taking a test that was a lot easier than they expected. They obviously found it difficult to take credit for their efforts. In teaching adults, it is important to make a point of stressing that the course is demanding and that the instructor has complete confidence in the ability of his or her students to succeed. When such a context is provided for a course (and it is in fact a demanding one) adult students gain a new level of confidence in their academic abilities.

PRACTICE WHAT YOU PREACH

The typical eighteen-to-twenty-year-old student is generally very accepting of the fact that adult authority figures often model the principle of, "Do as I say, not as I do." But this is not true for adult learners. They have been adult authority figures for many years, either as parents, or in a respected position in the work force, or both. If *they* are required to arrive on time for class, have their work turned in on time, and be organized and ready to participate in each class session, then it behooves the *instructor* of adult learners to do the same. Adult learners have little patience for instructors who are not prepared; or who take forever to return graded assignments that their students struggled to get in by the deadline, or who give the impression that teaching is not their first priority.

DON'T TRY TO FAKE IT

Adult students expect their instructors to have an in-depth understanding of their subject matter. Also, unlike many younger students, they have a great deal of experience in the work force with colleagues who have pretended to know what they don't know. Honesty is always the best policy. Adult learners feel comfortable in arguing with their instructors, and will even check up on the information given to them if it appears to be unsubstantiated. It is helpful to remember that they are not eighteen-year-old students who are in awe of their instructors. Instructors must earn the respect of the adult student. It doesn't come automatically because the instructor has the right credentials. In many cases, adult students will view the instructor as nothing more than an important colleague in their learning experiences. Adult students view themselves as both givers and receivers of knowledge.

FOCUS THE RELEVANCE OF COURSE MATERIAL TO THE GOALS OF THE STUDENTS

This is probably one of the most important issues to keep in mind when working with adult learners. The typical 20-year-old is less than thrilled as their junior year approaches. This is when they are finally forced to put their cards on the table. "What are you going to major in?" asks their faculty advisor, parent, and friends. "Surely you know what you want to do with the rest of your life." But, in truth, many don't, as readers may remember from their own personal experience. Adult students, on the other hand, know exactly where they are going. In many instances, they have given up highly successful positions in the work place to pursue higher education as a means toward other careers. They come to college with a well thought through vision of where they want to be when they have been validated by the educational community.

In the majority of cases, adult learners are paying for their own education. They are making huge financial and time sacrifices, and so are their families and friends, as they pursue a new dream. They look to each of their instructors to take them one step closer to that goal. Yes, they are impatient. Their concept of time, at the age of thirty, forty, or fifty, is not the same as that of the eighteen-to-twenty-year-old. They want to know how new knowledge fits into their personal and professional paradigms. This does not mean that instructors should not challenge their students' current paradigms. The adult learner enjoys the experience of engaging in lively debate and examining current issues that are the subject of controversy. The important thing to keep in mind is that the content of the course should prepare students to be successful in their future endeavors.

COMBINING DIALOGUE WITH LECTURES

The instructors at National University often look back with nostalgia at the number of fine-tuned lectures that we all had spent so many hours perfecting for our traditional students. Those lectures were considered an acceptable vehicle for transmitting information to students. The adult learner presented us with a new challenge: their need to be personally involved in the information they receive. Adult learners are not comfortable in the role of passive recipients of knowledge. They need to be given the opportunity to share their own opinions, challenge the instructor's assumptions, and have their personal experiences validated and/or openly explored. As a result, those who are most successful working with the adult learner provide their students with the opportunity to engage in cooperative learning activities, panel discussions, group or individual presentations, and formal debates. The lecture format has not been completely abandoned. There are times when "mini-lectures" are invaluable. Although some information is given in the lecture format, the focus is not on the instructor's ability to transmit information but instead on his or her skill in involving the class in active participation once the important concepts have been presented.

EMPHASIZING LISTENING SKILLS

Working with the adult learner presents a paradoxical challenge for the instructor. They want their voices to be heard, and an instructor who enjoys active participation will welcome this experience. At the same time, it needs to be noted that the adult learner is not openly receptive to the opinions of their colleagues if these opinions differ from those they have brought to the classroom setting. The younger student is still open to new ways of looking at important issues. Adult learners may be fairly well entrenched in their own points of view which have been reinforced over a longer period of time. They do not view their opinions as assumptions, but as truths which have weathered a lifetime of experience. Not surprisingly, they are very protective of their points of view and may become defensive when any fellow student tries to challenge them. The benefits that both the instructor and the students gain by engaging in dialogue can be undermined if this issue is not addressed. Taking the time to discuss the principles of effective communication can be invaluable. (See the chapter by Greene, this volume.)

It's a fact of human nature that we tend to spend time with those whose views are similar to ours. Adults returning to school find themselves suddenly in a new situation and with strangers who think very differently. In order to establish a learning community that is effective, instructors need to assist their students in developing their listening skills which entails encouraging them to suspend their beliefs long enough to listen to the opinions of their classmates. According to Covey (1990):

> "If I were to summarize in one sentence the single most important principle I have learned in the field of interpersonal relations, it would be this: Seek first to understand, then to be understood."

Imparting this knowledge will not only enhance the interpersonal dynamics of a class; it will have a long-range benefit for students whose paradigms will be constantly challenged in their future endeavors. Employers have nothing but praise for the skills and professionalism that the adult learner brings to their organizations. Adults who do not possess the humility necessary to realize that there are new things to learn, different ways to do things, and different attitudes and beliefs to be considered, soon find themselves isolated in spite of the wealth of experience they bring to the workplace.

RECIPE FOR SUCCESS: A CAUTIONARY TALE

Despite adult learners' need to protect their own paradigms, they have a desire to learn what will and what won't work when they graduate and start their new profession or return to an old position with a new set of skills they can share with their colleagues. This can put instructors in the uncomfortable position of having students who interpret their wisdom as a recipe for success. It's similar to the attitude that is manifested in their verbal communication: if the instructor just tells them how to get an "A," they'll do it. In this case, they are looking for specific skills that are guaranteed to work.

In order to illustrate this issue we will share a true story that happened to one of our instructors and is something that all of us have experienced. It occurred with a student teacher who had gained her knowledge in a teacher preparation program at National University, but it is a scenario that could apply to any discipline. It is not often that instructors get to see the results of what they have taught their students. In this case, the instructors who taught the courses also supervised the students during their first experiences in the workplace where they had the opportunity to implement what they had learned in the classroom.

Scenario

I'd like to introduce Kelsey, a former high school teacher that I worked with. I went to observe Kelsey as her university supervisor during her third day of student teaching to see how things were going. It only took five minutes of observation to realize that one of her students was a very uncooperative student who was more in control of the class than Kelsey was. His vocabulary seemed to be limited to four-letter words, and the class was getting a great deal of pleasure from the innuendoes of this handsome, popular sixteen-year-old. Kelsey, meanwhile, completely ignored his behavior. The class was a disaster. After the class, Kelsey and I met, and I discussed with her the positive things I had observed. I then asked her how she felt about the class. She said it had gone extremely well. I pointed out that one of her students appeared to be more in control of the class than she was. She told me, to my complete surprise, that I should not worry about this. Her instructors at National had told her that the best way to eliminate disruptive behavior in the classroom was to ignore it. Kelsey had taken a piece of information and accepted it as a recipe for success. She would continue to use it until the desired outcome was achieved.

The problem was that this particular approach was not working in this situation. The adult learner needs to understand that there are no simple solutions. Instructors can give them a guidebook, but they cannot stand in their shoes. The key to moving from student to active participant in the workplace is the ability to constantly assess the reality of the situation.

THE DIVERSITY CHALLENGE

One of the most significant challenges to instructors today, regardless of the age group they teach, is responding to the needs of a diverse population of students. More specifically, we are referring to the needs of students from different cultural and linguistic backgrounds. In the classroom, there is an additional and equally important issue: the broad differences in expectations and knowledge among students of varying ages. It is not just the difference between the younger student and the adult learner. It also includes the important differences among adult learners of widely varying ages. The challenge is to create a learning community by assisting students in examining their preconceived assumptions about a particular age group. Students often harbor resentment towards their colleagues who are twenty or more years younger or older. In the research project referred to earlier, those in their late twenties told us that they couldn't understand why their fellow students in their fifties were not getting ready for retirement instead of preparing to compete with them for a job. At the same time, the fifty-year-olds expressed an impatience with the younger students' comments in class. All of these students are "adults," but the gap in ages is often great enough that some of them take on a parenting role while others assume the role of a contentious child. Their personal perspectives, based on different generational experiences, need to be addressed.

The mixture of different age groups provides a perfect opportunity to help students understand and respect the different stages that we must all pass through. The older group of students needs to remember what it felt like to be in their late twenties, and the younger students need to see that they can learn from students who may be the same age as their parents. Creating a community of adult learners is likely to enhance the instructor's success. But a class of students divided by generational experiences with little respect for this diversity is likely to lead to frustration.

CLASSROOM MANAGEMENT

Adult learners do not throw spit balls or send love letters during class, and if the faculty member's expectations—academic and behavioral—are made clear, the students will respond in a professional manner. That is why we were so surprised when Helene, one of our colleagues in the adult learner journal research project, said that she was having classroom management problems. The most difficult thing for Helene was that she was teaching future teachers how to implement effective classroom management plans. She wasn't practicing what she was preaching, and her journals at the end of the class confirmed her suspicions. The students were upset that she allowed individuals in the class to participate in disruptive private conversations. Her dilemma was to tell a group of adult students, close to her own age, that they are being rude and need to get their acts together. We were somewhat skeptical of Helene's problem until we experienced the same situation. It is hard to reprimand an adult. Adult students frequently have side conversations, but more often than not they are related to the course material. They have a wealth of experiential learning to share regarding almost any topic. We decided to open up the issue to discussion whenever it occurred in a particular class. What we learned is that adult learners have an overwhelming need to share their ideas, which are based on their validated personal experiences. This necessitates giving them every opportunity to express their views, if not in open discussion then in a group learning format. Classroom disruptions through side conversations are no longer a problem for any of us. When they occur, we discuss it openly and respond to what we consider one of the most important needs of the adult learner: respect for and validation of their life experiences.

As instructors prone to reading everything in the fields we are teaching, it can be disconcerting when a student says, "Well, that person you are quoting may be a scholar in this field but in my experience..." Adult learners *do* have a wealth of experience, and giving legitimacy to only the knowledge that lies between the pages of the textbook can undermine instructors' relationship, and therefore their effectiveness, in working with the adult learner. More importantly, not responding to what they have to offer may keep instructors from reaping the greatest reward in being teachers of adult learners: to become students in their own classrooms. Not all learning comes about through the reading of scholarly articles and required textbooks. The adult learner, if given the opportunity, will bring a class alive with personal anecdotes, a fresh perspective, and the inevitable challenge of forcing everyone—instructor included—to personalize the material.

INSTRUCTOR AS ADULT LEARNER

If instructors want to understand what it means to be an adult learner, they can begin by becoming actively involved in the process. This entails responding to that inner voice that draws them to learn something that they never had the opportunity and/or confidence to pursue. It's what I, as an avowed technophobe, am experiencing trying to type this chapter on my first lap-top computer. I keep waiting for everything I've written to disappear from the screen because I've pushed the wrong key. My anxiety is great, and I keep telling myself that I should continue to depend on the word processing services offered by the University. It is unsettling to move out of one's comfort zone, and that is exactly what many of the adult learners in an instructor's course have done. I will continue to explore the benefits of computers, in part so that I can experience what it means to be a lifelong learner. Like my students, I will board the train because "Once the educational train has been boarded, it can contribute to the individual status of the passengers and possibly increase (the) degree of power in making life choices" (Fordham, Poulton, and Randell, 1979).

CONCLUSION

America's institutions of higher education face an uncertain future. After many years of unrestricted growth, colleges and universities are in the midst of a nationwide decline—in student enrollment, in economic circumstances, and in public confidence. With the 18-21-year-old residential student comprising a shrinking portion of higher education's clientele; with public and governmental confidence in higher education at an all-time low; with traditional funding sources unable or unwilling to underwrite further expansion; and with new information technologies poised to undermine the very foundations of "education" as we have known it during the past 100 years, America's colleges and universities clearly stand at a crossroads.

"Lifelong learning" is no longer a catchy phrase or an optional component of a university's community outreach program. Over the coming decades, a college's ability to understand and meet the needs of the adult learner may well be the difference between survival and extinction in a fiercely competitive marketplace.

We are confident that the community of scholars will be able to heed the "wake-up call" and respond to its changing student population. A substantial literature regarding the education of adult learners exists. We trust that the Academy will turn to that body of understanding as it faces the challenge of serving a new group of students.

AUTHORS

Kathleen Wagschal is Associate Professor in the School of Education and Human Services at National University's San Diego campus. Her most recent scholarly work has focused on helping instructors to improve their teaching of adult learners through personalized journals—work funded by a grant from the National Center for Adult Learning (NCAL). Dr. Wagschal is an NCAL fellow and received the President's Distinguished Teaching Award at National University in 1994.

Peter H. Wagschal is Vice-President for Research at National University and Director of the National University Research Institute which serves as a clearinghouse for research related to higher education and the adult learner. Dr. Wagschal is working to expand National University's distance education capabilities through video teleconferencing and INTERNET access, and to develop a "just-in-time" information system for use by faculty and administrators as part of the university's approach to continuous improvement of academic quality.

<h2 style="text-align:center">REFERENCES</h2>

Brookfield, S. (1989). Facilitating adult learning. In S.B. Merriam & P.M. Cunningham (Eds.), *Handbook of adult and continuing education*. San Francisco, CA: Jossey-Bass.

Brookfield, S. (1990). *The skillful teacher: On technique, trust, and responsiveness in the classroom*. San Francisco, CA: Jossey-Bass.

Covey, S.R. (1990). *The seven habits of highly effective people*. New York, NY: Signet.

Cross, K.P. (1981). *Adults as learners*. San Francisco, CA: Jossey-Bass.

Fordham, P., Poulton, G., & Randell, L. (1979). *Learning networks in adult education*. New York, NY: Routledge & Kegan Paul.

Houle, C.O. (1992). *The literature of adult education: A bibliographic essay*. San Francisco, CA: Jossey-Bass.

Knowles, M. (1978). *The adult learner: A neglected species*. Houston, TX: Gulf.

Merriam, S.B., & Carrarella, R.S. (1991). *Learning in adulthood*. San Francisco, CA: Jossey-Bass.

National Center for Education Statistics. (1993). *Projections of education statistics to 2003*.

U.S. Bureau of the Census. (1992). *Current population reports*.

TWENTY

CHAPTER SUMMARIES: RECOMMENDATIONS FOR IMPROVING COLLEGE TEACHING

Peter Seldin

This book offers a broad range of strategies for improving teaching in colleges and universities. These chapter-by-chapter key points and recommendations show how administrators and faculty members can effect needed changes for spreading teaching excellence throughout the institution. An advisory note is in order: the full meaning of each of these points can best be understood and appreciated by reading the chapters themselves.

Chapter One
IMPROVING COLLEGE TEACHING

(Seldin)

1. There has never been a more promising time to improve teaching. At last, after a decade of criticism and calls for reform, countless institutions are feverishly reexamining their commitment to teaching and exploring ways to improve it.

2. The rationale for improving teaching is found in four different but interconnected reasons. They are reasons related to institutions, to faculty members, to students, and to society and societal forces.

3. Activities to improve teaching include enlarging a faculty member's knowledge of learning theory and pedagogical practices, of increasing his or her interest in and commitment to teaching, of reinforcing and rewarding teaching excellence, and of providing opportunities to bring about their growth.

4. Successful teaching improvement programs share certain characteristics. Among other things, the most effective programs: are tailored to the institution, receive clear and visible support from top-level administrators, approach the improvement of teaching positively, stimulate faculty enthusiasm and a high rate of participation, result in tangible changes in courses, teaching strategies, and methods.

5. To bring about substantial improvement in college teaching requires concrete action by administrators. They must introduce and promote appropriate institutional policies and practices. They must change the campus environment to make it more responsive to teaching. That includes providing the proper setting and tools to support instruction and using appropriate rewards.

Chapter Two

Using Campus Culture to Foster Improved Teaching

(Armour)

1. It is possible to build a campus culture that encourages good teaching and insists that teaching be given at least equal attention when compared to research. Even institutions that already emphasize teaching, such as liberal arts colleges, can improve instruction through deliberate attention to the culture that fosters teaching on their campuses.

2. This chapter uses case studies from different institutions to examine campus cultures that contribute to good teaching. Among the important lessons learned from these cases are the following: a) a positive environment for teaching takes a committed president and provost or dean; b) the faculty have to be equally accepting of the emphasis; c) there must be clear statements in print that forcefully make public the institution's position on teaching, especially as it affects promotion, tenure, and salary; d) the hiring process is one of the most valuable points for establishing this culture; e) faculty members should be provided developmental opportunities to increase their skills as teachers.

3. Characteristics of a supportive culture include: a) attention to the process for change; b) opportunities for telling stories about good teaching on campus; c) high standards for teaching; d) recognition that faculty are motivated by both extrinsic and intrinsic rewards.

4. Innovations to look for in the future which will enhance the campus culture include entire departments accepting a collective responsibility for meeting the mission of the institution and teaching becoming a community activity which is openly discussed, openly valued, and openly evaluated.

Chapter Three
QUALITY TEACHING: WHAT ROLE FOR ADMINISTRATORS?

(Hecht)

1. The focus on the quality of education and in particular the quality of teaching demands change in administrative behavior as well as in faculty practice.

2. Administrators can strengthen the quality of teaching in their institutions by helping set the agenda and tone of dialogue on the campus for questions ranging from the nature and purposes of disciplines, to discussions of pedagogy, research, new technologies, and forms of assessment.

3. They can influence behaviors by encouraging the development of team skills and collaborative work within a context of institution-wide vision.

4. Administrators can help build connections between the campus and external community both locally and/or nationally and can open doors to innovative problem solving.

5. Enhancement of teaching must become a primary administrative goal.

Chapter Four
FACULTY MOTIVATION FOR TEACHING

(Austin and Baldwin)

1. Difficult working conditions in higher education threaten the intrinsic motivation faculty bring to the classroom.

2. Expectancy theory, need theory, and flow theory are theoretical perspectives on motivation which have implications useful to colleges and universities wishing to encourage faculty member's motivation as teachers.

3. Motivation theorists disagree on the relative usefulness of intrinsic and extrinsic rewards as a means for motivating individuals. Most would agree, however, that both intrinsic and extrinsic rewards can support faculty motivation. Environments that enable faculty to enjoy the intrinsic benefits of teaching promote effective instruction. At the same time, extrinsic rewards (e.g., teaching awards, salary increases) communicate that effort devoted to teaching is valued by one's institution and one's colleagues.

4. Different types of teaching opportunities and support may be needed to enhance the motivation of faculty at successive stages.

5. A comprehensive plan to support faculty motivation for teaching should include several key components: a) organizational culture strategies. A college or university's commitment to teaching excellence should be communicated clearly through symbols, rituals, ceremonies, and programs that convey the institution's core values; b) formal organizational structures and policies. The evaluation and reward system as well as other academic and personnel policies must directly reflect the institution's commitment to effective teaching; c) faculty development strategies. Opportunities to enhance teaching appropriate to professors' career stages and distinctive professional circumstances must be available; d) institutional leadership strategies. Academic leaders have a crucial role to play in articulating their institution's commitment to and support for teaching excellence. Another key administrative function is to find formal and informal methods to recognize professors' efforts to improve teaching.

Chapter Five

Creating a Culture of Commitment as a Foundation for Teaching Effectiveness

(Pastore)

1. Formal faculty development is important to the enhancement of teaching effectiveness, but it is sometimes fraught with budgetary and program management constraints as well as a level of indifference among those who can profit most.

2. Institutional policies and practices can help shape a campus climate conducive to teaching effectiveness, but policies and practices are

potentially dysfunctional, especially when politicized, malevolent or punitive in tone, poorly devised, or inappropriately administered.

3. Leadership is critical to teaching effectiveness because leaders can initiate and influence policies and practices supportive of teaching. But leadership today is often transient or distant, and a preoccupation with academic leadership, especially that which is transformational and heroic, often begs the need for more systemic, community-based commitment to teaching excellence.

4. The creation of a systemic culture of commitment, focus, or devotion to "teaching space," therefore, is foundational to any programmatic, policy, or leadership effort intended to enhance teaching effectiveness.

5. Colleges and universities, as systems affected by larger systems, appear to have been undermined and distracted from a commitment to "teaching space" by four sustained trends: popularized definitions of quality; changed perception of academic leadership; the marketplace; and forces which erode faculty commitment.

6. Efforts to create a culture of commitment as a foundation for teaching excellence will and should vary from campus to campus, but at the core of the effort must be a managed response to those forces which threaten to distract the academy from a focus on teaching and learning combined with a systemic (students, faculty, administration, governing boards) campus existence laced with values, conversation, storytelling, ceremony, symbols, policy making, and functions which place teaching and learning as active, not merely rhetorical, manifestations of institutional purpose.

Chapter Six

TA Training: Making a Difference in Undergraduate Education

(Black)

1. At large institutions, graduate student teaching assistants (TAs) have a unique opportunity to enhance undergraduate education. Since most of their teaching is done in small classes or in one-to-one situations, they are in a good position to personalize education and to get students actively involved, which encourages thinking in the discipline. TAs can help students to develop the skills necessary for

analyzing material, solving problems, and grappling with difficult questions. TAs also provide much of the assessment and feedback given to students. For these reasons, it is essential to provide teaching assistants with the training and support necessary to effectively fill their roles.

2. There are a number of different models of TA training across the country, and they work with varying degrees of success.

3. The bulk of TA training should be located in departments. It is important for new TAs to get critical information that affects what they do in their classrooms and to get training that focuses on what the TAs will actually be doing in their teaching: what they teach, how they are expected to teach, the students they will be teaching, the expectations of the faculty member in charge of the course, etc. Even generic teaching strategies can be learned best in the context of learning to teach a particular course.

4. Training should be an ongoing process with support available to TAs throughout their first years of teaching and whenever they are asked to do something different. Many TAs go through a fairly comprehensive training when they first start teaching, but their responsibilities change over the years, and they are often left to figure out on their own how to do the more difficult assignments.

5. Including faculty along with graduate students in departmental teaching development programs can make a difference in how teaching is viewed in the department. This may take the form of getting faculty members involved in the planning and facilitation of the training for TAs or having faculty participate in teaching development activities along with TAs. Including a teaching development program with course and curriculum revisions for faculty as well as TAs can make a big difference in the success of the changes.

6. Teaching and learning centers can be an important resource for TA training. While departments should have the responsibility of preparing their graduate students to teach, staff members from central teaching and learning centers can provide the assistance needed to help make these programs successful.

Chapter Seven

FITTING PROGRAMS TO INSTITUTIONAL CULTURES: THE FOUNDING AND EVOLUTION OF THE UNIVERSITY TEACHING CENTER

(Ambrose)

1. Whether creating a new faculty development program or maintaining an already established program, success in improving teaching depends in large part on how well the program is integrated into the institution. Thus, understanding the culture of the institution and creating a program consistent with that culture is vital to success.

2. Strategic planning during the early phases of the creation of a faculty development program helps to place it in a situation which contributes to success. Thinking through all aspects of the creation and implementation of such a program entails defining what your institution means by "faculty development," determining the goals of such a program, discussing a variety of ways to meet those goals, planning where the program fits into the larger institutional structure, figuring out where to begin and how to proceed in the most efficient and effective way, and identifying individuals who are important in building a power base.

3. Talking to a lot of people—deans, department heads, faculty members—helps in identifying problems to address or initiatives to take on and assures that these groups have input and thus feel ownership of the program. Constant contact with all of these groups reinforces the notion that this is not a "top down" initiative, but rather a "bottom up" one.

4. Faculty development programs must have administrators who fully believe in and support the program. These people need to publicly support the program at every possible opportunity and provide enough resources to make it work.

5. Starting slow and moving cautiously is important in establishing a faculty development program—test the waters to assure that you meet the needs of your faculty, build credibility and trust with early successes, and pilot different initiatives to determine what works best on your campus.

6. Opportunities for individual consultations should be an integral part of any faculty development program. Consultations enable faculty

developers to customize discussions, feedback, and suggestions to individual faculty, taking into account faculty personalities, specific domains, and types of courses. Consultations are among the most powerful methods for changing teaching behavior or practices.

Chapter Eight
LOW-COST OR NO-COST
INSTRUCTIONAL DEVELOPMENT ACTIVITIES

(Simpson and Jackson)

1. The key to an effective, low-cost program of individual consultation is the use of volunteer peer consultants whenever possible. Most well-established instructional development programs have access to a corps of faculty members who are especially skillful at certain aspects of their teaching.

2. A copy of McKeachie's *Teaching Tips* for each new faculty member is a relatively low-cost means of placing effective teaching tools in the hands of large numbers of instructors.

3. An instructional mini-grant of a few hundred dollars can serve as leverage to attract departmental support for an instructional activity. In addition, these grants can serve as seed money for future institutional or externally-supported instructional improvement grants.

4. "Faculty teaching faculty" is a wonderful concept and requires no money and little time to sponsor. From experience we have learned that most faculty members are pleased to be asked to share some area of their expertise with their peers.

5. If faculty development can be viewed as a career-span activity, then it must begin in graduate school. Teaching assistants are the professors of the future. An almost endless number of low-cost programs can be offered for TAs.

Chapter Nine
CAPITALIZING ON DIVERSITY IN THE CLASSROOM

(Greene)

1. Teaching college students to live successfully in a multicultural society requires that faculty recognize, value, and use diversity issues as an integral part of their teaching practices.

2. The impact of the changing mix of college students challenges faculty in very personal ways and requires that faculty learn both how to manage and how to raise difficult, controversial issues in the classroom.

3. We can no longer leave the work of creating appreciation for diversity or of reducing bias solely to special campus units.

4. Faculty who value diversity and use it and the emotions around it as a part of the teaching and learning "process" will produce positive cognitive and affective growth in students.

5. Research has shown that when students and faculty are given opportunities to participate in bias reduction courses and workshops, they experience positive changes in both cognitive and affective development.

6. Making use of well-developed bias reduction workshop models gives faculty and students additional skills for coping with difficult, emotionally charged issues in the classroom.

Chapter Ten

INSTRUCTIONAL DEVELOPMENT IN COMMUNITY COLLEGES

(Wadsworth)

Because teaching is the primary focus for community college faculty, instructional development is a matter of beginning and sustaining a conversation about teaching. Instructional development coordinators can do the following:

1. Create effective programs by working with division heads to increase their knowledge of and skill in evaluating teaching and to encourage them to use regular meeting times as a forum for discussion of teaching and learning issues.

2. Provide opportunities for faculty to meet with each other across disciplines to examine their own courses in light of new perspectives, to incorporate writing or thinking across the curriculum, or to create interdisciplinary courses.

3. Provide opportunities for faculty to share their expertise with new audiences through lecture series open to the public or through participation in celebratory occasions such as Women's History Month.

4. Use regular professional development opportunities to provide on-campus (or distance learning) graduate courses on teaching and learning topics.

5. Design new faculty orientation programs, mentor programs, and circulate print materials on teaching and learning.

Chapter Eleven

HOW MENTORING PROGRAMS CAN IMPROVE TEACHING

(Sorcinelli)

1. Studies of new and junior faculty find the initial years in academe to be a time of great stress as well as satisfaction. The challenges of teaching loom particularly large.

2. In exploring facets of teaching perceived by new faculty as most stressful, the following themes arise: time constraints, lack of collegial guidance and support, and inadequate feedback, recognition, and reward.

3. Mentoring programs have become a popular part of plans and programs for new faculty support. The goals of mentoring programs may vary and may include providing information on the institution, support for teaching and research, and collegial communications and interactions.

4. Mentoring programs that take teaching seriously have several common approaches: they find ways to help new teachers manage time for teaching; encourage collegiality in teaching across such variables as age, discipline, gender and rank; and recognize and reward good teaching.

5. Some important lessons on mentoring junior faculty members for teaching development include recognizing that : (a) a perfect "match" between mentor and mentee is not critical to the success of the pair; (b) every mentor needs to be a good teacher but need not have won major awards for teaching excellence; (c) while formal rewards for mentoring can serve as incentives, intrinsic rewards are at least as important; (d) mentoring programs need to create incentives—both intrinsic and extrinsic—that express appreciation for mentors and mentees; (e) mentoring programs need to be approached in a flexible manner; (f) mentors and mentees are well-served by an orientation to the responsibilities and possibilities of the

relationship; and (g) mentoring programs for teaching development are time intensive and need a coordinator to manage activities.

Chapter Twelve
ENHANCING TEACHING THROUGH PEER CLASSROOM OBSERVATIONS

(Millis and Kaplan)

1. The need for responsive, cooperative discussions about teaching among faculty is becoming more important as the student body becomes ever more diverse.

2. If well-conducted in an atmosphere of trust, peer classroom observations can engender reflective discussions that can strengthen teaching.

3. Placing the emphasis on teaching enhancement can eliminate some of the barriers that arise when peer classroom observations are conducted for summative purposes.

4. To develop an effective peer visit program, care must be taken to recruit as visitors those who have exemplary teaching records and strong interpersonal skills.

5. Visitors should agree on a systematic procedure and a viable standardized instrument to summarize observation data. A "focused narrative" report is often preferred, since it offers a holistic view of classroom activities without presupposing any one particular pedagogical approach.

6. Ideally, classroom observations should be part of an extended review of classroom performance which also takes into account such materials as the course syllabus, exams, and student evaluations.

Chapter Thirteen
THE DEPARTMENT CHAIR'S ROLE IN IMPROVING TEACHING

(Gmelch)

1. Department chairs believe their role as faculty developers is their most important responsibility, even more than their roles as leaders, managers, and scholars.

2. Chairs need to exhibit several types of behaviors necessary to build and maintain teaching performance: supporting, developing, recognizing, rewarding and reinforcing effective teaching.

3. Chairs need to model effective teaching and filter unnecessary stress from faculty lives.

4. Chairs need to share the responsibility for developing effective teaching with competent and experienced senior faculty mentors.

5. The stark absence of collegial support and networking, such as co-teaching and mentoring, reinforces the need for the chair to facilitate faculty interaction.

6. Chairs should not miss an opportunity to recognize and reward faculty for effective teaching. They should provide verbal commendation, expressions of appreciation, and tangible rewards for teaching accomplishments.

Chapter Fourteen
USING TEACHING PORTFOLIO STRATEGIES TO IMPROVE COURSE INSTRUCTION

(Zubizarreta)

1. Teaching portfolios effectively document teaching performance for assessment and evaluation but also provide professors with a powerful tool for improvement of a particular course when adapted as a concise course portfolio focused on the singular philosophy, methods, materials, evaluations, improvement efforts, learning outcomes, and goals of a specific course.

2. The course portfolio engages the professor in a process of continual research about the quality of teaching an individual course. As an ongoing result of the scholarship of teaching, the portfolio fosters intellectual and professional growth and prompts practical changes that provide the foundation for general faculty development and for decisive strengthening of classroom performance.

3. Four pages of selected critical description and reflective analysis with the necessary accompanying appendix materials provide ample opportunity for a teacher to include seminal information about a course. Such information should come from oneself, from others, and from products of student learning, diverse materials that become the recorded evidence of performance and the impetus for experimentation and genuine improvement. The compact dimensions of both the narrative and appendix promote trenchant examination of precisely what, how, and why we teach, keeping the professor

focused on the process of teaching. The result is a committed, self-conscious approach to instruction that sets the stage for renewal and success.

4. Collaboration is essential to the process of developing a valid portfolio. A mentor guides the process of course improvement by supporting the professor's efforts to focus on reflective study of teaching performance and student outcomes and by continually helping a teacher to provide strong evidence of improvement through vital assessment.

Chapter Fifteen

STUDENT PORTFOLIOS: THEIR OBJECTIVES, DEVELOPMENT, AND USE

(Annis and Jones)

1. A portfolio is a multidimensional and documented organization of either a student's or a teacher's work and includes a reflective discussion of the materials in the portfolio.

2. There are many parallel uses of portfolios for students and teachers. For example, students can use portfolios to improve their learning while teachers can use them to improve their teaching.

3. Student portfolios can be used for three basic purposes: (a) to evaluate individual performance in a classroom; (b) to evaluate performance in a program or for a specific purpose such as finding a job; (c) to evaluate an entire program or its components.

4. When using a portfolio assignment, instructors are urged to: (a) determine the portfolio purpose; (b) plan a systematic method of presentation; c) help students determine what items to include; (d) be sure students understand how to prepare a reflective essay; and (e) stress the importance of documenting statements made about performance by including sample work.

5. Organization, content, presentation, and overall effect of the portfolio are appropriate components of an evaluation instrument.

6. The preparation of student portfolios has a very positive impact on teaching and learning for both students and teachers. The portfolio also can serve as a useful assessment tool in determining student performance.

Chapter Sixteen
EVALUATING YOUR OWN TEACHING

(Fink)

1. Professors who want to improve their teaching have to evaluate carefully in order to determine which aspects of it need changing and which do not.

2. There are basically five sources of information to use in evaluation. All evaluation techniques are variations of one or more of these five sources. The sources are self-monitoring, audio and video recordings, student test results, information from students, and outside observations.

3. A comprehensive evaluation of one's teaching requires the use of all five sources of information because each one provides a kind of information that none of the others does.

4. Comprehensive evaluation takes time and effort, but not an excessive amount.

5. The benefits of comprehensively evaluating your teaching are: (a) it is the only way to know what changes are needed; (b) it is the only way of thoroughly documenting your teaching for others; and (c) it is the only way of providing a solid basis for knowing how well you have done as a teacher.

Chapter Seventeen
FACULTY COLLABORATION IN TEACHING

(Baldwin and Austin)

1. Many educators have discovered that collaborative teaching is an effective way to address complex issues and broad themes in the college classroom. Team teachers also find that they grow professionally as they learn new content and approaches to instruction from their colleagues.

2. Collaborative teaching arrangements exist on a continuum. At one extreme, the primary instructor has full responsibility for a course but invites others to lecture on special topics or assist with various instructional functions such as leading small group discussions and grading. At the other end of the spectrum, collaborative teachers equally share responsibility for the design and implementation of a

course. In this interactive mode, team members communicate on all aspects of a course and cooperate in the facilitation of class sessions.

3. Collaborative teaching poses distinctive challenges that educators must be prepared to address. These include: (a) increased time for course planning; (b) loss of autonomy; (c) the evaluation of individual contributions to team teaching efforts; and (d) complex dynamics occurring when people of different disciplines, levels of status, gender, and ethnicity work together closely.

4. Faculty interested in collaborative teaching should: (a) know their potential collaborators well and clarify what each brings to the partnership; (b) work out the details of the collaborative teaching arrangement in advance; (c) monitor the effectiveness of the team teaching effort and renegotiate roles and responsibilities periodically; (d) cultivate a spirit of camaraderie; and (e) especially for junior faculty, be cautious about collaborative teaching. It is important to establish an independent identity as a teacher and to determine how one's institution will credit team teaching.

Chapter Eighteen
DISTANCE EDUCATION:
THE EMERGENCE OF AMERICA'S VIRTUAL UNIVERSITY

(Arreola)

1. The use of telecommunication technology to deliver instruction (distance education) has emerged as an important, and potentially revolutionary, force in education especially in the form of live, two-way video connections that can bring "virtual" classroom experiences into students' homes or workplaces.

2. Today more than 300,000 people are taking for-credit distance education courses in over 125 fields offered by nearly 90 colleges and universities in more than 40 states, with some 30,000 enrolled in degree programs.

3. To be an effective distance education teacher, one must: (a) become familiar with the equipment used both at the teaching and remote receiving sites; (b) develop the course and presentations according to the principles of instructional systems design; (c) prepare all materials in advance and have in mind precisely where in the instruction each will be used; (d) prepare all handouts in advance and make sure

they have been mailed or otherwise distributed to remote learners before class; (e) pace the presentation to permit questions and comments from students; and (f) decide whether students should be in the classroom with the instructor during the broadcast.

4. The advent and spread of two-way interactive video instruction capable of being delivered virtually to any location in the country, or even the world, has profound implications and poses significant questions concerning: (a) defining mission, service area, and teacher productivity; (b) determining accreditation standards and procedures, registration and fee charges for remote students, and residency requirements; and (c) evaluating faculty performance.

5. In the same way that a university college may exist within a traditional academic organization wherein courses are drawn from various departments to form a specialized degree program, degrees comprised of distance education courses taught by faculty located throughout a state or even the country may form an electronic university college or a "virtual" university.

Chapter Nineteen
TEACHING ADULT LEARNERS

(Wagschal and Wagschal)

1. The participation of adult learners in higher education will continue to grow over the coming decades. This trend is a reflection of three ongoing phenomena in America: the aging of the baby boom generation; social changes that require lifelong learning opportunities; and the rapid pace of technological change.

2. Adult learners bring a variety of characteristics to the learning process that are not common to their younger counterparts. These features include a pragmatic, problem-oriented attitude; a wealth of prior experience that needs to be included in their learning experiences; and a substantial capacity for self-direction.

3. Though they often have anxieties about returning to school, adult learners benefit most from a learning environment that is challenging. They respond well to high expectations and gain increased self-esteem by accomplishing learning tasks that they did not think they could achieve.

4. Teaching adults requires a particularly high degree of honesty on the part of instructors. The adult learner expects teachers to practice what they preach, to admit what they don't know, and to understand what it is like to be engaged in the lifelong learning process. After all, instructors of adults are, like their students, lifelong learners.

5. Teaching adults requires a mixture of skills and techniques—lecture, dialogue, guided group projects—that take advantage of the adult learners' wealth of prior experience.

6. Although adult learners, aged 25 on, are typically viewed as a single group, there are substantial differences in motivation, life stage, interest, and educational needs among adult learners of different ages. Adult learners are extremely diverse and are best served by instructors who are sensitive to their individual educational needs and learning styles.

INDEX